The Eighteenth-Century London Upholder

Steven Sanders

The Eighteenth-Century London Upholder

A New Domestic Commerce

palgrave
macmillan

Steven Sanders
Lake Forest, IL, USA

ISBN 978-3-032-08659-4 ISBN 978-3-032-08660-0 (eBook)
https://doi.org/10.1007/978-3-032-08660-0

This Palgrave Macmillan imprint is published by the registered company Springer Nature Switzerland AG
The registered company address is: Gewerbestrasse 11, 6330 Cham, Switzerland

Preface

This book is a study of the eighteenth-century upholding trade in London. Although the word 'upholder' may be considered archaic today, upholders were very important contributors in furnishing eighteenth-century homes. Skilled in the manufacturing and assembly of furniture and in providing upholstery goods and services, by mid-century, the upholding trade evolved into providing other products, including funeral undertaking, appraising and brokering of household goods, and auctioneering. Upholders formed their livery company in 1360, and upon receiving their royal charter in 1626 from Charles I, they became known as The Worshipful Company of Upholders of the City of London. As will be seen in this work, not all upholders belonged to the Upholders' Company. From using eighteenth-century newspaper advertisements and news items, along with archives and manuscripts, it was possible to quantify key business aspects of upholders and how their trade evolved throughout the eighteenth century.

The Introduction provides context to the social and business lives of upholders. Many changes occurred during the eighteenth century that affected the lives of the British population, not just upholders. While upholstery and cabinet-making were the core product lines of upholders, their trade evolved over the century. Chapter 2 is devoted to how upholders came to dominate the funeral undertaking business. Chapter 3 details how and why upholders integrated brokering, appraising, and auctioneering into their businesses. Within these first chapters, the issues surrounding credit and bankruptcy in a growing consumer economy are examined.

Two case studies of financially successful upholders are included in this work. They were specialized, rather than general, upholders and became wealthy. Investigation of their business and social lives required primary and secondary research into diverse topics. The East India Company, banking, royal household tradesmen, and military contracting were among the topics researched to add context to their business and social lives.

Lake Forest, IL, USA Steven Sanders

Acknowledgements

Many people helped me along the way in completing this work. William Gibson, Joanne Begiato, and Matthew Craske were most generous with their time and advice. Robert Bucholz at Loyola University in Chicago was very helpful in advising me on researching the Royal Household records. Alex Werner, former lead curator at the Museum of London, Emma Miller, curator at Grimsthorpe Castle, Howard Rehs of Rehs Galleries, and Robert Hartle generously handled my inquisitiveness. I am especially grateful to Philip Williams and Timothy Powys-Lybbe for their help in researching their remarkable ancestors. Thank you to Jackie Williams, John Houston, and Wendy Shorter-Blake from The Worshipful Company of Upholders of the City of London for sharing their knowledge. Finally, completing this work would not have been possible without the support of my family.

Competing Interests The author has no competing interests to declare that are relevant to the content of this manuscript.

Contents

List of Illustrations

List of Tables

CHAPTER 1

Introduction

This introduction covers key issues that affected the social and business lives of eighteenth-century upholders. These issues and selective views about the importance of apprenticeship and livery companies, empire, material culture, consumption and consumerism, advertising, and credit are surveyed. There were significant shifts in several areas in the second half of the eighteenth century that shaped upholders' activities.

Upholders and Their Trade

Literature about upholders is somewhat limited. Two books published in 1747 are valuable in forming a basic understanding of an eighteenth-century upholder. R. Campbell's *The London Tradesman* is an apprenticeship advice book and describes the upholding trade by function and the goods they sold. Campbell was clear that upholders were more than upholsterers; they were furniture makers, too. More importantly, Campbell stated that upholders were central to supplying or 'fitting out' a residence with fashionable and tasteful furniture and upholstery goods.[1] He wrote:

> I have just finished my house, and must now think of furnishing it with fashionable furniture. The upholder is chief agent in this case; he is the man upon whose judgment I rely in the choice of goods; and I suppose he has

[1] R. Campbell, *The London Tradesman* (London: T. Gardner, 1747), 169–76.

S. Sanders, *The Eighteenth–Century London Upholder*,
https://doi.org/10.1007/978-3-032-08660-0_1

> not only judgment in the materials, but taste in the fashions, and skill in workmanship.[2]

This 1747 extract from Campbell's apprenticeship advice book recognized upholding as a trade that went beyond the manufacture and assembly of household furniture. The elite upholder was also the main adviser in furnishing a home with tasteful and fashionable furniture. When Campbell wrote of furnishings, he did not mean only chairs, tables, and other items constructed mainly from wood. Furnishings also included 'soft goods' such as curtains, upholstery, and carpets.[3] Thomas Waller's 1747 apprenticeship advice book added that upholding was a 'clean and genteel trade'.[4]

One of the first written uses of the word 'upholder', according to J.F. Houston, dates from 1258, when the word was spelled 'uphelder'. The word had various spellings for the next one hundred and fifty years, including 'upheldre', 'upheldere', and 'uphalder'. By 1500, 'upholder' had become the conventional spelling.[5] The spelling and etymology of upholder are of some interest because they indicate that the upholding trade was known as early as 1258. However, the context in which the word was used is more important. The *Oxford English Dictionary* considers the word 'upholder' obsolete and rare. The primary definition is: 'A dealer in small wares or second-hand articles (of clothing, furniture, etc.); a maker or repairer of such things'. A second definition is: 'Upholsterer'. A third definition is: 'An Undertaker'.[6] Karen Walton pointed out that

[2] Campbell, *The London Tradesman*, 169–70.

[3] It might be assumed that an eighteenth-century upholder is similar to a modern day interior decorator. After all, understanding fashion and taste were as important for the eighteenth-century upholding trade as they are to the modern day interior decorator. However, this comparison between the two ends there. Upholders manufactured, assembled, and installed much of what they sold; modern day interior decorators do few or none of these tasks and mostly provide an advisory and purchasing service.

[4] Thomas Waller, *A general description of all trades, digested in alphabetical order: by which parents, guardians, and trustees, may make choice of trades agreeable to the capacity, education, inclination, strength, and fortune of the youth* (London: Printed at Crown and Mitre, 1747), 214–15.

[5] J.F. Houston, *Featherbedds and Flock Bedds* (London: Three Tents Press, 2010), 21–22.

[6] *Oxford English Dictionary* "upholder, n.". OED Online. December 2018. Oxford University Press. http://www.oed.com.oxfordbrookes.idm.oclc.org/view/Entry/219963?redirectedFrom=upholder (accessed 6 January 2019).

medieval upholders were often called 'frippers'.[7] The *Oxford English Dictionary* defines 'fripper' as an obsolete term meaning 'to tear to rags'.[8] One can deduce from these sources that upholders were once rag sellers, dealers in used household goods, upholsterers, and undertakers.

Prior to the seventeenth century, upholders were often derisively referred to as sharpers and dealers in stolen goods. True respectability did not come until 1626, when Charles I granted the upholders a livery company charter as The Worshipful Company of Upholders of the City of London.[9] Upholders earned a reputation for being experts in the furnishing or 'fitting out' of residential interiors in the seventeenth and eighteenth centuries, though their livery company was not large, ranking around number fifty out of one hundred in membership size throughout the eighteenth century.[10]

A general historical definition of an upholder was someone who provided the household goods needed to furnish a residential interior. What Campbell and Waller provided was an analysis of how upholders were integral in furnishing residences, but they did not touch upon how upholders became influential in the furnishing of residences. A closer examination of the eighteenth-century society and economy in which they operated was needed.

At the beginning of the eighteenth century, upholders were known as dealers in new and used household goods, upholsterers, and funeral undertakers. The upholding business evolved in the first half of the eighteenth century, after which an upholder became known as someone who manufactured, assembled, and sourced interior household goods; could, on a full-time or part-time basis, broker and appraise household goods; participate in the auction business; provide funeral goods and services; and act as a client agent and intermediary.

Recently published academic works have provided additional information about upholders and are discussed below. Three studies specifically relate to eighteenth-century upholders in London. Karin Walton

[7] Karin M. Walton, "The Worshipful Company of Upholders of the City of London," *Furniture History Society* Vol. 9 (1973): 41–42.

[8] *Oxford English Dictionary* "fripper, n.". OED Online. December 2018. Oxford University Press. http://www.oed.com.oxfordbrookes.idm.oclc.org/view/Entry/74752?redirectedFrom=fripper (accessed 6 January 2019).

[9] Officially known as The of Worshipful Company of Upholders of the City of London. [hereafter Upholders' Company].

[10] Walton, "The Worshipful Company of Upholders," 41–42; Houston, *Featherbedds*, 77–78.

presented a brief history of the Upholders' Company and lists the members and apprentices by their joining dates and addresses. Her history gives an overview of how the Upholders' Company operated but provides little information about the products and practices of London upholders.[11] J.F. Houston produced a historical account of the Upholders' Company and the key events in its history. Of particular interest is the fact that upholders were the dominant, but not the exclusive, providers of funeral undertaking. Houston also explained how, early in the eighteenth century, a business feud occurred between the Upholders' Company and the United Company of Undertakers. The Undertakers' Company attempted, unsuccessfully, to create a new livery company exclusively for funeral undertaking.[12] The third study specific to the Upholders' Company is *Fripperers to Upholders*, authored in 2020 by David A. C. Ayres. This work provides short case studies of upholders from the sixteenth century to well into the nineteenth century. Ayres's short chapter about George Oakley is important to mention here because, even though the Upholders' Company had become mostly a social and charitable organization by the early nineteenth century, upholding as a trade was still thriving. Oakley was an elite upholder and furniture-maker who ran a prosperous business during the Regency. His clients included the aristocracy and the royal household.[13]

Geoffrey Beard's *Upholsterers and Interior Furnishing England 1530–1840* devotes an entire chapter to the upholding trade. Primarily focused on the upholstery facet of the upholding trade, Beard also provides valuable insight into their apprenticeships, furniture-making skills, workspaces, and sources of supply.[14] Furniture historian Adam Bowett provides little description of upholders in his detailed writing about the materials and construction techniques used in manufacturing late-seventeenth-century and early-eighteenth-century English furniture. In *English Furniture 1660–1714*, Bowett acknowledges the importance of upholders in producing over 200,000 upholstered chairs annually and writes about the Upholders' Company complaining to Parliament that the

[11] Walton, "The Worshipful Company of Upholders," 41–79.

[12] Houston, *Featherbedds*, 21–139.

[13] David A. C. Ayres, *Fripperers to Upholders* (London: Sustine Press, 2020), 95–101.

[14] Geoffrey Beard, *Upholsterers and Interior Furnishing England 1530–1840* (New Haven: Yale University Press, 1997), 4.

cane chair manufacturers were usurping work from established livery companies.[15]

Bowett's second book, *Early Georgian Furniture 1715–1740*, discusses how joiners and upholders were the main furniture-makers. He states that upholders were the largest group of furniture-makers represented in the *Dictionary of English Furniture Makers*. He recognizes that upholders became multi-faceted and began involvement in appraising and trading in second-hand goods. Bowett claims that these multi-faceted firms were comprehensive, a phenomenon of the second half of the eighteenth century.[16]

Another furniture historian, Pat Kirkham, explains in detail the manufacturing and business practices of the London furniture-making trade. Her research confirms that members of the Upholders' Company and the Joiners' Company manufactured the majority of London furniture. Another finding from her research was that by 1750, just under fifty per cent of the Upholders' Company membership was made up of upholsterers. Kirkham also traced the evolution of the furniture-making firms into comprehensive firms. A comprehensive upholding firm offered more than the manufacture, assembly, sourcing, and sale of furniture and upholstery goods for residential interiors. Although comprehensive upholders remained anchored in the upholstery and furniture-making trade, many diversified into other areas, including appraising, dealing in used household goods, and auctioneering.[17]

Clive Edwards provides a rich description of upholders and their importance to the furniture trade. In the seventeenth century, upholsterers (upholders) became arbiters of taste and skilled in introducing new furnishing styles. As furniture retailers, upholders had two relationships with their customers in the eighteenth century. First, upholders served their clients' furniture needs through manufacturing and sourcing. Second,

[15] Adam Bowett, *English Furniture 1660–1714 From Charles II to Queen Anne* (Woodbridge: Antique Collectors' Club, 2002), 31, 84. Bowett replaces the word upholder with upholsterer.

[16] Adam Bowett, *Early Georgian Furniture 1715–1740* (Woodbridge: Antique Collectors' Club, 2009), 12, 27–32.

[17] Pat Kirkham, *The London Furniture Trade 1700–1870* (Leeds: Furniture History Society, 1988), 57–68, 136–44. Valerie Hope, Clive Birch, Gilbert Tory, *The Freedom: The Past and Present of the Livery, Guilds and City of London* (Buckingham: Barracuda Books, Ltd., 1982), 198.

upholders were taste arbiters and advised their clients accordingly. Edwards is also clear that upholsters were dealers in second-hand goods.[18]

While it is apparent that upholders concentrated on two areas, namely upholstery and furniture-making, some sources mention ancillary services in which upholders were involved, such as brokers and appraisers of used household goods and auctioneering. Houston was the only author who devoted a large section to upholders being involved with funeral undertaking, which was an important product line for many upholders by the second half of the eighteenth century. These extra business lines were so important that one chapter in this work is devoted to upholders as funeral undertakers, and another chapter is devoted to upholders as brokers, appraisers, and auctioneers. Each of the above sources gives part of the picture of what an upholder was and, taken together, establishes an academic foundation for new analysis of the upholding trade.

Although this study is focused on London, there were upholders throughout Britain. The elite from the provincial areas who had town homes in London could purchase household goods from Chippendale, for instance, and from him commission furniture for country homes such as Harewood House in West Yorkshire and Dumfries House in Ayrshire, Scotland. These were extensive and expensive commissions that required shipping and workers travelling to the houses to install the furniture.[19] Those of lesser social status and financial means wanting stylish and fashionable household goods could visit upholder shops in the larger provincial cities. In York, for instance, Robert Barker and Richard Farrer were upholders who subscribed to Chippendale's *Director*.[20] Barker was also an appraiser and an undertaker. From using the online database of British and Irish furniture-makers that included upholders, it was found that about half of British upholders were from London. Clearly, London was the centre for British fashion and design. However, design books became widely available by the 1740s, allowing non-London upholders to manufacture, assemble, and copy fashionable household goods.[21]

[18] Clive Edwards, *Turning Houses into Homes: A History of the Retailing and Consumption of Domestic Furnishings* (London: Routledge, 2017), 31, 39–41, 71–4, 86.

[19] Christopher Gilbert, *The Life & Work of Thomas Chippendale* (New York: Tabard Press, 1978), 28–30.

[20] Thomas Chippendale, *The gentleman and cabinet-maker's director* (London: Thomas Chippendale, 1754), vii–viii.

[21] Beard, *Upholsterers and Interior Furnishing*, 161–63; Michael Snodin and John Styles, *Design & the Decorative Arts: Georgian Britain 1714–1837* (London: V&A Publications,

The upholder trade in London and the British provinces was similar in structure. Furniture-making and upholstery were core products. Using Robert Barker from York as an example, upholders outside London also practised funeral undertaking and appraising. How the apprenticeship system worked in provincial cities like York, Dorset, Bath, and Liverpool was not studied here, but their apprenticeship schemes were similar to those in London. This is reinforced by information noting that some upholders took out their freedom in their particular city.[22] Thomas Chippendale did not serve a London apprenticeship. He is thought to have learned the cabinet-making trade from Richard Wood, a cabinet-maker and joiner in York.[23] One can assume from using Chippendale as an example that there were capable furniture-makers and upholsterers in the provincial cities.

The manufacture, assembly, and retailing of furniture and providing upholstery services paralleled the role of Parisian *marchands merciers.* Their shops sold a wide range of residential interior goods similar to what London's upholders sold. They were also involved in the second-hand trade for interior goods. These merciers would often hire outside designers, and some were involved in the export/import business between France and Britain, especially through the trading centre at Dunkirk. Because of the shortage of hard currency, merciers, like upholders, relied on credit to purchase raw materials and inventory. Although credit and bankruptcy will be discussed later on, merciers faced credit and bankruptcy risk just as did London's upholders.[24] One significant difference between upholders and *marchands merciers* was that upholders often provided

2004), 76; Gilbert, *The Life & Work of Thomas Chippendale*, 77–78. Gilbert writes of the proliferation of design books; *The British and Irish Furniture Makers Online*, https://bifmo.history.ac.uk/about/project (accessed 12 October 2020). Using The British and Irish Furniture Makers Online database, a simple search was used to determine how many upholders were located in London and how many were from the provinces. The date range used was 1750 to 1780, the general active period of Thomas Chippendale. Using the search term 'upholder' for all locations, returned 986 upholders located throughout Britain and Ireland. Narrowing the search to London yielded 492 upholders. Subtracting the number of London upholders (492) from the total number of upholders in Britain and Ireland (986) equals 494 provincial upholders. This result confirms that upholders were spread throughout Britain and Ireland. It also confirms that London was the national hub for the upholding trade.

22 Beard, *Upholsterers and Interior Furnishing*, 5–8.

23 Gilbert, *The Life & Work of Thomas Chippendale*, 3–5.

24 Carolyn Sargentson *Merchants and Luxury Markets: The Marchands Merciers of Eighteenth-Century Paris* (London, Malibu: Victoria and Albert Museum in association with the J. Paul Getty Museum, 1996), 21, 23, 28–9, 33, 38, 81–2, 114, 118.

funeral undertaking goods and services, while merciers did not. They were similar in wanting to earn more money from consumer demand for fashionable residential interior goods. In London, it was livery companies, especially the Upholders' Company, that supplied this demand.

Livery Companies and Apprenticeship

Population growth increased demand for household goods in eighteenth-century London, which created a need for increased supply. Supply was provided in two ways: importation and domestic production. Formerly an importer of finished goods, Britain increasingly became an importer of raw materials and an exporter of finished goods.[25] London upholders were major suppliers of 'fashionable' household goods and either manufactured or acquired goods from wholesalers.[26] Upholders needed production employees who could meet consumer demand. Part of meeting demand was having a competent group of skilled employees and apprentices.

The Upholders' Company followed the same traditions as the other livery companies. When it came to labour, the tradition was that workers began as apprentices and, eventually, became members of the Upholders' Company as journeymen and 'free' to work as they pleased. The authority of City of London livery companies over their respective trades was absolute going into the seventeenth century. This iron-clad livery company control over their respective trades would not last.

The influence of livery companies over their membership and their trade was waning before the eighteenth century. Population growth is often the reason given for the demise of livery control over the trades and apprenticeship schemes. Joan Lane gives a logical reason for the decline in the importance of apprenticeships by the end of the eighteenth century. The sheer number of young people apprenticed into the manufacturing trades devalued the concept of apprenticeship as a way to learn a trade and become financially independent.[27] Was the decline in livery company

[25] Snodin and Styles, *Design & the Decorative Arts*, 25–26.

[26] Campbell, *The London Tradesman*, 169–70; Waller, *A general description of all trades*, 214–15.

[27] Joan Lane, *Apprenticeship in England, 1600–1914* (London: UCL Press, 1996), 3; Kirkham, *London Furniture Trade*, 215. See: T.K. Derry, "The Repeal of the Apprenticeship Clauses of the Statute of Apprentices," *The Economic History Review* Vol. 3, No. 1 (Jan. 1931): 67–87. Lane also points out that the apprenticeship system for the best careers and professions remained effective.

influence attributable to population growth? This was partially the case. What happened was that there was an increase in journeymen practicing a trade without a livery company affiliation, a situation that rankled livery companies. By the end of the seventeenth century, guilds were losing control over their respective trades because the population growth beyond the City walls and in the suburbs made it difficult to enforce livery company rules and oversee production. More importantly, J.R. Kellett detailed how livery companies lost legal cases that upended traditional customs and rules.[28] The implications from the Common Council (the City's legal authority) and livery companies losing court cases were great. The biggest implication was that the livery companies became mostly social and charity organizations by the first part of the nineteenth century.

The first case the Common Council lost was a 1599 ruling that the confiscation and forfeiture of goods from company searches was illegal. In that same year, a court ruled that company trade rules had to be 'constant to law and reason'. Also, in 1599, it was ruled that there was no binding force behind an ordinance prohibiting a freeman from sub-contracting work to non-freemen. In 1614, the Upholders' Company lost a case to compel a freeman from another company, but practising upholding, to seek admission to the Upholders' Company. Now, any freeman having served an apprenticeship in a trade could move to a different trade as they saw fit. Finally, in 1616, it was ruled that a tradesman trained outside London could not be compelled to join a livery company. Kellett cogently argues that these five cases, all decided before 1620, were responsible for the erosion of Common Council and livery company control over the craft and retail trades.[29]

[28] J.R. Kellett, "The Breakdown of Gild and Corporation Control over the Handicraft and Retail Trade in London," *The Economic History Review* New Series, Vol. 10, No. 3 (1958): 383. These five cases included: declaring as illegal searches made for banned or poorly made goods that were not consonant to law and reason [Watham v. Austin, C.P. 1599, Case of London, *8th Part, Reports of Sir Edward Coke125a*, Vol. IV, (J. F. Fraser's ed), 386–400]; overruling the rule that a freeman from a livery company could not practise another trade unless he joined the other company [J. Tolley v. Upholders' Company, W. Bohun, *Privilegia Londini* (1702), 115]; an ordinance preventing a freeman from sub-contracting work from a non-freeman was declared nonbinding [Davenant and Hurdis, *12 Coke, 86a*. W. Bohun, *Prinvilegia Londini* (1702), 115]; and two non-London cases that determined the Lord Mayor's Court forcing a non-freeman to join a livery company could be legally challenged [Pasch. 12 Jac, 9254 in Godbolt's Reports (1652), B.M. 6120, b6] and [Pasch. 14 Jac. 211 in Hobart's Reports (1641), B.M. 513, h19].

[29] Kellett, "Breakdown of Gild and Corporation Control," 383–85.

The impact of these legal decisions was not immediate and did not happen in lockstep. For instance, the Upholders' Company did not end searches for inferior (badly made) goods until about 1730. Even though company searches were ruled illegal in 1599, searches for inferior goods continued for some time. The livery companies had been very protective of the quality of the goods produced by their members. The fine for an upholder using sheep's leather in chairs was 20s. per chair, and the fine for using bad stuffing material was £5 for each offence. This rule fell by the wayside as, after 1726, searches for bad quality goods ended.[30]

Upholders' Company searches mostly involved the stuffing of bedding with improper materials. The best stuffing for mattresses, pillows, and cushions was dry-pulled and cleaned swan and goose feathers, but other waterfowl feathers and cleaned fleece were acceptable stuffing materials. Holly Fletcher's academic study of proper versus improper stuffing materials elaborated on the conflicts that arose among the Upholders' Company members. What some members considered improper was considered proper by other members. Population growth and a feeling that consumers generally understood what they were purchasing, whether new or used, led the Upholders' Company by 1730 to focus on other issues that threatened their livelihoods.[31] One of the problematic issues throughout much of the eighteenth century was bringing to heel upholders who had no livery company affiliation and, often, failed to register apprentices.

Originally controlled by medieval guilds, early modern government regulation over apprenticeships started during the reign of Elizabeth I. The government recognized that taxing apprenticeship agreements or 'bindings' was a new revenue source and, in 1709, extended this taxation by the Stamp Act. Because about a quarter of a million of these agreements were recorded between 1710 and 1762, the tax was an important revenue source. However, Joan Lane stated that there was probably a considerable amount of underreporting of bindings.[32]

The apprenticeship system had considerable advantages. The greatest was that good training provided a youngster with financial stability as an adult.[33] A fully trained youngster who became a journeyman was allowed

[30] Company of Upholders, *Financial History*, 5, 10.

[31] Holly Fletcher, "Making Beds in early modern England: sleep, matter and environmental change," *Historical Research* XX (2024): 1–22. Houston, *Featherbedds*, 29–34.

[32] Lane, *Apprenticeship in England*, 3; Kirkham, *London Furniture Trade*, 40.

[33] Lane, *Apprenticeship in England*, 2–3.

to work for wages. Generally, apprenticeship began at fourteen years of age and lasted seven years.[34] The tradition was that a youth's parents or guardian paid a premium to the master. In return, the master provided training in the trade and usually provided room and board. An apprenticeship indenture (also known as the apprenticeship agreement or binding) was signed that outlined the responsibilities of both parties.[35]

There were problems with apprenticeships, including unruly youths. A runaway apprentice was an occasional challenge masters faced in all the trades. Tradesmen sometimes placed newspaper advertisements asking for help in locating and apprehending runaway youngsters. William Brown was a nineteen-year-old who 'absented himself from his Master's Service'. His master was the Westminster upholder and undertaker William Horner, who advertised that anyone who returned him would be rewarded with a deal coffin and a wool shroud.[36] The number of advertisements concerning runaway youths is small, indicating this was a minor problem for upholders or, more likely, other methods of informing the public of runaways were used, including broadsheets and word of mouth.

Parents and guardians knew how apprenticeship schemes worked and were aware of the various routes for securing suitable training for a young man or woman. The youngster probably had some input into the selection process based on his/her aptitudes and preferences. Placing a younger son in a traditional scheme with a suitable master was a parental goal, even for the gentry. According to Kirkham, from 1712 to 1741, eight per cent of apprentice furniture-makers and twenty-two per cent of apprentice upholders were the younger sons of gentlemen.[37] Parents believed binding a younger son to a 'gentleman-tradesman' would help ensure that their son would retain the comportment taught to them at home.[38] Lane argues the most frequent way of finding an acceptable master was through

[34] Some apprenticeship age aggregations determine an average age of twenty. See: Robert Bucholz and Joseph Ward, *London: A Social and Cultural History 1550–1750* (Cambridge: Cambridge University Press, 2012), 79. Lane's research found that the average apprenticeship age depended on trade type, sex, and physical maturity. See: Lane, *Apprenticeship in England*, 12–14.

[35] Lane, *Apprenticeship in England*, 3, 12–17; Kirkham, *London Furniture Trade*, 40, 174–80.

[36] *Daily Advertiser*, 1 April 1743.

[37] Kirkham, *London Furniture Trade*, 172.

[38] Henry French and Mark Rothery, *Man's Estate: Landed Gentry Masculinities 1660–1900* (Oxford: Oxford University Press, 2012), 115.

personal connections. A parent sometimes knew a master, a relative, or a neighbour who could make a personal recommendation. Advertising by a master or a parent for training in a trade was another way of matching a youngster and a master. Non-London geographical connections were sometimes successful in securing a London apprenticeship.[39]

Gentry families apprenticed a younger son to an upholder because it could lead to financial independence and improved gentlemanly comportment.[40] Mr. Bradshaw, an upholder in Soho, advertised:

> Wanted an apprentice to an upholder. Parents or guardians wishing to establish a young man of good family and morals in a genteel business, where proper care will be taken care of him.[41]

Mr. Bradshaw, it appears, wanted a young man who would live up to the moral clauses of the standard indenture, which included promises not to gamble, fornicate, and drink alcohol. Mr. Bradshaw's responsibilities would have included providing room and board and the training needed to become financially independent. His advertisement characterized his upholding firm as a 'genteel business'. T. Waller's advice book from 1747 described upholding this way: '…the working part is not hard, but clean and genteel … therefore fit for smart youths, who have no strength to spare…'[42] Overall, securing a training arrangement with a respectable master enabled a younger gentry son, in a system of primogeniture, to enter a trade or profession that led to their financial independence. To this end, the apprentice system was integral in training competent employees as well as providing low-cost labour.

Tim Leunig, Chris Minns, and Patrick Wallis disputed the importance of social networks in searching for an apprenticeship. Their study found no overall evidence that placements were found through family or parental position.[43] These authors used data from sixty-five livery companies but admitted to missing data from some large companies, including the goldsmiths and the merchant tailors. With this data, they formed conclusions

[39] Lane, *Apprenticeship in England*, 9.
[40] French and Rothery, *Man's Estate*, 115.
[41] *Daily Advertiser*, 10 July 1777.
[42] Waller, *A general description of all trades*, 214–15.
[43] Tim Leunig, Chris Minns, and Patrick Wallis, "Networks in the Premodern Economy: The Market for London Apprenticeships, 1600–1749," *The Journal of Economic History* Vol. 71, No. 2 (Jun. 2011): 416.

about the apprenticeship system as a whole, rather than on a company-by-company basis. They concluded that formal training placements were found through indirect ties.[44] The work of Leunig, Minns, and Wallis is useful for understanding London employment demographics as a whole. Apprenticeship recruitment, in their opinion, was an open process where aptitudes were matched with opportunities, rather than a recruitment process based on personal ties.[45] In researching an individual livery company, the Upholders' Company in this case, the research of Leunig, Minns, and Wallis was helpful. However, with Kirkham and Lane's research in mind, personal connections among gentlemen did count in securing apprenticeships for younger sons and, occasionally, daughters.

It is possible to draw conclusions on how some upholder apprenticeships were found. The two case studies in this work indicate that a gentry background and familial connections were important factors in formal training placement. Robert Williams was from a Dorset gentry family and began his apprenticeship in 1749. His indenture cannot be located, which adds credence to Lane's statement that there was underreporting of apprenticeship bindings. However, there is much information about his upholding business and his entry into the banking and East India Company businesses.[46] John Trotter was from a Scottish gentry family and a cousin of the Coutts brothers, the founders of London's famous Coutts Bank. His indenture exists. He was bound to Henry Williams, the royal joiner.[47] These two cases illustrate that family and, possibly, geographic connections were important in finding apprenticeships for the Upholders' Company and the Joiners' Company.

For this study, Lane's research was more pertinent. Studying a specific livery company requires research into individuals, even those with common surnames such as Smith or Jones. A qualitative method rather than a quantitative approach helps us understand patronage or ties as a micro-study. As Margaret Ponsonby explains in her study of the nineteenth-century household, 'Whereas in quantitative analysis everything is reduced to averages and means and no individual household emerges, in the qualitative approach the analysis applies to the individual.'[48]

[44] Leunig, Minns, and Wallis, "Networks," 413–38.

[45] Leunig, Minns, and Wallis, "Networks," 436.

[46] See Chapter Four: Robert Williams. References 1, 3–9.

[47] See Chapter Five: John Trotter. References 1–3.

[48] Margaret Ponsonby, "Ideals, Reality and Meaning: Homemaking in England in the First Half of the Nineteenth Century," *Journal of Design History* 16, No. 3 (2003): 204.

By the last part of the eighteenth century, Paul Langford argued that training became 'dubious', as indicated by the training period being reduced to as low as three years.[49] Apprenticeship training may have been routinely lowered for some trades. However, Kirkham's study of the furniture trade challenges Langford's assertion and found that a seven-year training period was seen in at least eighty per cent of the cabinet-making and upholding apprenticeships between 1711 and 1779.[50] Relying on Langford's length of apprenticeship service as a proxy for the loss of livery control over all trades is suspect, which is especially true for the eighteenth-century furniture and upholding trades. These trades were largely unaffected by mechanical inventions and required substantial time to learn.[51]

It is difficult to pinpoint a specific reason for any particular high or low apprenticeship premium, often making conclusions from quantitative analysis somewhat speculative. The analysis of premiums for furniture-makers and upholders as a method to measure the loss of livery control is not useful in drawing meaningful conclusions. Even though quantitative information is available from the Tax Act records of apprenticeship premiums, it is difficult to determine significant upward or downward trends. The average premium for a trainee cabinet-maker was twenty-one pounds in the 1740s and twenty-four pounds in the 1780s. For the upholding trade, however, the average trainee premium rose from thirty-three pounds in the 1740s to fifty-two pounds in the 1780s, an increase that is not indicative of the loss of livery company control. There were even differences in apprenticeship premiums with the same master. The reasons for the differences in premiums are not often apparent, but it may be that a particular apprentice had a business sense that could be groomed for management. Or, it may be a family could not afford a higher premium. Kirkham mentioned that John Trotter received an unusually high £200 premium from the binding of Samuel Betts because of his management skills.[52] This high amount cannot be solely attributed to managerial talent. John Trotter's wife, Ann, was the illegitimate daughter of Mrs. Betts and

[49] Paul Langford, *A Polite and Commercial People: England 1727–1783* (Oxford: Clarendon Press, 1989), 180.

[50] For instance, a five-year apprenticeship was normal for lawyers, milliners, and mantua-makers. See: Lane, *Apprenticeship in England*, 15; Kirkham, *London Furniture Trade*, 174.

[51] Kirkham, *London Furniture Trade*, 109.

[52] Kirkham, *London Furniture Trade*, 44–45, 174–80.

John Locke, a member of the Turkey Company.[53] It is probable that Ann Betts Locke and Samuel Betts were sister and brother. Locke took responsibility for his illegitimate daughter and provided a £5000 marriage settlement.[54] He probably paid Trotter the high premium for Samuel's apprenticeship as another act of responsibility.

The Upholders' Company was male dominated, but women were admitted. Sarah Chapman, apprentice to Joseph William Thomas, was admitted free by servitude on 6 July 1737. She, in turn, bound Anna Hunt as an apprentice on 3 October 1737. Interestingly, Sarah Chapman bound her sister, Elizabeth, on 22 October 1747.[55] The upholding goods and services Sarah Chapman provided are not known. However, it is apparent that the Upholders' Company accepted women into their livery.

It was not unusual for women to run an upholding business, especially widows. For example, when upholder Peter Deschamps died, his widow and eldest son carried on the business.[56] Another example was Mrs. Ann Seabrook, widow of Samuel, who advertised that she 'intends to carry on the (upholding) business in all branches with the aid of a proper assistant'.[57] It is apparent that women were often knowledgeable of their husbands' businesses, enough that they could carry on the business. Hannah Farmborough is an example of a woman running a well-known upholding business. When her husband, William, died, she continued to run his upholding business, including continuing in the role as the royal upholsterer.[58]

The upholding trade probably relied on women for upholstery work. Robert Williams, for instance, met his wife, Jane Chassereau, while he was an apprentice upholder and she was working at the shop as an upholsterer.[59] It cannot be determined what type of upholding shop the women associated with Sarah Chapman worked in, but it may be that they

[53] Timothy Powys-Lybbe (heir general of John Trotter) et al., e-mail messages to author, 14 August to 17 August 2015; Trustees from the Turkey Company. http://www.british-history.ac.uk/survey-london/bk10/pp36-51 (accessed 23 November 2015).

[54] *London Evening Post*, 23–25 June 1752.

[55] Worshipful Company of Upholders in the City of London, *Meeting Notes of the Court of Assistants and Livery*, 6 July 1737, 3 October 1737, 22 October 1747. (Guildhall Repository) [hereafter Company of Upholders, *Meeting Notes*].

[56] *Gazetteer and New Daily Advertiser*, 23 July 1766.

[57] *Gazetteer and New Daily Advertiser*, 13 June 1768.

[58] *Public Advertiser*, 4 December 1773.

[59] Kenneth Holden et al., *Williams Deacon's 1771–1970* (Manchester: McCorquodale & Co. Ltd., 1971), 6–7.

specialized in fabric and upholstery work. There is also the possibility that they concentrated on the funeral undertaking business. Jane Whittle and Mark Hailwood's research into the female/male division of labour in south-western England found that in the craft and cloth industries is where women were frequently employed. Furthermore, their research concluded that in craft production there was a significant division of labour, where women predominately did certain tasks and men other tasks. Women, for instance, dominated the buying and selling of textiles.[60]

Although this research did not investigate how upholders' children carried on the business, some evidence emerged that the children of very successful upholders did not carry on the business. However, newspaper research did find examples of sons taking over their fathers' upholding businesses. When Mr. Carpenter died in 1775, for example, his son-in-law, who had managed the shop for several years, carried on the upholding business.[61] John Spurrier of Leadenhall Street announced he was opening his own business, following in the footsteps of his father, Jonathan, an auctioneer, appraiser, upholder, and undertaker of James Street.[62] When Mr. Weatherall retired, he announced 'his son will pick up the business'.[63] At Thomas Skerrett's death in 1789, his son carried on the business.[64] As for the daughters of upholders, nearly all news items were about marriages. However, there was one notable exception. Catherine Naish's father, Henry Williams, was the royal joiner, and after his death in 1759, she continued to supply furniture to the royal household.[65]

There was a defined route to becoming a member of the Upholders' Company, which included the area beyond the City's walls. The three main membership qualifications were servitude, patrimony, and redemption. Servitude was the most common qualification, followed by patrimony and redemption.[66]

[60] Jane Whittle and Mark Hailwood, "The gender division of labour in early modern England," *Economic History Review* 00, 0 (2018): 18, 23.

[61] *Daily Advertiser*, 17 September 1775.

[62] *Daily Advertiser*, 18 October 1777.

[63] *World*, 1 December 1788.

[64] *Morning Herald*, 19 January 1789.

[65] Kirkham, *London Furniture Trade*, 85. John Trotter was an apprentice for Henry Williams.

[66] Lane, *Apprenticeship in England*, 215. Parish and charity/pauper were other apprenticeship types. See: Stuart Raymond, *My Ancestor Was An Apprentice* (London: Society of Genealogists Enterprises Ltd., 2010), 13–26; Lane, *Apprenticeship in England*, 71–82.

It was an entrenched tradition among the City's companies to serve a seven-year apprenticeship known as servitude before becoming a journeyman member of the company and 'free' to work for pay. Upon completion of the apprenticeship by servitude, the master presented the aspiring upholder to the Court of Assistants (the membership) to become 'free' of the Upholders' Company as a journeyman. For the Upholders' Company, the standard practice for an apprentice accepting freedom by servitude was the presentation to the Company of a two-ounce silver spoon. In the eighteenth century, nearly all apprentices becoming journeymen paid a fine or fee of 10s. in lieu of silver plate.[67]

The Upholders' Company recognized that the children of livery members often learned the trade by growing up around the family business. The Company allowed these children to become free by patrimony. This method required the parent to be a member of the Company before the child was born. For instance, Robert Humphreys, son of William, was made free by patrimony on 3 May 1732, and Sarah Hallford, daughter of Samuel Hallford, was made free by patrimony on 29 October 1734.[68] Customary fees were still required to be paid at this time.

A third way of joining the Company was through redemption, which worked well for experienced tradesmen migrating to or immigrating to London. These trained tradesmen simply purchased their freedom. The total fees for redemption and, many times, the right to open a shop were 16s. 8d.[69]

A new livery membership enforcement method was developed by the 1750 Act of Common Council, which was responsible for governing the City of London and the surrounding seven miles. The Common Council and the livery companies tried as late as 1750 to regain their power. Finally, the Common Council of the City of London passed an act that reaffirmed the authority of livery companies, including the Upholders' Company, resulting in an increase in membership into the 1790s. (There were 1095 admissions into the Upholders' Company during the eighteenth century.)[70] This Act was passed because there was considerable concern within the

[67] The Worshipful Company of Upholders, *Worshipful Company of Upholders Financial History 1678–1939* (London: Printed for The Company, 1934. Reprinted 1999), 4.

[68] Company of Upholders, *Meeting Notes*, 3 May 1732, 29 October 1734.

[69] Company of Upholders, *Meeting Notes*, 21 September 1730.

[70] Kellett, "Breakdown of Gild and Corporation," 381–94; Walton, "The Worshipful Company of Upholders," 49–50; Houston, *Featherbedds*, 91–99; Kirkham, *London Furniture Trade*, 136–44.

Upholders' Company that a number of people practicing the upholding trade in the City and the surrounding seven miles were not freemen. With this in mind, the Upholders' Company petitioned the City's legal authority, the Common Council, for the passage of a law requiring practitioners of the upholding trade to be freemen of the Company.[71] The 'Act for Regulating the Company of Upholders in London' was passed in 1750 and recorded in the *Assistant's Book* on 30 July 1750. The aim was that non-freemen practising the upholding trade were required to join the Company under the Act, i.e. pay a fine (membership fee), or face legal consequences. Many joined, but one noted upholder who refused to conform was George Seddon of Aldersgate. Seddon ran the largest furniture company in London and consistently refused demands to become a Company freeman.[72] The Seddon situation must have been an embarrassment to the Company, and how best to get him to take his freedoms was discussed by the Court of Assistants on 4 July 1781.[73] For unknown reasons other than, perhaps, the threat of expensive legal action from the Company that he might have lost, George Seddon joined the Company in 1787 and began binding apprentices, including his nephew.[74]

The case of George Seddon is one example of what was happening to the livery companies. The tight control of apprenticeships and freedoms that they had known as late as 1700 was waning. Upholders often avoided Company rules by binding apprentices to other companies, and a few also purchased licences to hire non-freemen on a short-term basis, as long as at least one apprentice was properly bound.[75] The issues around the binding of apprentices were of minor concern. The real concern was tradesmen practising upholding but not being members of the Company. It is in this regard that the Upholders' Company was relentless in pursuing those who had not taken their freedom. On 7 January 1778, the Upholders' Company Court of Assistants ordered the Clerk to abstract and advertise in the *Daily Advertiser* 'The Act of Common Council from July 1750 "An Act for Regulating the Company of Upholders"'.[76] Still, as seen with George Seddon, there was resistance to joining the Company, and there were

[71] Company of Upholders, *Meeting Notes*, 30 July 1750.
[72] Kirkham, *London Furniture Trade*, 48.
[73] Company of Upholders, *Meeting Notes*, 4 July 1781.
[74] Kirkham, *London Furniture Trade*, 142–143.
[75] Kirkham, *London Furniture Trade*, 143.
[76] Company of Upholders, *Meeting Notes*, 7 January 1778.

upholders like John Cobb who successfully avoided taking his freedom in the Company.[77]

Even with the resolution of the Seddon situation, the Company continued to face challenges in bringing interlopers into the membership. The Company was losing its importance. Upholders without Company membership profited from the accelerating consumerism occurring in the last half of the eighteenth century. For upholding, the formal apprenticeship system had significantly declined by the early nineteenth century. This decline was not because of a surplus of young apprentices learning the trade elsewhere or because of mechanization, but because the Upholders' Company itself no longer had control over the upholding trade. Apprentices were still needed to learn the trade, but often they were taken on outside Company control. The economic benefits of livery company membership were less and less attractive, and by the nineteenth century, the Company became mostly a philanthropic and social organization.[78]

The Empire

Robert Williams (Chap. 4) was a beneficiary of commercial trading in the British Empire. After establishing and operating a successful upholding business, he became the managing partner of a prosperous bank and the owner of thirteen British East India Company (EIC) ships. Williams accumulated great wealth in his lifetime. The EIC stockowners were primarily from what can be called the 'commercial aristocracy'.[79] Williams's rise into the commercial aristocracy is an example of the trading opportunities available within the British Empire. Another upholder studied in this work, John Trotter (Chap. 5), also became commercially successful. In contrast to Williams, Trotter did not accumulate wealth from overseas trading. He was a military contractor and capitalized on supplying the army camp equipment needed by British troops stationed throughout the Empire. These are just two examples of the wealth that was created with the growth of the British Empire in the eighteenth century.

[77] Walton, "The Worshipful Company of Upholders," 50.

[78] Walton, "The Worshipful Company of Upholders," 50.

[79] H.V. Bowen, "Investment and Empire in the Later Eighteenth Century: East India Stockholding, 1756–1791," *The Economic History Review* Vol. 42, No. 2 (May 1989): 191–92, 194–95.

The British Empire grew throughout the eighteenth century because of war, mostly with France. The Royal Navy was formidable at the end of the War of the Spanish Succession (1701–13), when France and Spain agreed to a peace. Britain defeated France again in the Seven Years' War (1756–63). War started again in 1793 between Britain and France, this time lasting nearly twenty-five years. Britain's successes in these wars meant that it protected its colonies and trade routes, allowing the Empire to grow, despite losing colonies in the American Revolution. Through control of the sea, Britain had a free flow of trade to North America and the West Indies and growing trade with India. Formerly an importer of finished goods, Britain increasingly became an importer of raw materials and an exporter of finished goods.[80]

The East India Company trade with China and Japan created new opportunities for upholders selling furniture and tableware. While only the nobility and wealthy could afford genuine Chinese porcelain or lacquered cabinets, Europeans began to copy original works in a style known as 'chinoiserie'.[81] As the Chinese and Japanese kept porcelain and lacquer formulas secret, European craftsmen experimented with making their own.[82] Dutch and English blue-and-white earthenware ceramics called 'Delftware' were made and painted in the manner of genuine Chinese porcelain.[83] English-made furniture was lacquered in a Chinese style with homemade recipes, a process called 'japanning', which became a 'fashionable pursuit' in the late 1600s, lasting well into the mid-eighteenth century.[84] One can speculate about why the term 'japanning' was used rather than another term, but it may be that the European craftsmen did not distinguish between lacquered furniture from China and that from Japan because of the lack of complete geographical understanding at that time.[85]

Atlantic commerce brought opportunities to upholders in the furniture trade, not only for new furniture but for used furniture too. Mahogany, for instance, replaced walnut as the furniture wood of choice for English cabinet-makers, though it was not used exclusively. Mahogany was brought

[80] Snodin and Styles, *Design & the Decorative Arts*, 22–26.

[81] Snodin and Styles, *Design & the Decorative Arts*, 45.

[82] Percy MacQuoid, *A History of English Furniture* (London: Bracken Books, 1988), 305–309.

[83] Peter Ward-Jackson, *English Furniture Designs of the 18th Century* (London: HMSO – Victoria & Albert Museum, 1958), 131.

[84] MacQuoid, *A History of English Furniture*, 156–63.

[85] Adam Bowett, *Early Georgian Furniture 1715–1740*, 148–49.

back to English ports from the West Indies in enormous quantities after the import duties on timber were removed in 1733. So much was available that furniture was often made of solid mahogany, as opposed to being made with veneers, which was previously common with walnut. Mahogany was considered as beautiful as walnut in colour and figure, and it was relatively easy to carve compared to walnut and oak, allowing for finer details.[86] Along with new mahogany furniture, upholders could now sell used oak and walnut furniture.

While commercial and military interests made money from the British Empire's colonies, there were some who made their fortunes at a terrible human cost that was at play with British Imperialism. This is apparent in this 1773 advertisement by E. Smith, an upholder from Blackfriars:

> … To the Captains and Gentlemen trading to the East Indies a musical clock suitable for the slave trade.[87]

Approximately 1300 upholder news items and advertisements from the eighteenth century were examined, and this advertisement was the only mention of the slave trade. The EIC was not involved in the Atlantic slave trade.[88] However, the EIC had become more involved in the Indian Ocean slave trade when this advertisement was published. Richard Allen estimates that the English traded approximately 10,500–12,500 Indian Ocean slaves from 1628 to 1789. Of that total, 8000–10,000 slaves were traded from 1762 to 1781.[89] Allen's research corresponds with the end of the Seven Years' War and the British gaining control of the Indian subcontinent. It is probable that the upholder, E. Smith, knew that the EIC had increased its involvement in the Indian Ocean slave trade and believed the musical clock was a suitable barter item.

[86] MacQuoid, *A History of English Furniture*, 216–17.

[87] *Daily Advertiser*, 7 December 1773; Walton, "The Company of Upholders," 43, 62. E. Smith was probably Edward Smith who became free of the Upholders' Company by servitude in 1765.

[88] Kenneth Morgan, "Remittance Procedures in the Eighteenth-Century British Slave Trade," *The Business History Review* Vol. 79, No. 4 (Winter 2005): 716–17, 722. British slave ships were individual charters and did not sail in a convoy system.

[89] Richard B. Allen, "Satisfying the 'Want for Labouring People': The European Slave Trading in the Indian Ocean, 1500–1850," *Journal of World History* Vol. 21, No. 1 (Mar 2010): 62–3. The French, in comparison, traded approximately 335,000 to 384,000 Indian Ocean slaves from 1670 to 1848.

There is no evidence that any of the ships Robert Williams owned participated in transporting Indian Ocean or Atlantic slaves. Still, as pointed out by Allen, forced migrations and slavery were important in creating imperial networks within the colonies.[90] It was from these colonial networks that goods such as tobacco, mahogany, and Indian fabrics were imported into Britain at attractive prices. Most consumers at that time probably knew that the tobacco they smoked, the solid mahogany chair they sat in, or the Indian chintz shirt they wore had been largely gotten from colonial forced labour. The use of forced labour would have been especially known in the last quarter of the eighteenth century with the increased publicity of the Wilberforce and Wedgwood anti-slavery campaigns. Luxury came at a high moral price.

Not all the goods that upholders sold were domestically or colonial-produced, which made it important that upholders and other retailers understood the laws relating to imported goods. After the Seven Years' War, Britain instituted a variety of trade regulations that concerned the American colonies. Although the seventeenth-century Navigation Act, which allowed the importation of continental goods into the American colonies upon payment of a re-export tax at a British port, was still in place, the British government under George Grenville (1763–1765) began making rule changes. Subsequent governments amended, withdrew, or added new regulations, creating uncertainty among domestic and colonial manufacturers and merchants. One justification for these changing laws was that continental Europe was becoming more protectionist, a trade war mentality. However, the new regulations were probably not as much about protecting domestic production as they were about increasing tax revenues. Stephen Conway's points out that these regulations did not stop the colonists from buying both illegal and legal foreign goods.[91]

The high import duties on imported goods encouraged smuggling and duty-dodging. This was especially so with tea. The Commutation Act of 1784 dramatically lowered the tax on tea, resulting in increased tea consumption.[92] The reduction of the tea tax may seem like a shift in government policy from the reliance on heavy taxation in favour of increasing

[90] Allen, "The European Slave Trading in the Indian Ocean," 73.

[91] Stephen Conway, "British Governments, Colonial Consumers, and Continental European Goods in the British Atlantic Empire, 1763–1775," *The Historical Journal* 58, 3, (2015): 717–27, 729, 731–32.

[92] Jon Stobart, "Making the global local? Overseas goods in English rural shops, c. 1600–1760," *Business History* 59:7, (Mar 2017): 1138–41, 1148.

demand so much that the tax reduction was revenue-neutral, that is no tax revenue was lost. Neutrality was not the case, however, because the bill also included a tax on windows as a method to make up for lost tea tax revenue.[93] The relaxation of import duties would have allowed upholders to expand their offerings and give their customers more choices. Without the relaxation of import duties on furniture and household goods, some upholders resorted to duty-dodging and smuggling to satisfy client needs.

As was previously mentioned, goods were traded between France and Britain through the port at Dunkirk. There was demand for French furniture, and upholders endeavoured to meet this demand. British customs officials had the responsibility of inspecting cargos to ensure compliance with import rules and taxation. The following newspaper article describes an upholder who violated the rules:

> Friday afternoon a considerable seizure was made of French sofas, chairs, and other cabinet-work, at an eminent upholder and cabinet-maker's, not many miles from Soho, which goods yesterday evening conveyed in wagons, escorted by several journeymen, to the Custom House ...[94]

In this instance, the upholder had several French furniture items confiscated. Among these items were chair fronts, feet, side rails and stretchers, and cane seats. Apparently, these were imported as pieces and intended for assembly. The customs authorities also confiscated fully assembled chairs. Just how the customs officials discovered the illegal items is unknown. It may be that another upholder alerted officials of the violation. Importing goods in pieces for later assembly was not illegal; dodging customs to avoid duties and taxes was. The issue was resolved on 17 November 1772 when the upholder paid a fine of £137.4.6 for the pieces of French furniture. The fully assembled furniture was valued at £64.13.0, apparently not subject to a fine.[95]

[93] Hoh-Cheung and Lorna Mui, "William Pitt and the Enforcement of the Commutation Act, 1784–1788," *The English Historical Review* Vol. 76, No. 300 (Jul. 1961): 447–65. This act reduced the tax on tea from 119 to 19.5 per cent, which effectively ended the financial incentives associated with smuggling tea. At the same time, The British East India Company achieved trade dominance with China.

[94] *Gazetteer and New Daily Advertiser*, 6 July 1772.

[95] The National Archives, Kew. CUST 21/75. No. 50, 3 July 1772. Revenue Commissioners and Boards of Customs: Miscellaneous Books. Register of Seizures. The upholder was John Brookege or Brookeye, depending on the interpretation of the handwritten name.

Thomas Chippendale was also among the upholders caught trying to evade import duties on French furniture. After having visited Paris the year before, customs officials seized sixty French chair frames in 1769 that he illegally imported. He undervalued the chair parts, probably reporting them as lumber. Illegally imported textiles were also seized from him, including Indian chintz owned by Mrs. Garrick and meant for her bedroom suite.[96]

Upholders probably did not care much about what made the Empire grow. What mattered to them were the business opportunities it brought to their shop doors. The Empire was not just a commercial exchange enterprise, nor just about exchanging commodities. The British Empire, according to Natasha Glaisyer, was comprised of many different networks: scientific, political, cultural, commodity, and other networks that interacted together.[97] Cain and Hopkins argued that the driving force for the growth of the Empire was not industrialization or a combination of networks as Glaisyer suggested. British Empire growth was initially driven by a small group of elite landowners, sometimes called 'rentier capitalists' because their income was derived from rents. Manufacturers had little political influence because they were occupied with running their businesses and, located in cities such as Manchester and Birmingham, were generally isolated from the City's commercial networks. Gentleman capitalists were not burdened with work, understood the market economy, wielded political influence, and drove the Empire forward. Aristocratic dominance was challenged by the 'monied interest' during the eighteenth century. Among the 'monied interests' were the merchants, bankers, and shippers, located in the City.[98] Whether or not it was aristocratic or the commercial wealth that upholders most sought out as customers is not known, but their wealth certainly attracted high-end upholders.

Cain and Hopkins's belief that aristocratic landowners and 'monied interests' drove British colonial expansion is compelling. However, Glaisyer's argument that the Empire grew because of the interlocking of various networks should not be dismissed. The case studies of Robert Williams and John Trotter highlight the importance of family and social

[96] Gilbert, *The Life & Work of Thomas Chippendale*, 16, 36–7.

[97] Natasha Glaisyer, "Networking: Trade and Exchange in the Eighteenth-Century British Empire," *The Historical Journal* Vol. 47, No. 2 (Jun. 2004): 467–76.

[98] P.J. Cain and A.G. Hopkins, "Gentlemanly Capitalism and British Expansion Overseas I. The Old Colonial System, 1688–1850," *The Economic History Review* Vol. 39, No. 4 (Nov. 1986): 503–25.

networks in achieving commercial success. Both men benefited from the Empire. By coming from minor gentry families, they had the social connections and access to the money needed to enter the upholding business and, eventually, other business enterprises. Much of their initial success can be attributed to their familial networks.

Material Culture

Studying material culture gives insight into behaviour, social rank, and residential interiors. Upholders were important contributors to the material culture of eighteenth-century London through the materials, ornamentation, and designs they used. It may be that many of them did not fully understand the historical meanings of, for instance, neoclassical ornament and merely copied furniture made in that style. Nonetheless, to make a profit, upholders needed some understanding of the material culture that their business depended on.

Karen Harvey argued that the historical study of material culture is a way to understand the multi-faceted lives of people.[99] Archaeologists studying material culture, according to Helen Berry, ask questions about an artefact's form and function, which are classified into two areas: the *material* and the *contextual*. The material questions archaeologists ask about an artefact's form can include such things as the material used and its source, the construction methods employed to create it, and its production date. Contextual questions are asked about an object's function, including who used it and how and when it was used.[100] Answering material and contextual questions requires our mind to process the information and make judgements. This mental processing allows us to understand an object's function and gives it context. Determining social standing is complex, and scholars have shown that studying material culture offers insights into social status.

Social standing depended on numerous considerations: family, property, profession, and less definably 'connections', 'politeness', and 'breeding'.[101] Paul Langford opines that applying these considerations to

[99] Karen Harvey, "Introduction," in *History and Material Culture*, ed. Karen Harvey (Abingdon: Routledge, 2009), 12.

[100] Helen Berry, "Regional identity and material culture," in *History and Material Culture*, ed. Karen Harvey (Abingdon: Routledge, 2009), 141–42.

[101] Paul Langford, *A Polite and Commercial People*, 62.

a material item creates contextual information. Ultimately, this played a large part in determining a person's social rank. Langford's considerations, however, go beyond the messaging associated with material culture, and, for instance, are among the conditions considered for an acceptable marriage. Harvey's point that the historical study of material culture aids in understanding the complexities of people's lives and experiences is an important one, and the archaeologist's method of breaking down the study of material culture into the *material* and the *contextual* is a reminder that even an everyday object can have significance.

Chairs were everyday items sold by upholders, but by adding upholstery, the chair might have more significance. A simple object with significant contextual meaning is the eighteenth-century clay tobacco pipe. Mostly men used them in a social context in settings like pubs and coffee houses. Pipes subtly changed over time and usually had a maker's mark, which makes dating them easy. They were inexpensive and disposable, making them common archaeological finds. Pipes are not of much intrinsic interest to the archaeologist as a tobacco-smoking implement, but they are useful in dating when the pipe and other objects were disposed of in the area being studied. The clay pipe and other objects found in the study area can be put into a material context for a certain date. Material study helps scholars understand whether there was previously a pub, a residence, or a rubbish pit on the site, and how frequently the poor, middling sort, wealthy, or military frequented there.[102]

A recent excavation of a building site that was used by eighteenth-century upholders illustrates how archaeologists can determine the material culture and social lives of the occupants. From 2011 to 2015, Museum of London Archaeology undertook the excavation and study of New Church Graveyard and the surrounding areas as part of the Crossrail Central project. An area bordering the graveyard was formerly known as 1 Brokers Row, located near modern-day Liverpool and Blomfield Streets, City of London. The building and shops of 1 Brokers Row were razed long ago, but two cess pits at the building site were uncovered and excavated. The first cess pit was cleaned and filled in during the 1770s, and the

[102] Sara Pennell, "Material Culture in Seventeenth-Century 'Britain': The Matter of Domestic Consumption," in *The Oxford Handbook of The History of Consumption*, ed. Frank Trentmann (Oxford: Oxford University Press, 2012), 74–76; Sara Pennell, "Mundane materiality, or, should small things still be forgotten?," in *History and Material Culture*, ed. Karen Harvey (Abingdon: Routledge, 2009), 178.

second pit was cleaned and filled in during the early 1780s. The fill in the pits included unwanted and often broken household goods. The bulk of the excavated objects were used for drinking and eating. Parts from wine glasses, including small shards, were found and dated. The bulk of the eating and dining vessels and plates were of Chinese porcelain, although some English and Continental pieces, usually broken, were also found and dated. Several wine bottles were uncovered, and pipes for smoking were a common find. Several pipe bowls were marked, some manufactured by known makers and others by unknown makers. There were a handful of items that would have been used by an upholder, including what is probably a lathe turning tool, furniture handles, and a shop bell. Most of the artefacts dated from the middle decades of the eighteenth century.

From using a variety of sources, including land tax and parish records, trade directories, and advertisements, the occupants of 1 Brokers Row were identified as upholders and brokers of household goods. Two of these occupants, Henry Hall and James Bolter, were members of the Upholders' Company. The archaeology study concluded that the bulk of the artefacts most likely belonged to the families that lived there, rather than being business remnants. These families owned fine porcelain and glassware, indicating their households lived a comfortable lifestyle. From a material culture standpoint, these items represent the households of good taste and social standing of tradesmen at the top end of the middling rank.[103]

There can be a regional interpretation of material culture, as pointed out by Helen Berry in her case study of north-east England glass manufacturers. There existed a bias that goods manufactured in or imported into London were the most prestigious. In north-east England (Tyneside), the Beilby family was noted for sourcing goblets and bowls from Newcastle lead glass manufacturers and adding white enamel and other decorative elements to them. Within its region of manufacture, Beilby glass was considered ordinary glassware. In London, however, Beilby glass was seen as sophisticated and used on special occasions. Beilby glass was expensive and difficult to make, which highlighted the wealth and status of the owner. While the enamel work and engraving were recognized as artistic achievements, the status of owning this glassware was increased by the use of

[103] Robert Hartle, Nigel Jeffries, and Jaqui Pearce, "Household Assemblages Discarded by Moorfields Brokers: Material Culture in 18th-Century", *Transactions of the London & Middlesex Archaeology Society* Volume 72–2021: 301–348.

familiar symbols seen by young aristocrats and wealthy gentry sons during their Grand Tour of classical Italy and Greece and through adding British iconography. These decorations made Beilby glassware appropriate for a sophisticated London dinner party.[104]

This regional bias against local manufacturers applied to regional upholders. Although many provincial upholders could craft furniture and upholstery goods according to the latest designs, there was a bias that only imported or London-made goods were socially sophisticated. Using Chippendale as an example, he developed the necessary skills from his York apprenticeship to become an esteemed London cabinet-maker. His *Director* and other design books allowed regional upholders to manufacture stylish furniture. If there were regional upholders capable of manufacturing fashionable furniture and upholstery goods, why was Chippendale's firm and not a York upholder hired to furnish Harewood House? Vanity may have played a large part in the decision, but there were practical reasons, too. An expensive commission like Harewood House needed the best materials, which were readily available from London's mercers and timber merchants. The commission required a large shop of experienced tradesmen and access to specialist sub-contractors. Finally, the contracted upholder needed the ability to produce drawings of the proposed furnishings and sketch out how the room would appear. There were disadvantages in using a London upholder for a country estate like Harewood House. Shipping the finished goods and sending shop workmen to install the commission at Harewood were added expenses. Using a competent local upholder would avoid much of these expenses.

British eighteenth-century material culture had many forms. Upholders, for instance, provided a range of residential interior goods. Luxury goods in the mid-to-late century included the furniture and goods associated with dining.[105] There are, however, problems with drawing conclusions from studying eighteenth-century luxury items. Sara Pennell points out that the main problem in studying items in museum collections is that they are usually luxury objects that lack provenance, meaning that the conclusions about how they fit into the material culture of the time are mainly speculative. Furthermore, she argues that the poor had a material

[104] Berry, "Regional identity and material culture," 145–53.

[105] Maxine Berg, "Luxury, The Luxury Trades, and Industrial Growth," in *The Oxford Handbook of The History of Consumption*, ed. Frank Trentmann (Oxford: Oxford University Press, 2012), 186.

culture as well as the elite. Finally, Pennell points out that even repurposed second-hand clothing was part of the overall material culture.[106] Her position that the worn and used could be repurposed is confirmed by Jon Stobart's study of the recycling of goods from country houses and Olivia Fryman's writing about how the Stuart Court's out-of-fashion and broken furniture was often remade or altered.[107] An upholder's shop had the ability to repair and alter furniture and the talent to repurpose upholstery goods.

Considering that it was not just luxury materials that had an attached cultural meaning validates Harvey's belief that comprehending the complexities of people's lives and experiences is a critical endeavour in the study of material culture. Eighteenth-century material culture was complex because the consumers of material goods were from differing social status levels and moved between them on occasion. Pennell's belief that worn and used material had its own culture adds to the complexity. In studying material culture, argues Richard Grassby, the most effective method is to combine written literature, both primary and secondary, with the physical evidence.[108] This is true, but, as Pennell points out, the link between the literature and the material is usually missing.[109]

The material of objects and their iconography do not necessarily provide information about past personal and social lives, according to Grassby. He warns that attaching meaning to an object that is no longer in its original context is speculation, as people thought differently in the eighteenth century than they do today.[110] Following Grassby's line of thinking would appear to make it impossible to find context for nearly any eighteenth-century image or artefact, given that documentation is scant. His theory highlights the need for cultural historians to develop cogent opinions based on the best information they have.

[106] Pennell, "Material Culture in Seventeenth-Century," 67–70, 78–83; Richard Grassby, "Material Culture and Cultural History," *The Journal of Interdisciplinary History* Vol. 39, No. 4 (Spring 2005): 597–98.

[107] Jon Stobart, "Luxury and Country House Sales in England, c. 1760–1830," in *The Afterlife of Used Things: Recycling in the Long Eighteenth Century*, ed. Ariane Fennetaux, Amélie Junqua, and Sophie Vasset (New York: Routledge, 2015), 31–2, 34; Olivia Fryman, "Recycling Furniture in the Late Stuart Court (1689–1714)," in *The Afterlife of Used Things: Recycling in the Long Eighteenth Century*, ed. Ariane Fennetaux, Amélie Junqua, and Sophie Vasset (New York: Routledge, 2015), 89–92.

[108] Grassby, "Material Culture and Cultural History," 602–3.

[109] Pennell, "Material Culture in Seventeenth-Century," 78–83.

[110] Grassby, "Material Culture and Cultural History," 598–601, 603.

Andrew Morrall provides a good contrast to Grassby's thinking, at least when it comes to decorative art. He claims that ornamentation was responsible for proclaiming a decorative art object as something with 'definable social, political, ideological, or cultural values'.[111] Morrall's belief that ornamentation could turn a decorative art object into one with various meanings should not be taken at face value for two reasons. First, the ornamentation of an object must be purposeful and transform it by assigning it a meaning beyond that of being a well-made item of decorative art. 'Viewers' (those who see the object) must also be able to 'read' (understand the meaning) the object, although they may disagree on its meaning. Reading an object assumes the viewer understands the creator's intended message, which can be subject to various interpretations. Nonetheless, cultural historians continually develop opinions about the meanings of objects' ornamentation.

There were also different levels of viewers. Considering that Campbell believed upholders understood what made a fashionable interior, it follows that they also knew what was fashionable and stylish for their customers' social rank. The social elite and the country gentry were the highest level of viewers, many of whom experienced the Grand Tour. These were the high-end customers sought by elite upholders. The middling sort was another type of viewer. Lorna Weatherill considered the middling sort as being comprised of 'lesser gentry, professions, merchants, shopkeepers, farmers, yeomen, husbandmen, and tradesmen'.[112] The middling sort could read and write, but many were not aware of iconographic meanings. Jon Stobart believes that fashion distinguished the elite from the other ranks. Elite taste was 'exclusive rather than inclusive' and 'insulated them from democratization of consumption'.[113] Could this exclusiveness be attributed to the elite's desire to maintain control and retain power over the lesser ranks? Perhaps, but being wealthy in itself also contributed to the elite maintaining control and retaining power over the middling sort and poor rather than merely owning an elite interior object, which only

[111] Andrew Morrall, "Ornament as evidence," in *History and Material Culture*, ed. Karen Harvey (Abingdon: Routledge, 2009), 47.

[112] Lorna Weatherill, *Consumer Behaviour & Material Culture in Britain 1660–1760* (Abingdon: Routledge, 1996), 13–14; Lorna Weatherill, "The meaning of consumer behaviour in late seventeenth- and early eighteenth-century England," in *Consumption and the World of Goods*, ed. John Brewer and Roy Porter (London: Routledge, 1993), 210.

[113] Jon Stobart, "Gentlemen and shopkeepers: supplying the country house in eighteenth-century England," *The Economic History Review* Vol. 64, No. 3 (Aug. 2001): 897.

the elite could properly see and understand. Wealth and elite objects were connected to each other and wielded power. It was not only interior objects that expressed power, but exterior objects, too. Objects of wealth like carriages and home exteriors, for instance, were seen as an expression of taste and status.[114]

If the middling sort were unable to read the meaning of an object, then why would they purchase it? Again, upholders determined fashionable and stylish interior furnishings for the middling ranks and probably explained material meanings to their customers. Some historians believe the middling sort purchased fashionable and stylish objects because they wanted to emulate the elite. Cynthia Wall argued that the non-elite purchased fine and decorative art at auctions as a way to project themselves into a higher social order.[115] Wall's argument from 1997 probably emanated from Neil McKendrick and Grant McCracken's claim from the 1980s that consumerism was driven by status emulation.[116] In contrast, Weatherill disagreed with this assertion because there was no proof that the middling ranks approved of emulating the social elite.[117] Jon Stobart's recent study on the auctions of the household goods of Northamptonshire area country homes found no convincing proof that consumers of second-hand goods were motivated to emulate a higher order. It was purchasing a quality item at a reduced price or obtaining an item that could not be gotten elsewhere that appealed to buyers of used goods at country home auctions.[118] Although some emulation by the middling sort of the elite's household goods probably happened, the middling rank bought stylish and fashionable home furnishings for a variety of other reasons, which could include the attractiveness of the object's materials, seeing the item as a conversation piece, or that the buyer simply enjoyed its appearance.

In the last half of the eighteenth century, the middling sort had choices of how to spend their money. They acquired items that defined their own

[114] Anne Laurence, "Using buildings to understand social history," in *History and Material Culture*, ed. Karen Harvey (Abingdon: Routledge, 2009), 115–17.

[115] Cynthia Wall, "The English Auction: Narratives of Dismantling," *Eighteenth-Century Studies* Vol. 31, No. 1 (Fall, 1997): 1–15.

[116] Neil McKendrick, John Brewer, J.H. Plumb, *The Birth of a Consumer Society: The Commercialization of Eighteenth-Century England* (Bloomington: Indiana University Press, 1982), 11; Grant McCracken, *Culture and Consumption* (Bloomington: Indiana University Press, 1988), 19–21, 40.

[117] Weatherill, *Consumer Behaviour*, 20, 194–97.

[118] Stobart, "Luxury and Country House Sales," 31–2, 34.

identity and tastes. Would a consumer purchase a decorative or furniture item because sweeping C- and S-scrolls, chinoiserie decoration, or exotic materials were visually attractive and created conversation? Simply enjoying an item because of its beautiful appearance, rather than its possible social meaning, could have applied to the middling order, especially those at the lower end. Perhaps those at the lower end purchased used and worn items that gave them enjoyment, whether or not they could understand the material culture meanings. One must also consider that an upholder selling new and used interior goods to the middling sort provided some information to customers about an item's meaning.

Probate and appraisal analysis is sometimes used to determine which occupations and social groups owned certain goods. Lorna Weatherill noted that probate studies are useful to the study of material culture, but not perfect. Problems with using probate inventories occur because they were not done in a standardized way.[119] For instance, appraisals were often done at low valuations because, if the goods did not sell at the appraised value, the appraiser could be required to buy the items at the appraised value. Also, household goods were often valued on a lump sum basis rather than itemized, making it difficult to interpret what individual objects were worth, which makes conclusions based on probate inventories somewhat subjective.[120] Within this scholarship, the emulation argument to explain aspects of consumerism is subjective. However, Jon Stobart's research into eighteenth-century country house sales provides valuable and verifiable insight into how luxury items were purchased for recycling, rather than for emulation of a higher social order.

Taste, Fashion, and Style

Britain was a laggard in design at the beginning of the eighteenth century, but by the time the century ended, it was among the world's leaders in artistic development and style. One reason for this rapid change in artistic competency was the relocation of French and other continental artisans to countries throughout Europe, including England, during the late-seventeenth and early-eighteenth centuries. Many of these artisans were

[119] Weatherill, *Consumer Behaviour*, 201–207.

[120] Joshua Montefiore, *A Commercial Dictionary: Containing the Present State of Mercantile Law, Practice, and Custom* (London: For the Author, 1803), APP. No page number; indexed by subject.

Protestant refugees from Catholic France. These French Huguenots, many of whom were skilled craftsmen from the state-sponsored workshops of Louis XIV, had learned about French design. Part of their artistic education was in drawing, a requirement for rococo design. Along with drawing, designing required an understanding of classical architecture and its emphasis on proportion.[121]

St. Martin's Lane Academy and Old Slaughter's Coffee House were where many London artists and craftsmen congregated. It is likely that Matthew or Matthias Darly (c.1720–1778?) was the master who taught Chippendale the intricacies of rococo drawing because he collaborated with Chippendale on the *Director*, engraving ninety-eight of the one hundred and forty-seven plates. Darly was primarily an engraver and well known to London cabinet-makers. He engraved plates for pattern books and produced some of his own designs. In 1748, he advertised his own chair designs and drawing lessons for tradesmen in St. Martin's Lane.[122]

Drawing was a necessary skill for upholders, especially those considered elite.[123] In the first part of the eighteenth century, architects were the main furniture designers.[124] By mid-century, furniture-makers often created their own designs.[125] Some upholders had warehouses (showrooms) where clients could see examples of how a furnished room would look.[126] Those with drawing ability could sketch out how a suite of furniture would look, even an entire room. John Linnell produced many drawings, and

[121] Snodin and Styles, *Design & the Decorative Arts*, 14, 27; Kirkham, *London Furniture Trade*, 96–101; Amanda Vickery, *Behind Closed Doors at Home in Georgian England* (New Haven & London: Yale University Press, 2009), 279–283.

[122] Gilbert, *The Life & Work of Thomas Chippendale*, 5–7; Matthew or Matthias Darly (c.1720–1778?) published *A New Book of Chinese, Gothic and Modern Chairs* (1751), *A New Book of Chinese Designs* (1754), and *The Chair-Makers' Guide* (1766). His Chinese designs were used in the production of chinoiserie linens and wallpaper. Darly and his wife, Mary, became known for their political satire prints after 1760. See: Kirkham, *London Furniture Trade*, 97; Snodin and Styles, *Design & the Decorative Arts*, 47, 79, 86–7, 93; Christopher Gilbert, "The Early Furniture Designs of Mathias Darly," *Furniture History* Vol. 11 (1975): 33–39; Timothy Clayton, "Darly, Matthias," in *Oxford Dictionary of National Biography*. 23 September 2004. For a discussion of Chippendale, Darly, designers, and Old Slaughter's Coffee House, See: Heckscher, Morrison, "Chippendale's Director: A Manifesto of Furniture Design," *The Metropolitan Museum of Art Bulletin* Vol.75, No. 4 (Spring 2018): 1–50.

[123] Campbell, *The London Tradesman*, 172, 175.

[124] Gilbert, *The Life & Work of Thomas Chippendale*, 94–98.

[125] Kirkham, *London Furniture Trade*, 96–101.

[126] Edwards, *Turning Houses into Homes*, 44–50.

Chippendale often produced coloured sketches.[127] For an upholder's clients, visualizing furniture was an important part of the sales process. Sketches of furnished interior spaces, along with showrooms, were critical to selling new, tasteful designs.

It is difficult to determine who were the arbiters of 'modern taste', but the royal court was not the main leader in taste, as it was in France. The royal court was not very influential in defining eighteenth-century English taste, not because they were unsophisticated, but because the early Georgian kings had to be frugal. They simply had limited funds provided by Parliament that had to be allocated across several areas. The architect William Kent designed a new royal mews, but St. James's Palace remained a ramshackle mess in contrast. Maintenance and renovation of the royal residences took precedence over expensive furniture and upholstery commissions.[128] Even British court clothing, as Hannah Greig points out, was out of date and attached to traditional clothing.[129] Rather than being a leader in style and fashion, the British court's role was seen as being an important part of the political process.[130]

In Britain, a more open and meritocratic elite dispersed taste-making to a wider audience than royal circles. For society's elite, Lord Burlington and the Society of the Dilettanti certainly were influential, but so was Horace Walpole. William Hogarth made comedy of the elite British copying French fine taste in his engraving *Taste in High Life*, but at the same time, in 1753, wrote about the 'serpentine line of beauty' in *The Analysis of Beauty*, where he praised the lines of the rococo.[131]

Taste in fashion was not only of concern for the social elite. The middling sort developed their own sense of taste, and, rather than emulating

[127] Beard, *Upholsterers and Interior Furnishing*, 2, 6. Gilbert, *The Life & Work of Thomas Chippendale*, 98–9.

[128] Hannah Smith, *Georgian Monarchy: Politics and Culture, 1714–1760* (Cambridge: Cambridge University Press, 2006), 59–120.

[129] Hannah Greig, "Faction and Fashion: The Politics of Court Dress in Eighteenth-Century England," *Apparance(s)* (6 August 2015): Abstract and Section 6, no page numbers. https://journals.openedition.org/apparences/1311#tocto1n (accessed 19 October 2021).

[130] Hannah Greig and Amanda Vickery, "The Political Day in London, C. 1697–1834," *Past & Present* Vol. 252, Issue 1 (August 2021): 119.

[131] Snodin and Styles, *Design & the Decorative Arts*, 11, 44–45, 70–82; Jeremy Black, *Culture in Eighteenth-Century England: A Subject for Taste* (London: Hambledon Continuum, 2007), 38. According to Black, artistic patronage came from landowners and the middling orders.

the elite, they bought what appealed to their own senses, not what appealed to others.[132] The middling rank was growing as was their consumption, and a middling sense of taste emerged by the mid-eighteenth century. They were exposed to new tastes through newspapers, shop windows, and outdoor venues, like Vauxhall Gardens.[133]

According to John Brewer, by the 1780s, the middle ranks of society were the new audience for the arts, and women were very much involved. Women were avid readers of periodicals and novels, attendees of the performing arts, collectors of fine art, and frequent visitors of the pleasure gardens, and they often drove the process of acquiring interior goods.[134] They were more associated with shopping on a regular basis than men.[135] The importance of women in making consuming decisions was not lost on the upholding trade.

One indicator that the upholding trade recognized the importance of women as decision-makers in the purchase of furniture and decorative art comes from Waller. He was direct in writing that upholders had to be 'clean' and 'genteel' for the ladies.[136] One can argue that in this context, these descriptors were gendered words that indicated an upholder's goods needed to appeal to a female clientele. One feminine selling technique upholders often used was displaying framed needlework beside mahogany furniture.[137]

When it came to manufacturing and selling tasteful, fashionable, and genteel household goods, upholders were the main providers. A comprehensive upholder provided upholstery goods, furniture, rugs, curtains, wallpaper, and more. They were, in Campbell's words, '...set up as a connoisseur in every article that belongs to a house'.[138]Few upholders served the aristocracy and elite exclusively, like Chippendale.[139] The majority probably sold most of their goods to the middling sort. It was the wealthier

[132] Weatherill, *Consumer Behaviour*, 20, 194–97; Richard H. Randall, Jr., "The French Taste," *Bulletin of the Museum of Fine Arts* Vol. 60, No. 320 (1962): 54.

[133] Black, *Culture in Eighteenth–Century England*, 105, 114, 121, 150.

[134] John Brewer, *The Pleasures of the Imagination* (London: Routledge, 2013), 9, 72–73.

[135] Amanda Vickery, "Women and the world of goods," 281.

[136] Waller, *A general description of all trades*, 214–15.

[137] Vickery, *Behind Closed Doors*, 254, 256.

[138] Campbell, *The London Tradesman*, 171; Waller, *A general description of all trades*, 214–15; Kirkham, *London Furniture Trade*, 57–68. Kirkham devoted a chapter to the comprehensive manufacturing firm.

[139] Kirkham, *London Furniture Trade*, 82–93. Kirkham emphasizes that an entrepreneurial furniture-maker was also a designer, not just a craftsman who made and sold furniture.

among the middle rank who owned an array of household goods and often purchased new and decorative items. New and decorative goods were displayed in the domestic spaces where they could be seen by visitors and interpreted as social markers.[140]

While the upholder was the main provider of new household and decorative goods for the middling sort, the market for used luxury goods must be considered, as upholders also were sellers of used household items. The challenge for an upholder aspiring to become wealthy was to manufacture and sell fashionable and tasteful goods, rather than new goods that were ordinary. Campbell believed that business success was dependent on designing and manufacturing something new and fresh that appealed to the consumer. He added that an upholder waiting to replicate a new style produced in Paris or by a competitor would never grow rich or eminent.[141] R.S. Clouston challenged Campbell in 1906. In his opinion, Chippendale was not an inventor, but an adaptor, as were other designers.[142] Clouston's opinion has some credibility because English furniture evolved throughout the first half of the eighteenth century, mostly from modifying French styles.[143] However, a new distinct style change occurred in the second part of the eighteenth century. This style change was the neoclassical style and was not invented by upholders and cabinet-makers.

The neoclassical style came into vogue in Britain, mostly through the designs of the architects Adam, Stuart, and Chambers.[144] Because of his overall impact, the time period of this furniture design is often called the 'Adam Period', and for cabinet-makers, it marked the 'taking back' of interior design elements by the architects. There was some uneasiness in the role between Chippendale and Chambers, but for the most part, architects, especially Adam, simply charged clients for drawings and allowed the

[140] Lorna Weatherill, "The meaning of consumer behaviour in late seventeenth- and early eighteenth-century England," in *Consumption and the World of Goods*, ed. John Brewer and Roy Porter (London: Routledge, 1993), 210–14.

[141] Campbell, *The London Tradesman*, 171.

[142] R.S. Clouston, *English Furniture and Furniture Makers of the 18th Century* (London: Hurst and Blackett, Ltd., 1906), 24.

[143] Gilbert, *The Life & Work of Thomas Chippendale*, 109–113; Randall, "The French Taste," 47–48; Snodin and Styles, *Design & the Decorative Arts*, 44–48, 120. It was not only furniture-makers adapting French designs. The silk designers and weavers in Spitalfields developed a distinct English interpretation of French rococo.

[144] Snodin and Styles, *Design & the Decorative Arts*, 50; Black, *Culture in Eighteenth-Century England*, 51–52, 182–183, 185.

cabinet-maker to carry out the work.[145] Because Chippendale continued to receive commissions, lost business from architects and interior designers was negligible.

The initial Adam period designs were meant for the elite. The middling ranks probably were interested in new designs, but it would have taken some time for upholders and cabinet-makers to adapt to neoclassical design. The upholders selling to the middling sort first needed to adapt production and procure suitable materials. At the same time, the new designs created a supply of older style furniture that upholders would have sold. Design changes increased business for upholders willing to find innovative ways to produce less expensive versions of expensive furniture. Opportunities also arose to increase sales of used furniture.

Consumption and Consumerism

Upholders operated in a society in which consumption habits were changing after the first half of the eighteenth century. Upholders were supplying the growing demand for fashionable and stylish residential interior goods for the elite and the growing middling ranks by the mid-eighteenth century, when over half of the population was in the middle rank.[146] Amanda Vickery found that in the last half of the eighteenth century, the average age for middling first-time marriages was about twenty-six for men and about twenty-five for women. Marrying at this age allowed the couple to save enough money to have their own residence, which validated their independence. Upon marriage in the eighteenth century, a middling couple usually established their own separate household. Vickery added that marriage was the time when the newlyweds began to make renovations and acquire the interior furnishings for their new home.[147] Upholders were in the business of 'fitting out' residential interiors, and they could provide a middling family the needed furnishings. Disposable income rose for many in the middling rank from working longer hours or from commanding higher wages. The choices offered in comfort and quality mattered in purchasing decisions. Upholders' expertise in producing and

[145] Gilbert, *The Life & Work of Thomas Chippendale*, 94–98.

[146] Lorna Weatherill, "The meaning of consumer behaviour in late seventeenth- and early eighteenth-century England," in *Consumption and the World of Goods*, ed. John Brewer and Roy Porter (London: Routledge, 1993), 210.

[147] Vickery, *Behind Closed Doors*, 6–7, 89, 291.

stocking household goods put them in a position to meet the increased demand from the middling sort. At the same time, some upholders found other sources of revenue from undertaking and funeral management, dealing in used household goods, auctioneering, and property agency.

The increase in personal spending on household goods in the last half of the eighteenth century was not a sudden event and should not be thought of as a revolution. Rather, it was an evolution that began in the seventeenth century. Neil McKendrick maintained that the increase in English consumerism in the last half of the eighteenth century was a revolution, as opposed to a gradual process beginning in the seventeenth century. This consumer revolution was the result of an increase in spending by the middling sort to emulate the materials and fashions of their social superiors. McKendrick also argued that the importation of colourful calicos by the East India Company set off a fashion revolution. Finally, he believed that it was in clothing that the lines of social distinction became blurred. To support his analysis, he used a rather tidy way of explaining supply and demand by proposing that social expectations rose with family income.[148] There are differing opinions in naming increased industrial output and consumer purchasing a 'revolution'.

Sara Pennell argued against the idea of a consumer revolution. Consumption trends happened over time, not in compressed time periods. Using thimbles as an example, Pennell pointed out that mechanical production was not an eighteenth-century event. The mechanical production of thimbles actually began in the late seventeenth century.[149] McKendrick does believe that consumerism had its roots in the seventeenth century, but he argues it was the middling ranks and their imitation of the rich that created the eighteenth-century commercial revolution.[150] Jan De Vries also countered the consumer revolution argument. Rather than a consumer revolution, it was an 'industrious revolution' that increased consumer purchasing of goods and services. The allocation of household leisure time from producing goods for direct or internal consumption to the production of goods for the outside markets created extra income that could be spent on consumer goods.[151]

[148] McKendrick, Brewer, Plumb, *The Birth of a Consumer Society*, 9, 11, 14, 53.

[149] Sara Pennell, "Material Culture in Seventeenth-Century," 76–78.

[150] McKendrick, Brewer, Plumb, *The Birth of a Consumer Society*, 14.

[151] Jan De Vries, "The Industrial Revolution and the Industrious Revolution," *The Journal of Economic History* Vol. 54, No. 2, (Jun. 1994): 255–66.

The word 'revolution' connotes a sudden and complete change. There were changes in production methods and purchasing habits, which were permanent rather than temporal or cyclical. However, these changes did not happen within a limited period, such as in the last half of the eighteenth century. Rather, the changes that created manufacturing efficiency and supply and increased consumerism were evolutionary, not revolutionary, and began in the seventeenth century. Grant McCracken agreed in principle with McKendrick and argued that fashion was no longer concerned with utility, but with aesthetic and stylistic considerations. The clothing of the elite and wealthy was disposed of when styles changed in the eighteenth century. This disposal of the unwanted and out-of-fashion created a turnover in goods and made shopping a social experience. In other words, [fashion] obsolescence resulted in increased [fashion] consumerism.[152]

McKendrick's and McCracken's arguments have been challenged. The argument that social emulation of the upper ranks' material culture by the middling sort was responsible for increased consumption is problematic. Lorna Weatherill disputed whether people of the middle rank approved of copying the fashions of the higher orders of society.[153] Amanda Vickery's analysis of the diaries, account ledgers, and correspondence of Elizabeth Shackleton, a Lancashire gentlewoman, found that Shackleton, though not opposed to expressing social status through 'things', disapproved of those who attempted to use 'things' to imply they were from a higher social order.[154]

Ben Fine and Ellen Leopold argue that wage growth, not emulation, created demand. For instance, they found that servants did not use their wages to purchase work clothing to emulate their employer; rather, the employer purchased their work clothing for them.[155] Recent research also disputes that obsolescence created increased consumer purchasing. Jon Stobart's work, for instance, showed that the lower ranks often bought second-hand goods and repurposed them. Furthermore, Stobart argued

[152] McCracken, *Culture and Consumption*, 16, 9–21, 40.

[153] Weatherill, *Consumer Behaviour*, 20, 194–97.

[154] Amanda Vickery, "Women and the world of goods: a Lancashire consumer and her possessions, 1751–81," in *Consumption and the World of Goods*, ed. John Brewer and Roy Porter (London: Routledge, 1993), 286.

[155] Ben Fine and Ellen Leopold, "Consumerism and the Industrial Revolution," *Social History* Vol. 15, No. 2 (May 1990): 167–69.

that the luxury goods associated with high status were seldom sold in the secondary market.[156]

Repairs, modifications, and repurposing of clothing were everyday activities.[157] Clothes of quality were passed down, and garments were easily altered. In this regard, taste was passed on to others through alterations and by adding small accoutrements.[158] The innovative research into household thefts by Horrell, Humphries, and Sneath determined that price and fashion were important in residential thievery, but so was quality and comfort. For instance, thieves standing trial at Old Bailey preferred stealing quality feather beds and cotton counterpanes to cheaper versions. These authors conclude that it was prosperity evidenced by disposable income that created consumer purchasing.[159]

One key theme in this work is that the middling sort had choices in how to spend their money. If one accepts that there was increasing demand for fashionable clothing, both new and used, then Fine and Leopold are correct that the incomes of tailors and seamstresses rose because their skills were in high demand.[160] Skilled workers, along with those putting in longer hours, had extra money. For the most part, consumer goods for the middling sort were household goods. This included items such as bedding, clothes, and household utensils. Carole Shammas estimated that these household items made up from fifty to seventy-five per cent of the total value of consumer purchases, with wealthier households spending a smaller proportion of their wealth on this consumption.[161] As consumerism increased, the shortage of coinage required the wider use of purchasing on credit.

[156] Stobart, "Luxury and Country House Sales," 31–32, 34.

[157] Pennell, "Material Culture in Seventeenth Century," 73–83.

[158] Fine and Leopold, "Consumerism and the Industrial Revolution," 174–75.

[159] Sara Horrell, Jane Humphries, and Ken Sneath, "Consumption conundrums unraveled," *Economic History Review* 68, 3, (2015): 830, 833, 849–50, 854–55.

[160] Fine and Leopold, "Consumerism and the Industrial Revolution," 173–74.

[161] Carole Shammas, "Changes in English and Anglo-American consumption from 1550 to 1800," in *Consumption and the World of Goods*, ed. John Brewer and Roy Porter (London: Routledge, 1993), 185–88.

Credit

The growth in consumerism after 1760 was fuelled by personal credit.[162] The expansion of credit that was tied to consumerism paralleled the increase in upholder bankruptcies. Economic downturns and war created credit risk.[163] Despite the risks, upholders were obliged to use credit.

The increasing demand for fashionable household goods was not lost on upholders. Although some upholders expanded their businesses before 1760, opportunities grew to expand their businesses after then. Upholders increased stock and added new products and services with the expectation of increased sales. Because of the limited number of coins in circulation, this expansion was possible by utilizing personal credit. While using credit for business expansion provided a convenient way for cash-strapped upholders to take advantage of perceived opportunities for more profits, it carried risks because their income had to expand to cover the loan costs. The biggest risk in using credit was insolvency, which often led to bankruptcy. Research found that 163 London upholders were declared bankrupt in the last half of the eighteenth century. Forty-two per cent of these upholder bankruptcies occurred in the twenty years between 1760 and 1779. While it is not always possible to determine the reason(s) for any bankruptcy, the fact is that upholder bankruptcies increased during this period of accelerated consumerism. This suggests that upholders either relied too much on credit to conduct their business or offered goods and services that no one wanted.

Searching eighteenth-century newspapers with the term 'upholder' yielded fifty-three upholder bankruptcy notices for the period between 1751 and 1770. For the period between 1771 and 1800, the number of upholder bankruptcy notices increased to 110. Interestingly, in the period from 1776 to 1781, during the American War of Independence, there were forty-two upholder bankruptcies. These six years accounted for

[162] Julian Hoppit, *Risk and failure in English business 1700–1800* (Cambridge: Cambridge University Press, 1987), 102, 162, 166–67.

[163] Hoppit, *Risk and failure*, 98–99, 122–39. Upholder bankruptcy numbers were derived from counting bankruptcy notices found in the Burney Collection of Eighteenth-Century British Newspapers. Bankruptcy notices were generally published three times, followed by a notice of the issuance of the bankruptcy certificate of conformity. Because this was a manual counting process, there is the possibility a few notices were double counted or not counted at all.

about twenty-five per cent of all upholder bankruptcies in the last half of the eighteenth century.

Joiners also had bankruptcy experiences similar to upholders. From 1770 through 1779, upholders and joiners each had forty-six bankruptcies. In contrast to upholders and joiners, linen drapers had 184 bankruptcies in those ten years (Table 1.1). Hoppit found that nearly one in four eighteenth-century bankruptcies involved the textile and clothing trades. Inventory speculation in new cotton fabrics was one reason linen drapers experienced high rates of business failure.[164]

Prior to the mid-eighteenth century, the two most common forms of credit were government and corporate. The government borrowed money and issued bonds to fund large expenses, most notably wars. Repayment of these loans was predicated on future tax revenue and was a method of deferring large expenses. Large corporate entities, such as insurance companies and turnpike trusts, borrowed money to fund their operations, with repayments to be met from immediate profits. Private credit was used on a smaller, localized scale. After the Seven Years' War ended and consumerism increased, smaller business owners, including upholders, increasingly used private credit to purchase raw materials and increase stock. Purchasers of their goods and services often favoured using private credit over paying

Table 1.1 Upholder, joiner, and linen draper bankruptcies by year 1770–1779

Year	*Upholders*	*Joiners*	*Linen Drapers*
1770	5	3	3
1771	4	3	0
1772	4	2	8
1773	2	3	13
1774	3	11	34
1775	2	1	43
1776	10	14	4
1777	5	4	3
1778	6	5	53
1779	5	0	23
Total	46	46	184

Source: Burney Newspapers Collection

[164] Hoppit, *Risk and failure*, 75–87, 103.

in cash, presumably as a way to help manage cash flow. One of the most common forms of private credit was promissory notes.[165]

Consumers often purchased small goods on credit and settled their bills when they had money. By 1760, consumers were purchasing more expensive items on credit.[166] Extending credit had now become more complicated than merely making an entry in a shopkeeper's ledger. Promissory notes were commonly used to pay for goods. Because a shopkeeper often wanted more immediate payment, the note would be assigned or endorsed over to another party at a discount and used to pay for goods that the shopkeeper needed.[167] Upholders used credit in this way to sell more goods and, in turn, to purchase raw materials and stock. The private credit system worked well until there was a market disruption.

The main problem with private credit was that promissory notes were usually assigned to others, often more than once. This created a chain of responsibility from one note owner to another. It was a convenient way to conduct commercial activities when hard currency was scarce. It was ideal until a disruption occurred, whether a real or an imagined economic crisis. A matured note was presented to the original issuer, and hard currency was demanded, rather than the note being renewed. If the issuer did not have hard currency, the note holder lost out on the principal value plus any accrued interest. More importantly, the holder of the worthless note was often unable to make good on any notes he had issued. When this happened, credit chains were broken, and bankruptcies ensued.[168]

The American War of Independence (1775–1783) had a deleterious effect on the ability of those in the upholding trade to pay back debt. Hoppit described the economic dislocations that resulted from the war. War initially drew money from the private credit markets to government bonds, and customs duties and taxes were raised to cover government spending shortfalls, while international monetary settlement mechanisms

[165] Julian Hoppit, "Financial Crises in Eighteenth-Century England," *The Economic History Review* New Series, Vol. 39, No. 1 (Feb. 1986): 41–3; John Smail, "Credit, Risk, and Honor in Eighteenth-Century Commerce," *Journal of British Studies* Vol. 44, No. 3 (Jul. 2005): 442–45.

[166] Joanna Innes, "The King's Bench prison in the later 18th century: law, authority, and order in a London debtor's prison," in *An Ungovernable People*, ed. John Brewer and John Styles (New Brunswick: Rutgers University Press, 1980), 251–53; Hoppit, "Financial Crises in Eighteenth-Century England," 41–3; Smail, "Credit, Risk, and Honor," 442–45.

[167] Hoppit, "Financial Crises in Eighteenth-Century England," 52–54.

[168] Hoppit, *Risk and failure*, 162–63, 166–67.

were disrupted, putting any upholder involved with overseas trade at risk of bankruptcy.[169]

Just one creditor could initiate bankruptcy proceedings in the eighteenth century. Other creditors could join the bankruptcy process if they felt the debtor's financial circumstances had gone beyond hope of repayment of owed debt. The creditor initiating the bankruptcy would petition the Lord Chancellor and provide a £200 bond to assure the petition was not malicious. A Commission of Bankruptcy was appointed and would examine the petition's merits. The Commission looked for three requirements to approve the petition, which were: was the debtor involved in the business of buying and selling; did the debtor owe at least £100 to one party, £150 to two, or £200 to three or more; and had the debtor committed an act of bankruptcy by refusing to pay debts? If the requirements were met and the petition was approved, the debtor's assets were seized and sold, and the proceeds were paid to the creditors in the form of dividends. Upon completion of the process, the debtor would receive a 'certificate of conformity', which freed the bankrupt to start a new business.[170]

At the individual level, an upholder was at risk of bankruptcy if the promissory notes accepted from sales became uncollectable. An upholder carrying a large stock of unwanted goods was also at risk, which made controlling stock and selling fashionable goods important.[171] Although many upholders carried fire insurance, there was business risk if the business was underinsured.[172] Even the untimely death of a partner could cause financial distress, as was the case with Chippendale when his main financial backer suddenly died and the family demanded the return of the partner's invested capital.[173] Of all the reasons for bankruptcy at the individual level, it was the assignment and trading in promissory notes that was the most dangerous credit risk because it cast a wide net.

Relying on credit for business expansion was, according to Julian Hoppit, dangerous.[174] Loan interest was costly, and solvency depended on

[169] Hoppit, *Risk and failure*, 122–29.

[170] Hoppit, *Risk and failure*, 35–7.

[171] Peter Earle, *The Making of the Middle Class: Business, Society and Family Life in London, 1660–1730* (Berkley: University of California Press, 1989), 118–23.

[172] Earle, *Making of the Middle Class*, 78–79.

[173] Gilbert, *The Life & Work of Thomas Chippendale*, 11–15, 30–33; *London Chronicle*, 8–11 February 1766. This notice announced the partnership dissolution between Chippendale and James Rannie; Thomas Haig was named as Chippendale's new partner.

[174] Hoppit, "Financial Crises in Eighteenth-Century England," 53.

confidence in continued economic growth and on uninterrupted repayment among the various parties. A loan repayment disruption, or even a perceived one, could result in a loss of confidence in the private credit network. A disruption occurred in 1772 and was the first financial crisis that resulted from an excess of private credit rather than public or corporate credit. Because London's banks, provincial banks (numbering over 400), and major merchants were closely linked by paper credit, loan defaults spread throughout Britain. This financial crisis led to an increase in bankruptcies.[175] This explains the surge in upholder bankruptcies in the 1770s.

Despite the risks of using credit, upholders aspiring for financial success had to use it to compete with other upholders. Financially prudent upholders probably aimed to organically grow their business by using profits to expand. Most upholders beginning their business probably started modestly and eschewed a large stock of goods. Campbell estimated the required capital for an upholder setting up business at between £100 and £1000 in the late 1740s.[176] Establishing an upholding business at the lower end was not too difficult for someone who was thrifty and able to borrow money from family members. Starting the trade at the upper end was more difficult because it required more capital to establish a comprehensive stock of goods and hire capable workers. Issuing a promissory note was a possibility to acquire stock in trade.

For some upholders, a marriage settlement from a wealthy woman gave the upholder the extra money needed to set up a business or expand an existing one.[177] News about important marriages often reported the amount of the marriage settlement. The *General Evening Post* reported a 1751 marriage as follows: '... an eminent Upholder (Thomas Burnett) in The Strand to Miss Jenny Parker of Fleet Street; an agreeable young Lady with a Fortune of £10,000'.[178] Samuel Seabrook's 1763 marriage announcement included, 'Eminent Upholder, married Miss Nancy Butler of Clerkenwell Green, an agreeable young Lady with a real fortune of £5,000 and all other necessary qualifications'.[179] 'Other necessary qualifications' meant that the bride was qualified to organize and run a household.

[175] Hoppit, "Financial Crises in Eighteenth-Century England," 52–54.
[176] Campbell, *The London Tradesman*, 340.
[177] Earle, *Making of the Middle Class*, 190.
[178] *General Evening Post*, 7–9 May 1751.
[179] *Gazetteer and London Daily Advertiser*, 7 June 1763.

She also had the ideals for a genteel man that included conversation, discretion, and chasteness. The use of the terms 'eminent', 'lady', and 'gentleman' indicated that these were marriages between people of good social standing. In the search of newspaper marriage announcements for upholders, some marriage announcements did not include financial details. For instance, Richard Secombe's bride, Patty Kemp, was 'a young lady possessed of every virtuous and polite qualification with a very handsome fortune'.[180] Whether or not these upholders used their settlement money to fund their businesses is not known, but it could have helped them to expand an existing business.

London retailers grew their businesses through reinvesting profits and borrowing money. Most upholders probably used credit prudently, but they still could become bankrupt because of circumstances outside their control. Small business owners with no intention of expanding their operations were exposed to the credit markets through the use of the credit instruments they issued to suppliers and received from their customers. Thomas Mortimer published advice on how to lower bankruptcy risk. Mortimer's advice included presenting the note to the issuing bank before day's end, verifying valid dates on the note, and not allowing the customer to take goods until the payment cleared the bank.[181] His practical advice did not eliminate bankruptcy risk, but it did help mitigate it.[182]

Some upholders chose to pool capital and create partnerships to expand their businesses. It may seem that the pooling of capital would spread the business risk among the partners, but partnership arrangements were not without risk. A bad decision by one partner could require the other partners to make good on a debt.[183] Sometimes misfortune, rather than bad decision-making, caused financial stress. As previously mentioned, misfortune happened to Chippendale when his partner unexpectedly died. The firm was saved when a junior partner put up additional capital, but Chippendale never financially recovered.[184]

[180] *Read's Weekly Journal or British Gazetteer*, 4 August 1753.

[181] Thomas Mortimer, *Every Man His Own Broker*, 4th ed. (London: S. Hooper, 1761), 128–29.

[182] For a contemporary description of the bankruptcy process, see: Thomas Mortimer, *Merchant's Directory, Being a Guide to all Men in Business*, 4th ed. (London: J. Rivington and Son, 1783), 527–612.

[183] Smail, "Credit, Risk, and Honor," 439.

[184] Gilbert, *The Life & Work of Thomas Chippendale*, 11–15, 30–33; *London Chronicle*, 8–11 February 1766. This newspaper notice announced the partnership dissolution between Chippendale and James Rannie; Thomas Haig was named as Chippendale's new partner.

Small shops extending credit to their customers had no quantifiable method by which to determine risk.[185] Understandably, provincial shops in smaller towns had an advantage in personally knowing their customers and whether or not they were honest, responsible, and trustworthy. Uncertainty creates risk, and London retail shops were often in the position of having to decide whether or not to extend credit to a customer they knew little about. For upholders, especially those selling to the higher end of the middling sort and to the elite, extending credit on a large scale could be risky. An upholder extending credit to the nobility for expensive commissions was in a particularly difficult position because, although selling a large amount of household furniture to a country house owner could yield a large profit, the nobility were notoriously late paying and, in some cases, exempt from lawsuits. Chippendale's firm frequently had problems in collecting payment on expensive commissions.[186] While waiting for payment, workers and suppliers had to be paid. The personal conditions of customers in large cities sometimes changed, and it was difficult for business owners to stay informed of increased risks. To counter this problem, trade protection societies appeared in the last quarter of the eighteenth century. These societies, such as the Society for the Protection of Trade against Swindlers and Sharpers, informed their subscribers about London fraudsters and provided legal assistance.[187]

Margot Finn argued that it was the competition for customers from the 'right class' that allowed cheats to flourish.[188] Her research relied on written material that often described what could go wrong when someone's character was misjudged. Hoppit detailed how bankruptcy filings ebbed and flowed with certain macroeconomic events, especially with the uncertainties that surrounded war.[189] Despite the risks, consumer purchasing on credit burgeoned after 1760.

[185] Margot Finn, *The Character of Credit – Personal Debt in English Culture, 1740–1914* (Cambridge: Cambridge University Press, 2003), 288.

[186] Gilbert, *The Life & Work of Thomas Chippendale*, 11–12.

[187] Finn, *The Character of Credit*, 288–294. Established in 1776, the Society for the Protection of Trade against Swindlers and Sharpers or Guardians, was the first trade protection society. Their 1799 membership list represented over eighty different trades, including the upholder George Oakley. Prior to this, the trades would have relied on *Public Advertiser* bankruptcy listings, news stories and obituaries from the newspapers, and word of mouth to monitor the personal conditions that affected the credit worthiness of their customers.

[188] Finn, *The Character of Credit*, 294.

[189] Julian Hoppit, *Risk and failure*, 122–29.

Rather than writing about what could go wrong in extending credit, like Finn and Hoppit, John Smail described what it was that made credit work in most instances. Trusting a borrower was important, but trusting implies accepting risk. A borrower's reputation, both financial and moral, was considered, but it was difficult to monitor a borrower's reputation from afar. It was the linking of honour to credit and masculinity in the eighteenth century that reduced lending risks. For the commercial rank, according to Smail, it was playing to the sense of honour that allowed lenders to successfully negotiate with distressed borrowers.[190] Reputation was a key element in the underwriting process, but the physical characteristics of a potential borrower were sometimes important underwriting elements. Physical characteristics included such things as clothing, cleanliness, and mannerisms.[191]

Eighteenth-century consumerism relied on a credit system that was based on trust, character, and honour. Smail and Pearson described these subjective assessments in different ways. Smail's argument that honour was critical to extending credit is compelling because of its emphasis on dutifully paying back debts. Pearson's view that physiognomy assessments (judging someone by looks, dress, and speaking skills) were important is also compelling because often there was little objective information that could be assessed, sometimes making extending credit in the eighteenth century more of an art than a science. Using credit to sell more products, however, was not always a prudent choice. Extending credit with a reasonable expectation of being paid back was the ideal. Recovering money through the courts was costly, and it often yielded a settlement that was much less than the original loan.[192]

Upholders often advertised credit availability for their household goods. John Mayhew and William Ince informed the public, '... they would be pleased to honour them with their commands that shall be executed with the neatest taste, at the most reasonable rates, and exact punctuality'.[193] Terms like 'most favourable rates' and 'most reasonable rates' advertised a willingness to sell goods or services on credit. Finn was correct in stating that cheats were a persistent problem for shopkeepers.

[190] John Smail, "Credit, Risk, and Honor," 445, 451–56.

[191] Robin Pearson, "Moral Hazard and the Assessment of Insurance Risk in Eighteenth- and Early-Nineteenth-Century Britain," *The Business History Review* Vol. 76, No. 1 (Spring 2002): 1–2, 34.

[192] Smail, "Credit, Risk, and Honor," 445.

[193] *London Evening Post*, 18–20 January 1759.

One upholder experienced a sharper who used credit to furnish an empty house. Once the furnishings were delivered, the sharper began to remove them. The upholder was alerted and immediately came to secure his property.[194] Nevertheless, upholder bankruptcies increased as the so-called 'consumer revolution' gained momentum. Credit was the main ingredient for increased household consumption. Upholders used credit to grow their businesses and increase their stock of goods, and selling on credit was a tool to increase sales. Using credit wisely could result in the accumulation of great wealth. Robert Williams, for instance, accumulated great wealth through using credit on a commercial scale to provide household goods to East India Company ship officers.

Advertising

The analysis of upholder advertisements is an important component of this book, especially newspaper advertisements. There were three main advertising methods upholders used during the eighteenth century: advertising bills, trade cards, and newspaper advertising. Their purpose was multi-faceted. First, advertising was a way to get prospective customers to visit an upholder's shop, where salesmanship could be applied. Second, advertising was a way to inform current and prospective customers of new product and service offerings. Finally, advertising could be used for a specific purpose, such as notifications of markdowns on specific goods or a shop's relocation. The overall goal of advertising was to increase sales revenue.

Advertising bills, sometimes known as broadsheets, were common throughout the century. They were printed on single sheets of paper and handed out to potential customers or affixed to a window or wall (billposting). Easy to produce, trade bills often included a product image. Although they may have been unsophisticated in their content compared to trade cards and newspaper advertisements, they did reach a wide audience of potential customers.

Trade cards were another advertising method that was popular throughout the eighteenth century. The printing plate was often engraved with rococo flourishes that framed the card's text. Upholder trade cards regularly included illustrations representing their goods, such as chairs or tables. Ashley Sims surmised their purpose was twofold. First, trade cards

[194] *Gazetteer and New Daily Advertiser*, 2 December 1768.

were advertisements and a way for shop owners to build a social connection by giving them to valued clients, creating a sense of exclusivity. Second, the reverse side of trade cards was blank and conveniently used by a shopkeeper to make notes of an estimate or detail extended credit and politely remind the client of their financial obligation.[195]

An example of an eighteenth-century promotional trade card is Robert Legg's (Illustration 1.1). The card was engraved by Matthias Darly and his wife of Chandois Street. (This is the same Darly, or his son by the same name, previously mentioned as having engraved several plates for Chippendale's *Director*.) As can be seen from the image, this card uses a mixture of fashion tastes, primarily artistic flourishes referencing the rococo and Chinese styles. The top medallion features a human leg, an obvious reference to Legg's surname. The address for Legg's business is at the Sign of the Leg, Southampton Street, Holborn. There is no exact date of when this card was printed, but it was probably printed between 1750 and 1760, possibly after the *Director* was published in 1754. Even though house numbering in London had started as early as 1708, the numbering process was somewhat haphazard and evidently had not yet reached Southampton Street in Holborn.[196] Legg presents himself as an upholder, appraiser, and undertaker. Furthermore, he states that he is the son of the late Robert Legg, whose business was located opposite Bloomsbury Market. He uses his father's name as a selling tool, implying that he is an honest and respectable tradesman following in his father's footsteps. Robert Legg was not a member of the Upholders' Company and is an example of an upholder belonging to another livery company or to no company at all. Trade cards and broadsheets were effective methods of advertising as long as they were seen by a prospective customer. In order to reach a wider audience of potential customers, upholders turned to newspaper advertising.

Newspaper advertising became especially popular with the upholding trade in the last half of the eighteenth century. T.R. Nevett affirms a measurable increase in newspaper advertising after 1740 by analysing the duty newspapers paid to the government. One shilling was paid per advertisement until 1757, when the rate was doubled to two shillings. The duties

[195] Ashley Sims, "'Selling Consumption': An Examination of Eighteenth-Century English Trade Cards," *Graduate Journal of Visual and Material Culture* Issue 5, 2012: 5–8.

[196] For a general discussion of house numbering in London, See: The Postal Museum. https://www.postalmuseum.org/blog/house-numbering/ (accessed 9 July 2025).

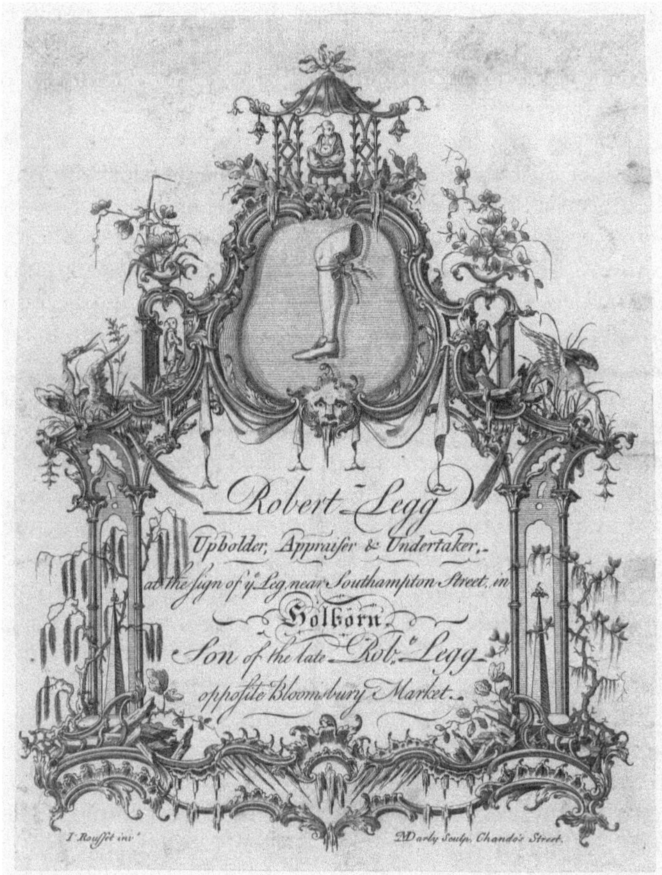

Illustration 1.1 Trade card of Robert Legg, Upholder. (By permission from Bridgeman Images)

amounted to £2969 in 1740 and rose to £4941 in 1750, an increase of over sixty-six per cent. Advertising duties in 1760 were £11,239. This duty amount must be halved to compare it to 1750 to account for the 1757 doubled rate. Comparing the 1760 adjusted duty amount of £5620 to the 1750 duty amount of £4941 yields a nearly fourteen per cent increase in advertising duties over the ten-year period. Unlike bills and trade cards, newspaper advertisements usually did not include images of the goods offered for sale because of the difficulties in doing this on large printing plates. Consequently, newspaper advertisements were artfully written to emphasize words and phrases that would attract the attention of potential customers.[197]

An analysis of newspaper advertising found a noticeable transformation in the upholder business model after 1760. This transformation indicates that upholders were now more than upholsterers and cabinet-makers. The advertisements show that funeral undertaking had become an established business line for many upholders by 1760. They also began advertising additional services that included appraising, brokering, and auctioneering. Thomas Chippendale and other upholders considered eminent rarely advertised, probably because they already had established a book of business with wealthy clientele.[198] Upholders who did advertise were probably targeting the middle ranks and their growing disposable income. For example, newspaper advertisements that stated 'prices on the most reasonable terms' probably were meant to appeal to the middling sort, perhaps allowing for purchases on credit. Many upholders probably operated part-time in some of these additional business services, as it does not seem possible to be competent in every one of them. The larger point here is that newspaper advertisements after 1760 were indicative of a growing consumer market and competitive economy in which upholders were looking to capture as much revenue as they could.

In summary, this introduction highlights the key factors that made eighteenth-century upholders what they were. These factors must be linked together, rather than seen individually, to create an overall understanding of what was occurring within and outside their trade. The growing British Empire brought new designs, styles, and materials into the realm of household interior goods, to which upholders adapted production. Losing court cases diluted the power of livery companies, while population growth beyond the City's walls made enforcement of livery company rules difficult. This loss of control was not immediate; rather, it evolved over the course of one hundred years. The upholding trade was an ideal business for the younger sons of gentry families because it could lead

[197] T.R. Nevitt, *Advertising in Britain: A History* (London: William Heinemann Ltd., 1982), 15–24.

[198] Gilbert, *The Life & Work of Thomas Chippendale*, 25–27. Chippendale and Rannie advertised the *Director* and their workshop on six consecutive June days in 1754. Gilbert considered this very clever as a new Parliament opened on 31 May.

to financial independence. A handful of upholders amassed fortunes. Nonetheless, most upholders remained in the middling rank of tradesmen. The rise of consumerism evolved during the first half of the eighteenth century as the middling rank began having the disposable income to purchase new and used household interior goods, notably couples at marriage. By 1760, increased consumer demand led upholders to rely more and more on personal credit to maintain and increase sales revenue, which increased bankruptcy risk.

Marriage often anchored an upholder in business. The marriage partnership was important to tradesmen, especially those having a financial settlement. Although mostly a masculine business, the wife played many roles, including running the household and helping with the business when needed. Wives often learned the business by helping in the front of the store, and given that widows often took over the business when a husband died before retirement, it is apparent that many wives were more than passive participants in the business.

One theme that cannot be ignored is that London upholders had choices in how they defined their own businesses. Should they join a livery? Should they be a general upholder selling furniture and upholstery goods and services, a comprehensive upholder with multiple business lines, or specialize in only one specific area? Was expanding stock through using credit a worthwhile business risk? These were among the choices that upholders and other tradesmen had to make. The next chapter examines the ways upholders participated in the funeral undertaking business.

CHAPTER 2

Upholders and Funeral Undertaking in London

Here I lie on my back,
S, the partner of Slack,
Upholder, and Undertaker,
Now I've finish'd my trade,
And my beds are all made,
I'm gone to take rest with my Maker.[1]

Upholders provided funeral materials and services to the elite and middling ranks in the eighteenth century. They were part of a funeral undertaking trade which had emerged by the end of the seventeenth century with a handful of full-time suppliers of funeral goods and services. The establishment of funeral undertaking as a trade meant that, rather than contracting with multiple suppliers and tradesmen, the deceased's family could have an undertaker 'undertake' all the arrangements. Moreover, funeral goods could be purchased or rented, which gave the consumer choices and purchasing power. Consumerism in the funeral undertaking trade had grown rapidly by the middle of the eighteenth century, and upholders became a main provider in London. This chapter establishes the reasons why the funeral undertaking trade began emerging in the last decades of the seventeenth century. It also explains why upholders were

[1] 'An EPITAPH on an Upholsterer'. *Middlesex Journal or Chronicle of Liberty*, 8–10 October 1771.

S. Sanders, *The Eighteenth-Century London Upholder*,
https://doi.org/10.1007/978-3-032-08660-0_2

often associated with this trade and considers the changes to the commercial environment after 1760, which attracted more upholders to this business. Finally, it examines upholders' business practices and business risks specific to funeral undertaking.

A New Business Opportunity: The Funeral Trade

Political, legal, economic, and social changes created a new business opportunity in the last quarter of the seventeenth century, the management and furnishing of funerals. Although these changes occurred by 1690, they did not happen suddenly. Rather, these changes evolved over the course of the final decades of the seventeenth century.

There were legal and political changes that supported the creation of the funeral trade. The first change occurred when the College of Arms lost its control over heraldic funerals in the late seventeenth century. Heraldic funerals were for armigers, those who held grants from the College of Arms. The College experienced challenges to its authority over elite funerals after the Glorious Revolution.[2] A confluence of factors occurred that led to challenges to their authority. First, the tradesmen who provided the approved funeral furnishings for the College of Arms's funerals had an expertise that appealed to the growing middling rank. Second, the wealthier among the middling sort wanted to have more elaborate funerals that included materials that replicated a heraldic funeral. Third, tradesmen experienced in supplying aristocratic funerals challenged the College of Arms by supplying funeral goods and services outside heraldic control. Ralph Holmes, for instance, was a banner maker for the College, who furnished an elite funeral outside of heraldic control in 1667. The College of Arms considered tradesmen like Holmes interlopers and threatened them with legal action.[3]

The court case that ended the College of Arms's monopoly over elite funerals occurred in 1691. The Court of Chivalry brought a legal action against a cheesemonger, Charles Domville, for managing and furnishing heraldic-styled funerals without a licence from the College of Arms. (How

[2] Ralph Houlbrooke, "The age of decency: 1660–1760," in *Death in England: An Illustrated History*, ed. Peter C. Jupp and Clare Gittings (New Brunswick: Rutgers University Press, 2000), 190.

[3] Paul Fritz, "The Undertaking Trade in England: Its Origins and Early Development, 1660–1830," *Eighteenth Century Studies* Vol. 28, No. 2 (Winter, 1994–1995): 246.

a cheesemonger became knowledgeable in funeral management is unknown.) Domville successfully challenged the Court of Chivalry's action by appealing and winning his case in the Court of Exchequer. The College then appealed to the House of Lords to void the Court of Exchequer's ruling. The House of Lords refused the appeal and upheld the decision by the Court of Exchequer.[4] The Painter-Stainers' Company had agreed with the College to not paint inauthentic devices in 1686, but the loss of the Domville case made this agreement ineffectual.[5] (Inauthentic devices were painted plaques and banners with coats of arms and crests that were not approved of by the College of Arms.)

Losing legal oversight over an emerging and unlicensed undertaking trade was not the major setback for the College of Arms. Although the College survived the Puritan policies against ostentatious displays of wealth, the major political setback came when William III refused to renew the College's royal commission to issue funeral certificates for the elite.[6] The government now wanted the money the College of Arms collected from funerals to help fund its war with France. The College petitioned the government for an act by which it would be the official source of baptismal and death certificates and marriage licences. Parliament refused the petition and instead passed an act that authorized the government to collect taxes and fees on issuing these documents. This was the Birth, Marriages, and Burials Duty Act of 1695.[7] Losing the Court of Exchequer case, the non-renewal of the College's royal commission, and the government's takeover of certifications essentially opened the way for the commercialization of funerals.

The economic change that was responsible for the commercialization of funerals was the burgeoning of the middling ranks. No matter the demand from the middling sort for more exclusive funerals, it was the breaking of the College's monopoly over elite funerals that allowed suppliers to freely supply the demand. Paul Fritz argued that the commercial consequence from the loss of the College of Arms's monopoly over elite funerals was indicative of Britain's movement from a feudal society to a

[4] Fritz, "The Undertaking Trade," 242–44.

[5] Julian Litten, *The English Way of Death: The Common Funeral Since 1450* (London: Robert Hale Ltd., 1991), 193–94.

[6] Ralph Houlbrooke, *Death, Religion, and the Family in England 1480–1750* (Oxford: Oxford University Press, 2006), 278–79.

[7] Fritz, "The Undertaking Trade," 244. Also see: Colin Brooks, "Political Arithmetic and the Act of 1695," *English Historical Review* Vol. 97, No. 382 (Jan. 1982): 31–53.

commercial society increasingly based on competition and profit.[8] Major economic change takes time, and Fritz's argument seems even more compelling when one considers Mark Noble's suppositions about a growing profit-motivated middling sort during the reign of Charles I. He claimed that from the reign of Elizabeth onward, a middling rank emerged. Though the middling rank was considered respectable, Charles I essentially ignored the contributions they brought to the kingdom's wealth. These riches came from commerce. The middling ranks were a valuable part of the community, and they considered it degrading that their plate was confiscated and their seals destroyed for unauthorized heraldic use after visitations from the local heralds. They also were forbidden to use a velvet funeral pall.[9] (A pall is a large cloth that covers a casket.[10]) The growing middling sort had the disposable income that could take advantage of choices in funerals. The wealthier among them could now afford the social prestige of an elite funeral, while those of more modest means had less expensive choices. Funeral undertakers, including upholders, offered families a range of options in material quality and service complexity to match their financial wherewithal.

In 1949, Robert Aubin presented his version of the establishment of the undertaking and funeral trade. There developed a sense of needs for the dead that were linked with the increasing middling family social desires. The middling rank by 1700 wanted embalmment and accessorized funerals. This created a new business opportunity for full-time funeral furnishers.[11] William Russell was the driving force in establishing the undertaking business around 1680, and, contrary to what some contemporary historians, including Fritz, Houlbrooke, and Litten, have written, Russell was not a member of the Painter-Stainers' Company. Aubin believed that Russell was a member of the Joiners' Company and was backed by members of the Painter-Stainers' Company to create a commercial funeral business. No matter his livery affiliation, Russell's business model combined embalming, coffin-making, and the furnishing of accessories, including inauthentic devices (those not approved by the College of Arms) that were previously reserved for heraldic funerals. At the same time, a few apothe-

[8] Paul Fritz, "The Undertaking Trade," 246.

[9] Mark Noble, *A History of the College of Arms* (London: J. Debrett, 1804), 222–24.

[10] Geoffrey Beard, *Upholsterers and Interior Furnishing England 1530–1840* (New Haven: Yale University Press, 1997), 325.

[11] Robert A. Aubin, "Behind Steele's Satire on Undertakers," *Modern Language Association* PLMA, Vol. 64, No. 5, (Dec. 1949): 1016–17.

caries like Thomas Warren were developing inexpensive embalming methods, methods probably practised by Russell.[12]

Contemporary authors are correct in recognizing William Russell as one of the first comprehensive undertakers. Fritz, Houlbrooke, and Litten rightly argue that the Painter-Stainers' Company played a role in the creation of the undertaking trade. Although all the authors generally agree on how the undertaking trade grew, Aubin's supposition that Russell was a joiner leads to two questions about how comprehensive undertaking began. Was the Painter-Stainers' Company as a whole conspiring with outside tradesmen in an attempt to create a monopoly over the commercial funeral business? If this was their intention, they failed. Or, were a handful of heraldic device painters partnering with members of other livery companies to profit from a new business opportunity? That is probably what happened.

Aubin concluded that by 1700, upholders began practising what by then was known as the 'undertaking' trade. He stated that upholders practised the trade in all respects, except for, maybe, embalming. Aubin was unsure how upholders came to dominate the undertaking trade, apparently because it was non-upholders who first established the trade. He did not ignore the fact that the funeral trade largely depended on fabric and that upholders had expertise in upholstery.[13] Whereas more contemporary historians saw that entering the undertaking business was a natural progression for upholders because of their expertise in upholstery and cabinet-making, Aubin ignored this natural progression. Where Aubin fell short was in not recognizing that upholders were more than craftsmen and artisans and that they were astute, profit-motivated business owners.

The Undertaking Trade in the Eighteenth Century

The commercialization of undertaking began in the first quarter of the eighteenth century, but quantitatively measuring the involvement of upholders in the trade is difficult. Thomas Waller's advice book and Richard Rolt's trade dictionary give weight to the consensus that upholders dominated the undertaking trade.[14] Although quantifiable information

[12] Aubin, "Behind Steele's Satire on Undertakers," 1015–19.

[13] Aubin, "Behind Steele's Satire on Undertakers," 1023–26.

[14] Thomas Waller, *A general description of all trades, digested in alphabetical order: by which parents, guardians, and trustees, may make choice of trades agreeable to the capacity, education,*

to support these conjectures is lacking, there were a handful of newspaper advertisements for undertaking and funeral services in the late-seventeenth century. These advertisements often were narrative in form and not as succinct as they were fifty years later.

A coffin-maker, James Morris in Cheapside, advertised funeral goods and services in 1682. He promoted his ability to preserve a body without any sign of physically invading the corpse. The second part of Morris's advertisement stated that he provided woollen dresses (shrouds) for the dead, velvet palls, mourning cloaks, black hangings, sconces, a hearse, and coaches, all 'fit for persons of quality'. Significantly, he stated that items such as palls and mourning cloaks were for hire.[15]

Some of those who began practicing the undertaking trade, at least initially, had a previous connection with the College of Arms. William Russell was a London provider in the emerging funeral trade. He had opened his London undertaking business by at least 1682. He managed funerals for London's elite and upper middling rank, eventually providing services in the provinces. According to Fritz and Litten, Russell was a member of the Painter-Stainers' Company, which explained how he acquired the knowledge to manage an elite funeral.[16]

Russell placed a narrative newspaper advertisement on 1 July 1682. He told the readers that he had skill in preserving dead bodies 'without emboweling, embalming, cutting, mangling, or defacing'. According to him, he had invited numerous parties to come to his home to view a corpse that he had preserved. After displaying the body for thirty-seven days, he sent it to the deceased's friends in Germany. Russell ended this section of the advertisement by reminding the readers that others '... have egregiously failed on the bodies of some persons of quality of late, to the annoyance of their relations'.[17]

inclination, strength, and fortune of the youth (London: Printed at Crown and Mitre, 1747), 214–15; Richard Rolt, *A new dictionary of trade and commerce, compiled from the information of the most eminent merchants, and from the works of the best writers on commercial subjects, in all languages. ... By Mr. Rolt, with the assistance of several eminent merchants.* (London: T. Osborne and J. Shipton; J. Hodges; J. Newbery; G. Keith; and B. Collins, 1756), Undertakers. No page number; indexed by subject.

[15] *Impartial Protestant Mercury or Occurrences Foreign and Domestick*, 28 April–2 May 1682.

[16] Fritz, "The Undertaking Trade", 242; Houlbrooke, "The age of decency," 190; Litten, *English Way of Death*, 17.

[17] *Loyal Protestant and True Domestick Intelligence*, 1 July 1682.

The last section of Russell's advertisement was more direct. He stated that all funeral furnishings and necessities were available from his Aldermanbury home. This included woollen dresses of all sorts, mourning attire, hangings for rooms, cloaks, rings, gloves, funeral tickets, velvet palls of all sorts, and choices in coffins. He ended by telling the reader that these items were available at reasonable rates. Russell's list of funeral goods and corpse-preserving services was wide-ranging and indicates that he was a large provider. His narrative was very similar to Morris's, but it was placed two months later. The two narrative portions were so similar that it appeared that Russell plagiarized Morris's advertisement.

The opening sentence of Russell's advertisement stated that he was licensed by his most gracious majesty, something Morris either could not say or inadvertently omitted. He also added that he provided whatever clients desired in heraldic items. If Russell was a member of the Painter-Stainers' Company and a heraldic device painter, it is interesting that in this advertisement he called himself a coffin-maker and not a painter. It appears that he was positioning his business as a funeral provider rather than as a painter. This advertisement is evidence that he began this business about six years before the College of Arms lost its dominance over elite funerals. By stating that he held a royal licence, he may have been appealing to the vanity of wealthy merchants and the upper middling sort. He was promoting exclusiveness, but he was careful in his wording not to overtly offer heraldic funerals to those without heraldic status. Just how the College reacted to Russell's advertisement is unknown. Nonetheless, it had to be uncomfortable to the College and seen as another threat to its dominance. This discomfort probably extended to surgeons who considered embalming their exclusive domain.

These two advertisements show there were large, if not full-time, funeral providers in the early 1680s. Letting or renting certain funeral goods, as Morris did, was not an eighteenth-century development, but an established business practice by at least the late-seventeenth century. Finally, each man identified himself as a coffin-maker, rather than as an undertaker or funeral furnisher. The convention at this time probably was to use the term coffin-maker. However, funeral undertakers only identifying themselves as coffin-makers rather than as a painter-stainer, joiner, or upholder makes it difficult to determine livery membership, if any.

Among the earliest newspaper mentions of an 'undertaker' is a news item from 1701. This reported that William Lewis Anwyl, Esq., a Welsh gentleman, had died in his lodgings at St. James's and that his body was taken to The Strand home of Mr. Evans, 'undertaker of funerals'. The corpse lay at Evans's premises in a room hung with velvet. Other rooms were hung in cloth, where several members of the House of Commons were entertained before attending Mr. Anwyl's funeral. This news item described Mr. Anwyl's funeral as 'very splendid'. Many dukes and lords attended, arriving at Westminster Abbey in coaches lit with 160 branch wax candles. Anwyl was interred in the Abbey with his ancestors.[18] Anwyl was a member of the Welsh gentry, with the rank of esquire. He amended his will shortly before his death at age twenty-five, and the bequest of his Montgomery estate was subject to lengthy litigation.[19] It appears that Anwyl's funeral was elite or heraldic in style, given the attendance of the social elite and his burial in the Abbey. Also, it is probable that the funeral was an evening affair because of the candles used for the coaches.

Little is known about Mr. (Edward) Evans, 'undertaker of funerals'. Given that the surname Evans was common in Wales, he may have been selected to furnish Anwyl's funeral because of this.[20] Nonetheless, Evans had the knowledge and skill to furnish and manage an elite funeral. No information has been found about his livery affiliation or trade background, which would indicate how he acquired the necessary knowledge and skills to manage elite funerals. After Evans died in 1722, there appeared in the *Evening Post* an announcement for the auction of his burial stock in trade. The auction notice clearly indicates that Evans's undertaking business was of significant size. This can be concluded from the list of items to be auctioned, including: black and grey cloth, beds (possibly coffin interiors), hangings and chairs for mourning, several velvet palls, velvet hangings for rooms, velvet coverings for hearses and horses, cloaks, silvered candlesticks, sconces, all manner of goods to be used in funerals, and a large quantity of cloth fit for salesmen or others.[21] The fact that Evans owned several velvet palls indicated that he offered clients choices and probably rented them out to other undertakers. In addition, the 1701 news item stated Anwyl's body was taken to the Evans home. His business would have probably been at street level, and he and any family members

[18] *Post Boy*, 8–11 February 1701.

[19] Philip Hugh Lawson, *Dictionary of Welsh Biography*, Anwyl family, of Park, Llanfrothen, Merionethshire. http://yba.llgc.org.uk/en/s-ANWY-PAR-1500.html (accessed 13 March 2017).

[20] See: Emrys Jones, ed., *The Welsh in London 1500–2000* (Cardiff: University of Wales Press, 2001).

[21] *Evening Post*, 5–7 April 1722.

may have lived either on the upper floors or elsewhere. The auction of Evans's stock in trade demonstrates that the funeral trade was recognized as a distinct occupation in the first quarter of the eighteenth century. There was, however, minimal newspaper advertising for funeral undertaking services at the beginning of the eighteenth century, when funeral undertakers promoted their services by using trade cards.[22]

Upholders noticeably increased their use of newspaper advertising after 1760. Many promoted funeral undertaking as a business line, along with their traditional lines of furniture-making and upholstery. It is apparent that upholders faced credit problems as the number of bankruptcies also increased. The following is a sampling of upholder newspaper advertisements and bankruptcy notices placed from the 1760s through the 1770s, a period when upholders were increasingly adding funeral undertaking to their product offerings. An example of an upholder advertising undertaking services after the end of the Seven Years' War was that placed by John Hewitt in 1766. He announced he was an upholder, appraiser, and undertaker and had taken over the business of Thomas Dobyns, deceased.[23] Hewitt became a freeman through servitude in the Upholders' Company in 1767 and established his business in fashionable Great George Street, Hanover Square. He served his apprenticeship with Dobyns and took over the business when the owner died.[24]

Another newspaper announcement, this one a news item from 1768, reported that an eminent upholder and undertaker, Mr. Watkins of Chancery Lane, had his horse stolen by a sharper.[25] Though seemingly a minor event, the theft of a horse from an undertaker could have serious consequences. The loss of a horse that was used to transport corpses or for a coach rented out to a funeral would represent the loss of working capital and future income.

An additional newspaper advertisement from the 1760s was that of Robert Barker. He was the late foreman of Mr. Lenn, and he announced in 1769 that he was taking up business as an upholder, appraiser, and undertaker in North Audley Street, Grosvenor Square, also a fashionable area, to serve the nobility and gentry.[26] Barker, evidently, had enough

[22] Litten, *English Way of Death*, 16–17.

[23] *Gazetteer and New Daily Advertiser*, 12 November 1766.

[24] Karin M. Walton, "The Worshipful Company of Upholders of the City of London," *Furniture History Society* Vol. 9 (1973): 62.

[25] *Gazetteer and New Daily Advertiser*, 4 February 1768.

[26] *Public Advertiser*, 14 April 1769.

confidence in the business climate at that time to risk his own capital to serve the higher-end of the upholding and funeral undertaking business. It is also possible that he purchased Mr. Lenn's business. Whether or not he used private credit in opening his business is not known, but he probably did because a third notice of bankruptcy appeared in 1774 for a Robert Barker, an upholder formerly of Goodge Street, and then living in Dublin.[27] This probably was the same Robert Barker who announced he was taking up business in North Audley Street in 1769.

Hannah and William Farmborough, mother and son, announced in 1773 that they were carrying on the upholding and undertaking business of William Farmborough, deceased. He was Hannah's husband and the father of William, the younger.[28] The elder William had been the royal upholsterer and upholder, and Hannah succeeded him in this role.[29] Farmborough would have provided upholstery services for royal funerals and used this knowledge in providing funeral undertaking as part of his upholding business.

William Brown was an upholder, cabinet-maker, undertaker, appraiser, and auctioneer in Founders Court, Lothbury. His 2 February 1776 newspaper advertisement made it apparent that he was a full-service upholder. He furnished funerals to any part of England, either public or private, and on the most reasonable terms.[30] Brown's ambitions to run a comprehensive upholding business probably relied on private credit, explaining why he was declared bankrupt on 25 November 1777.[31] On 27 November 1777, an auction notice appeared announcing the sale of Brown's household furniture and stock in trade.[32] America declared its independence from Britain less than six months after Brown first promoted his business. The ongoing war in America and the subsequent Declaration of Independence eroded national confidence in the private credit system, making Brown's business ambitions even riskier.

Brown's willingness to furnish funerals anywhere in England could have meant that he actually managed funerals outside London, or it could have meant that he sent funeral furnishings to a provincial undertaker. It

[27] *London Gazette*, 12–17 December 1774.

[28] *Public Advertiser*, 4 December 1773.

[29] The National Archives, Kew. Lord Chamberlain's Appointment Books–Series II, 1760–1793.

[30] *Daily Advertiser*, 2 February 1776.

[31] *London Gazette*, 25–29 November 1777.

[32] *Gazetteer and New Daily Advertiser*, 27 November 1777.

took time for London funeral fashions to reach the provinces.[33] The larger provincial towns often had an upholder who practised funeral undertaking at least on a part-time basis. Having a dedicated funeral undertaker was often not the case in smaller towns and rural areas, where undertaking was practised on a less formal basis. Fritz used Thomas Turner as an example of this. Turner was a shopkeeper, grocer, draper, mercer, tax collector, and undertaker from East Hoathy, Sussex. Turner was not an undertaker who managed funerals. Fritz wrote that he merely carried out the family's instructions for the funeral and burial.[34]

Upholders Dominate the Eighteenth-Century Funeral Trade

Although funeral furnishing was not the exclusive purview of upholders and upholsterers, they dominated this burgeoning business.[35] Their dominance did not necessarily emerge in the late-seventeenth century. There was much business acrimony that developed among the College of Arms, the Painter-Stainers' Company, the Upholders' Company, undertakers with no livery affiliation, and surgeons (embalmers) because funeral undertaking was a financially attractive business. The first quarter of the eighteenth century saw attempts to form a new livery company, called the United Company of Undertakers. A leading member of this new company was Robert Legg, Sr., an eminent undertaker from Bloomsbury. The United Company of Undertakers was unsuccessful in gaining livery status from Guildhall in the 1720s and 1730s, and little was heard of them afterwards. Litten speculated that the Upholders' Company mounted a vigorous defence against these interlopers' growing influence in the funeral trade and prevented the formation of a new livery company representing undertakers.[36] John Houston agreed with Litten and elaborated further on this complicated business feud. The College of Arms and Painter-Stainers' Company lamented the loss of their monopoly over heraldic funerals. Independent undertakers wanted to protect their business inter-

[33] Houlbrooke, *Death, Religion, and the Family*, 287.

[34] Fritz, "The Undertaking Trade," 249–50, citing: David Vaisey, ed., *The Diary of Thomas Turner, 1754–1765* (Oxford: Oxford University Press, 1984), 7.

[35] Fritz, "The Undertaking Trade," 248; Houlbrooke, "The age of decency," 190; Litten, *English Way of Death*, 19.

[36] Litten, *English Way of Death*, 22–23.

ests in the growing funeral trade by joining the Upholders' Company, which rejected their membership. When the independent undertakers tried to charter their own livery company, the Upholders' Company conspired against them. Finally, surgeons wanted protection from non-surgeons practising any aspect of embalming.[37] One pamphleteer at this time, T.T. Merchant, argued that the commercialization of middling rank funerals would hurt not only the woollen trade but other trades because renting goods meant that a funeral item could be used multiple times, rather than purchased.[38]

There was one main reason for this acrimony: money. Given that elite funerals were available to anyone who wanted to pay the costs, there were funeral furnishers available to meet the demand. Even non-elite funerals could be expensive. Litten fittingly wrote:

> There were plenty of outlets for one's cash: printed invitations, mourning rings, hatbands, scarves, gloves, complete suits of mourning for pall-bearers, plus as many mutes and attendants, feathers, plumes, lights, and carriages as one would care to hire.[39]

This competitive environment among the various trades for control of the undertaking business at the end of the seventeenth century can also be linked to the breakdown in the livery system. As previously stated, the traditional protections London's livery companies enjoyed were not upended by one sensational change in crown policy, act of Parliament, or court ruling. The loss of livery company control over their respective trades evolved over a period of time. The authority of the livery companies declined through a series of court cases from the late-sixteenth century to the early-seventeenth century. The cumulative effect of five court rulings *against* various livery companies limited their power in the seventeenth century. Also, the growth of London beyond the City walls, exacerbated by the Great Fire and the Plague, greatly weakened livery company control over their respective crafts.[40] The diminished power of the livery companies became very apparent early in the eighteenth century. Now, nearly

[37] J.F. Houston, *Featherbedds and Flock Bedds* (London: Three Tents Press, 2010), 84–86.

[38] Fritz, "The Undertaking Trade," 246.

[39] Litten, *English Way of Death*, 161.

[40] J.R. Kellett, "The Breakdown of Gild and Corporation Control over the Handicraft and Retail Trade in London," *The Economic History Review* New Series, Vol. 10, No. 3 (1958): 381–85.

anyone with enough money, livery company member or not, could practise the undertaking trade.

Without livery control, the funeral undertaking trade was largely unregulated. However, one act that Parliament passed did have a direct impact on undertaking. First passed in 1666, An Act for the Burying in Woollen Only was intended to protect domestic woollen production from imported textiles. The Act required that corpses should be buried in wool, including the burial clothes, the shroud (or winding sheet in the case of the poor), and the fabrics used on a coffin's inside and outside. Violators were subject to a £5 fine, but plague victims were exempted from the Act.[41] The 1666 Act was quickly amended. A revised Act for Burying in Woollen was passed in 1667 and became effective in 1668. This Act improved the discovery and prosecution of violators. Executors and families were required to obtain a sworn affidavit, at no cost from their parish authority, stating that the deceased was buried only in wool and then present it to the parish where the deceased was buried. Churchwardens were required to keep track of burials and collect the affidavit for each burial. Fines for violating the Act remained at £5, and plague victims were still exempted.[42] It was common practice by the time of these Acts that even the poorest were shrouded.[43] The wealthy often ignored the Act, paid the £5 fine, and were buried in more luxurious material than wool.[44] One example of where a fine would have been levied is the 1772 funeral of Lady Heathcote, which was managed by Chippendale Haig & Company. Her shroud was made of superfine crape, and the coffin mattress, pillows, sheet, and quilt made of rich sarsnet (silk). The coffin was covered in black velvet.[45] These silk and velvet fabrics violated the Act, and a £5 fine would

[41] "Charles II, 1666: An Act for Burying in Woollen," in *Statutes of the Realm: Volume 5, 1628–80*, ed. John Raithby (s.l: Great Britain Record Commission, 1819), 598. *British History Online*, http://www.british-history.ac.uk/statutes-realm/vol5/p598a (accessed 27 March 2017).

[42] "Charles II, 1677 & 1678: An Act for burying in Woollen," in *Statutes of the Realm: Volume 5, 1628–80*, ed. John Raithby (s.l: Great Britain Record Commission, 1819), 885–886. *British History Online*, http://www.british-history.ac.uk/statutes-realm/vol5/pp885-886 (accessed 27 March 2017).

[43] Clare Gittings, "Sacred and secular: 1558–1660," in *Death in England: An Illustrated History*, ed. Peter C. Jupp and Clare Gittings, (New Brunswick: Rutgers University Press, 2000), 157.

[44] Gittings, *Death, Burial and the Individual*, 113.

[45] Christopher Gilbert, "Chippendale as Undertaker," *Furniture History* Vol. 9 (1973): 116–18.

have been imposed. There is no indication that the Act of Burying in Woollen was a controversial burial requirement, probably because a woollen shroud was not expensive and was an expected element of a decent funeral. Upholders overseeing the interment provided the sworn affidavit and ensured it was properly recorded with the local parish. They would also pay the fine for using non-woollen material and add it to the client's bill.

Fritz concluded from examining trade cards that undertaking became a separate trade in the first quarter of the eighteenth century. He also believed that there were a substantial number of undertakers in the last half of the seventeenth century. He based this opinion on the number of surviving trade cards from this period but gave no quantitative evidence to support what 'substantial' meant.[46] As for undertakers catering to the lower middling funeral market, some of them may not have used trade cards. Awareness of individual funeral providers was probably increased through broadsheets, word of mouth, and from attending the services of relatives and friends.

Another way to determine the scale of the undertaking business is by using probate records. Teerapa Pirohakul analysed records of over one hundred deceased undertakers between 1702 and 1800. Some in her list were also involved in other trades such as carpentry, painting, and joinery. This list identified only one upholder, Richard Browning.[47] At least one other of the undertakers on Pirohakul's list was also an upholder but not described as one—Peter Deschamps, who became a member of the Upholders' Company in 1725.[48] Unfortunately, the lack of a full description of the other occupations and livery membership of the deceased undertakers makes it difficult to use probate research to accurately determine how many undertakers were also upholders. There were, however, some mid-eighteenth-century publications that associated undertakers with upholders.

R. Campbell's apprenticeship advice book from 1747 did not associate undertaking with upholders, making no mention of it in the extensive upholders section. Undertaking had no general heading in his book and

[46] Fritz, "The Undertaking Trade," 243, 248.

[47] Teerapa Pirohakul, *The Funeral in England in the Long Eighteenth Century* (London: PhD Thesis at London School of Economics, 2015), APPENDIX 3, 212–14, http://etheses.lse.ac.uk/1076/1/Pirohakul_The_Funeral_in_England_in_the_Long.pdf (accessed 17 January 2016).

[48] Walton, Company of Upholders, 58.

was only mentioned as a minor trade. He wrote that undertakers were generally carpenters and heralds, and he characterized them as hard-hearted and needing more money than brains to practise their trade.[49] Thomas Waller's apprenticeship advice book differs from Campbell. He described undertaking as work often performed by upholders, though he wrote that box-makers, coffin-makers, carpenters, and joiners also practised undertaking.[50] Richard Rolt's commercial dictionary from 1756 stated that the word undertaker '... is chiefly used for upholders, or persons who furnish out funerals...'.[51]

The stage was set at the beginning of the eighteenth century for upholders and other tradesmen to earn money from the funeral undertaking trade. Upholders were positioned to dominate this new opportunity because of their experience in working with fabric. As the eighteenth century progressed, more and more upholders looked to business opportunities in funeral undertaking.

Operating a Funeral Undertaking Business

An upholder furnishing funerals required two competencies to succeed. First, upholstery and cabinet-making skills were required. Goods not made by the upholder were sourced from specialist tradesmen. Except for the coffin, shroud, and coffin equipment (handles and name plate), most funeral items could be rented.[52] The second competency any funeral undertaker needed was managerial skills. Along with the traditional upholding and organizational skills, an upholder furnishing and managing funerals required knowledge of a number of different areas. Ensuring that the corpse had been properly prepared for viewing and burial, supplying mourning clothing and accoutrements, transportation of the body, and helping coordinate religious services and the interment could have many permutations. All required a reliable network of suppliers to deliver the correct goods and services at the right time, at the right place, and at the right cost. The furnishings were provided by a supply system made up of tradesmen, among them other upholders, carpenters and coffin-makers,

[49] R. Campbell, *The London Tradesman* (London: T. Gardner, 1747), 169–176, 329–30.

[50] Waller, *A general description of all trades*, 214–15.

[51] Rolt, *A new dictionary of trade and* commerce, Undertakers. No page number; indexed by subject.

[52] Houlbrooke, "The age of decency," 190.

tailors, and mercers. Finally, the importance of credit must not be overlooked. An upholder furnishing funerals needed to negotiate payment terms in advance. Whether or not payment was made upon delivery of the goods and services or through credit, outside suppliers of fabric and accoutrements, hearse owners, coachmen, and so forth would have expected timely payment.

There were three ways by which an upholder could enter the funeral undertaking business in eighteenth-century London. First, an upholder could participate in the business by simply referring funerals to a funeral furnisher for a fee. Referring a funeral to another party would have been easy. Obviously, this had little financial risk, but the profits would be limited to just the referral fee, and any price mark-ups on goods and services were forgone. In a case of 'some money was better than none', referring funerals to another firm would have appealed to an upholder having substantial business in other areas or limited capacity or financial means. A second way of participating in the business was to supply some of the goods and rent some of the required goods, such as the pall and hearse. Finally, upholders could treat funeral undertaking as a main business line.[53]

Upholders were in a position to furnish and manage funerals as a specialty or full-time business if they wanted. Many upholders probably avoided practicing full-time undertaking because of the financial risks from maintaining a large stock of goods or a lack of capital. The decision of whether or not to enter the undertaking business was based on expected profits and personal choice. Expected undertaking profits, as compared to other product-line profits like cabinet-making and upholstery, would have been estimated. Any upholder entering the funeral undertaking trade on more than an intermittent basis needed to identify their target market, which could be the higher-end elite market, the middling sort market, or a combination of the two. Entering the elite market would have required maintaining more expensive stock than the middling funeral undertaking market required. Presuming that many upholders used private credit to expand, financial success would have depended on managing inventory and credit risk.

There was naturally a cost distinction between elite and common (middling) funerals. The previously mentioned funeral of Lady Heathcote, which was furnished and managed by Chippendale Haig & Company in May 1772, is an example of an elite funeral. She died in London and

[53] Fritz, "The Undertaking Trade," 247.

required transportation of her body to the family's Normanton country home. The invoice for the goods and services provided by Chippendale's firm survived and was broken down into sections. The first section, totalling £47, pertained to supplying the basic funeral furnishings, including the inner lead-lined coffin, the pillow and other textiles for the corpse, the outer coffin covered in black velvet and attached with brass nails, gilt brass coffin handles and a brass plate, six men carrying the coffin, and other accoutrements like cloaks, hatbands, and scarves. The silk hatbands and gloves provided for twenty-six tenants and similar items for other attendees totalled nearly £27 in the bill's second section. The third section of the bill pertained to the transportation of the body from London to Normanton, a distance of over one hundred miles. This part of the invoice added about £22 to the total bill and included ostrich feathers and velvet coverings for the hearse and horses, mourning attire for the coachmen and horsemen, a painted heraldic hatchment, and Mr. Haig's travel expenses. The invoice's fourth section was for disbursements paid out for various expenses totalling nearly £24. The final section of the invoice was for additional expenses and added an additional £1 to the invoice. The total paid to Chippendale Haig & Company for goods and services was £121.15.11.[54]

All in all, Lady Heathcote's funeral required considerable administrative coordination and expertise. According to Gilbert, Chippendale's firm made the outside elm coffin, covered it with fabric, and attached the hardware. Gilbert also rightly surmised that many of the items provided by the firm, including the lead-lined inner coffin and coffin hardware, were got from the stock of specialist tradesmen.[55]

If one considers the Heathcote funeral as an elite funeral, Robert Williams, who is discussed in Chap. 4, furnished what can be described as a common or middling funeral. Documentation proves Williams could furnish and manage a funeral, but he did so only once in 1765 for about £7. It seems fair to describe it as a decent but not expensive burial. The deceased was provided with an elm coffin, the standard coffin because it was thought to be water-resistant and not prone to splitting.[56] The outside of the coffin was covered with fine flannel, which was attached with burnished buttons (nails). A nameplate and three pairs of handles were also provided. A shroud was included, probably flannel, because the 1668 Act

[54] Gilbert, "Chippendale as Undertaker," 114–18.
[55] Gilbert, "Chippendale as Undertaker," 115.
[56] Litten, *English Way of Death*, 90.

for Burying in Woollen imposed a fine for using shrouds made of imported material. The inside of the coffin was lined, and a ruffled pillow was provided. The bottom of the coffin was filled with bran to prevent the body from shifting in the coffin during carriage and to absorb the body fluids of the decomposing corpse. The best pall, six cloaks, two crepe hatbands, and four pairs of ribbon-bound black gloves were provided, which were probably rented by Williams, as there would be no practical use for them after the burial. His charges included arranging for a hearse, one coach, four bearers, and a gravedigger. Williams also charged for drinks for the coachman and other workers and for turnpike fees, along with the affidavit that the corpse was buried in wool.[57] The funeral goods and services delivered by Williams were modest when compared to those provided by Chippendale Haig & Company, £7 versus £121.

There was a wide range of choices in funeral furnishings from which the executor and family could choose. The Heathcote funeral had many extras when compared to the common funeral furnished by Robert Williams. The deceased's family would meet with an undertaker or funeral furnisher to decide what kind of funeral they wanted and if it was within their financial means. Funeral expense was generally determined by wealth and status.[58]

There were upholders who managed funerals by selling some items and renting the other needed items from suppliers and passing on the costs to the family.[59] Upholder newspaper advertisements from the last half of the eighteenth century often listed undertaking as one of their services. The fact that they also listed upholstery, cabinet-making, and other businesses in their advertisements indicated that funeral undertaking was not their main business line. Rather than specialty or niche upholders, they were generalists. Although renting the required accoutrements on behalf of a client and hiring transportation may have diminished profits, there were, undoubtedly, price mark-ups for the occasional undertaker. An upholder renting the required funeral items also had the advantage of requiring only enough capital to pay the rental costs, rather than maintaining a stock of goods. Upholders practicing funeral undertaking on a part-time basis

[57] London Metropolitan Archives, City of London. Reference Code: ACC/0426. Account Book of Robert Williams. 1765 account entry for undertaking expenses charged to Mr. Chassereau, Sr. by Robert Williams.

[58] Peter Earle, *The Making of the Middle Class* (Berkeley: University of California Press, 1989), 311.

[59] Houlbrooke, "The age of decency," 190; Litten, *English Way of Death*, 21–22.

would have had considerable latitude in renting versus owning. They could own some items, palls, for instance, and rent them out multiple times.

Peter Earle believed that the commercialization of funerals resulted from the profit motive. Funerals had become fashionable with the middling ranks as a way to emulate elite funerals.[60] The middling sort that emerged in London had sufficient capital accumulation (savings) to engage the services of a funeral undertaker. At the lower end of the middling sort, funeral expenses would have been considerably lower when compared to the expenses paid for a more elaborate funeral at the upper end. Thus, the undertakers and funeral furnishers were offering families in the middling station choices in how to spend their savings.

Historically, one of the benefits of livery company membership was assistance with burial costs, a custom established by the medieval guilds from which the London livery companies evolved.[61] For those without livery company membership, a basic common funeral was available. By the mid-eighteenth century, most in the middling ranks could afford a £5 burial or at least could borrow enough for one. There was assistance available for those who did not have the means to arrange for a decent funeral. Although parishes provided free burials for the poor, some in this rank wanted more decent funerals, which were provided by the burial clubs. A small number of undertakers established burial clubs where one could pay a few pence per week to assure that they and their family members could receive a decent burial.[62] It was mostly the poor who subscribed to burial clubs. Joining a club sponsored by an undertaker would have required confidence that the undertaker would remain financially solvent when it came time to draw upon the contracted burial services. Because the funeral undertaking trade was not regulated in the eighteenth century, it would have been necessary to sue in court for any breach of contract or file a criminal complaint for fraud if the burial club failed to meet its obligations.

Earle created distribution groupings of funeral expenses using the value of the deceased's estate. These groupings were based on a sample of 207 inventories. Using the lower and upper ends from Earle's distribution

[60] Earle, *The Making of the Middle Class*, 79, 332.

[61] City of London Livery Companies Commission. "Report of the Commissioners: Part 1," in *City of London Livery Companies Commission. Report: Volume 1*, (London: Eyre and Spottiswoode, 1884), 7–20. *British History Online*, http://www.british-history.ac.uk/livery-companies-commission/vol1/pp7-20 (accessed 17 April 2017).

[62] Litten, *English Way of Death*, 164–65.

table, he showed that funeral expenses increased with wealth. For those having wealth of less than £1000, sixty-six per cent of the funerals cost under £50. When the deceased had wealth of more than £10,000, seventy-seven per cent of the funerals cost more than £200.[63]

Pirohakul gave more detail on funeral costs by social rank. Her extensive research into probate accounts that listed funeral expenses showed a drop in funeral expenditure for the aristocracy, gentry, and middling sort in the last forty years of the eighteenth century. For the period 1761–1800, the mean funeral expenditure for the aristocracy was about £60, the gentry about £40, and the middling sort around £20. Although Earle was correct in that the wealthy spent more on funerals, Pirohakul's research showed that the least wealthy spent a higher percentage of their wealth on funerals than when compared to the amount spent by those with higher-than-average wealth. She pointed out that competition in the funeral trade lowered costs. Though the lower middling family spent a higher proportion of their wealth on a funeral, they could get more for their money through renting.[64]

There was an increase in fully managed funerals by undertakers in the eighteenth century. Pirohakul's research showed that for the period 1711–1740, fully managed funerals by undertakers comprised eleven per cent out of the sample of 679 funerals. For the period 1741–1770, fully managed funerals by undertakers represented twenty per cent of the sample size of 633 funerals. Finally, from 1771–1800, fully managed funerals by undertakers were thirty per cent of the 528 sample funerals. This research also showed that funerals partially managed by undertakers also increased during the eighteenth century, other than for a slight drop after 1770. By 1800, undertakers either fully or partially managed fifty-four per cent of the funerals in Pirohakul's sample.[65] Economies of scale were at work in encouraging families to hire an undertaker. Pirohakul found that goods and services purchased separately for a £5 funeral included a shroud, coffin, burial services, and wine for the attendees. Alternatively, a £5 fully managed funeral by an undertaker often included extra items, such as gloves and hatbands. Undertakers also provided textiles of a higher quality.[66] Upholders probably manufactured coffins and fabric goods, purchas-

[63] Earle, *The Making of the Middle Class*, 312.
[64] Pirohakul, *The Funeral in England in the Long Eighteenth Century*, 69–77.
[65] Pirohakul, *The Funeral in England in the Long Eighteenth Century*, 178.
[66] Pirohakul, *The Funeral in England in the Long Eighteenth Century*, 182.

ing non-stock items at favourable rates from sub-contractors. Their own shop production, along with the practice of renting out items multiple times, were key components of a profitable pricing scheme.

The most important attribute of a successful business is profitability. Existing upholder and undertaker account books, though illuminating in regard to stock in trade purchases, names of suppliers, and funeral charges, do not give a clear picture of profitability. Pirohakul challenged Litten's estimates that an average funeral could yield a 175 per cent profit and even over 500 per cent at the upper end as unrealistic. Pirohakul wrote that Litten's estimates did not account for overhead expenses, which would include labour, any rents and interest, bad debt, and coal for heating. She estimated the average profits earned by Robert Legg, a milliner turned undertaker practicing in the first three decades of the eighteenth century, were less than fifty per cent. Her research also showed that Legg's customers spent over forty per cent on milliner items, which meant that the more expensive the funeral, the more profit Legg made from his milliner business.[67] Pirohakul's estimate that Legg's profits were less than fifty per cent, though more accurate than Litten's, lacks preciseness. Accounting for overhead, as John Trotter surely did in 1759 for Princess Elizabeth Caroline's coffin, is why his seven and one-half per cent price mark-up is compelling to accept as a profitability target.[68] This precision indicated confidence in knowing his overhead costs in calculating expected profit. This exactness was not unknown. By 1770, Josiah Wedgwood was using an overhead cost accounting system to understand the nuances of supply and demand in managing his manufacturing business's expenses and profits.[69]

The two main business risks for upholders in the funeral business were credit and stock in trade or inventory. Credit was the riskiest of all, and financial success depended on managing this risk. Keeping stock levels as low as possible would have helped. Increasing revenues through the ability to raise prices, known as pricing power, was always a possibility for a business owner. However, this was not possible in the funeral undertaking trade in the last decades of the eighteenth century. Pirohakul found that

[67] Pirohakul, *The Funeral in England in the Long Eighteenth Century*, 182–84.

[68] Lord Chamberlain's Department, Records of Special Events, Funeral of Princess Elizabeth Caroline. Reference: LC 2/27.

[69] See: N. McKendrick "Josiah Wedgwood: An Eighteenth-Century Entrepreneur in Salesmanship and Marketing Techniques," *The Economic History Review* New Series, Vol. 12, No. 3 (1960): 408–33.

funeral expenditures dropped in the last forty years of the century, perhaps indicating that the funeral trade was competitive and that there was little pricing power. Ideally, the more risk, the higher the price. The lack of pricing power probably meant that upholders who were using credit to finance undertaking goods were unable to offset the additional credit default risk with higher revenues. At the beginning of the eighteenth century, the undertaking trade was a growth business and, probably, very profitable. Pirohakul also pointed out that between 1770 and 1800, fully managed funerals grew by ten per cent. The lack of pricing power in a growing business meant that funeral undertaking was competitive and high-risk. This resulted in a consolidation of funeral undertakers by the end of the century, either from dropping this line of business or bankruptcies.

There was a fall in upholders advertising undertaking services in the 1780s, probably indicating their consolidation into separate specialty trades. It could also indicate that upholders had to choose whether they were in the undertaking business full-time or not at all. The number of upholders becoming bankrupt also declined in this period, although there were six found in 1780 and eight in 1781. It appears that the private credit crisis of the 1770s, when ten upholders went bankrupt in 1776, probably created a more cautious approach to not only taking on credit but also to extending it. The prudent upholder would have avoided the funeral undertaking business or been in it only part-time or intermittently.

Social Desire for Funeral Display

The funeral trade thrived because many families in the growing middling ranks had the disposable income that enabled them to hire a funeral manager if they chose. Over the course of the seventeenth century, families became increasingly willing to allow the undertaker to assume responsibility for what had traditionally been done by the family and servants, from preparing the corpse for burial to acquiring the needed goods. Known as 'dressing and trimming' the corpse, undertakers began taking over this task from the family, usually by hiring poor women to perform the washing and dressing of the body.[70] Coffin-makers, who began 'undertaking' what was traditionally a family's task, were later known as undertakers. By the end of the seventeenth century, middling families could afford lesser versions of the goods and services used for elite funerals. According to

[70] Litten, *English Way of Death*, 72.

Houlbrooke, those most successful in managing funerals were upholders. It was expected that the family provide funerals that were commensurate with the deceased's social status, but family wealth and personal choice were also on display.[71] In the first quarter of the eighteenth century, undertakers began offering the middling sort choices in the goods and services needed for a 'decent' funeral that corresponded to the deceased's social status. Engaging the services of a funeral undertaker had two advantages for the family. The family no longer had to contact multiple suppliers. Different pricing schemes that included renting items allowed the family to provide a 'decent' funeral that emulated an elite one but at a lower cost. These advantages gave the family more time to concentrate on mourning their loss. Also, not having to handle the corpse fit in with the rise of the sense of sentimentality in the upper and middling ranks. Julie Rugg explained that sentimentality emphasized the individual in the last part of the eighteenth century. Known as Romanticism, love was celebrated among family members, and openly mourning the death of a loved one was considered honourable.[72] Family members could properly grieve after hiring a funeral manager.

The consumer demand that was necessary for the growth of the undertaking trade came from social desire. Eighteenth-century funerals were meant to convey family status and had little to do with the transfer of political power from one heir to the next in line.[73] The executors and family of the deceased decided how elaborate the funeral would be. The funeral was often a show of the family's wealth and status (or lack of it), rather than just an event to mourn the loss of a family member.[74] Families aimed to provide what was called a 'decent funeral'. Ralph Houlbrooke characterized the time period 1660–1760 as the 'Age of Decency', defining decency as 'appropriateness, fitness, seemliness, order, comeliness, good taste and the avoidance of vulgarity or excess'.[75]

Defining what contributed to a 'decent funeral' is difficult, however, just as it is defining the meaning of 'good taste', though one can

[71] Houlbrooke, *Death, Religion, and the Family*, 286–287, 293.

[72] Julie Rugg, "From reason to regulation: 1760–1850," in *Death in England: An Illustrated History*, ed. Peter C. Jupp and Clare Gittings (New Brunswick: Rutgers University Press, 2000), 210.

[73] Clare Gittings, *Death, Burial and the Individual in Early Modern England* (Beckenham: Croom Helm Ltd., 1984), 88–89, 135, 181–82,197.

[74] Houlbrooke, *Death, Religion, and the Family*, 293.

[75] Ralph Houlbrooke, "The age of decency," 174.

historicize its meaning. Christians at that time may have thought that, at least in the eyes of God, an expensive funeral was no better than an inexpensive one. Puritans, for instance, considered ostentatious displays of wealth as sinful. From a religious standpoint, all that mattered was that the funeral was done in a Christian manner. Requesting a modest funeral in one's will was probably meant to save the survivors the angst of burdensome expenses.[76] It was also an expression of piety. Just what 'a decent but not expensive funeral' meant was left to executors to determine. However, according to Fritz, the family largely had control of the funeral.[77]

The will of Soho upholder John Trotter, for example, requested a decent but not expensive burial inside the vault beside his wife at St. Ann's Church, Soho.[78] An act of Parliament prohibited vault burial beneath a church for sanitary reasons, not the least of which was offensive odours. Burial beneath a church and in a churchyard were socially popular and brought money to the church, making the law impossible to enforce.[79] Gittings pointed out that requesting burial beside a loved one, as John Trotter did, was common in the eighteenth century. For example, George II made arrangements for the facing sides of his and Queen Caroline's coffins to be removed so that their decaying remains would intermingle.[80]

Trotter's wife had died nearly thirty years before him, and it may be that he wanted to ensure that his financial legacy was not spent on a lavish funeral, but rather passed on to his three children. Or, he may have had a pious aversion to ostentatious displays like those he had furnished as the royal upholsterer. Therefore, it may be that the executors provided him with the decent but not expensive funeral that he requested.

More importantly, Gittings pointed out that the large majority of executors arranged funerals that were commensurate with the deceased's social rank.[81] Houlbrooke wrote that a decent funeral could have different con-

[76] Litten, *English Way of Death*, 87.

[77] Fritz, "The Undertaking Trade," 250.

[78] The National Archives, Kew. PROB 11/1194/170. Will of John Trotter of Soho Square, Middlesex. 24 July 1790.

[79] Mark Jenner, "Death, Decomposition and Dechristianisation? Public Health and Church Burial in Eighteenth-Century England," *The English Historical Review* Vol. 120, No. 487 (Jun. 2005): 628–29.

[80] Jeremy Black, *George II: Puppet of the Politicians?* (Exeter: University of Exeter Press, 2007), 253; Andrew Thompson, *George II: King and Elector* (London & New Haven: Yale University Press, 2011), 125, 290.

[81] Gittings, *Death, Burial and the Individual*, 86–87, 94.

textual meanings, including 'appropriate to the rank of the deceased, free of ostentation or excess, sober, sufficient, respectful, and dignified'.[82] Social standing usually determined funeral expenses, and funeral undertakers were more than willing to help families err on the side of spending too much money rather than spending too little.[83]

Upholders Face Reputational Challenges

Even though funeral undertaking providers promoted convenience and savings, there was resistance to their growing influence. There were instances when the deceased's wills were explicit with regard to funeral arrangements. When Norfolk's Peter Le Neve, Esq., a herald and, therefore, knowledgeable in such things, died in 1729, he instructed in his will that he be buried where he died with a service held in the parish church. A hearse, his coach, and one other coach were allowed and no more. He specifically directed, '... that no Undertaker, *alias* Cold Cook, or Upholder, shall have the management thereof'.[84] Obviously, the loss of power by the heralds over elite funerals still rankled him until his death.

Le Neve's attitude toward the undertaking profession was extreme enough for him to be specific. There was, apparently, an underlying discomfort with the undertaking services that upholders provided, perhaps because, as Litton pointed out, the funeral trade was more than willing to charge as much as possible. In a 1764 newspaper opinion, an anonymous writer, using the initials Y.N., expressed dislike of upholders in the undertaking trade. The author wrote that undertaking was of no use to the deceased, enriched the upholder at the wish of the living's vanity, and that the upholder's profits come from a dead man's estate. The author likened an upholder embalming the dead to a politician politically embalming the living.[85]

Negative opinions of undertaking like Y.N.'s were not new. Over sixty years earlier, in 1701, Sir Richard Steele wrote a comedy about the undertaking trade called *The funeral: or, grief a-la-mode: A Comedy*. Steele created a comedic setting in Act One, Scene One, when Mr. Cabinet opened with, 'I burst into laughter! I can't bear to see writ over an undertaker's

[82] Houlbrooke, "The age of decency," 188.
[83] Houlbrooke, "The age of decency," 189–91.
[84] *Country Chronicle*, September 1729.
[85] *Gazetteer and New Daily Advertiser*, 17 September 1764.

door, dresses for the dead, and necessaries for Funerals! Ha! Ha! Ha!' Mr. Sable, the undertaker, responded, 'Well Gentlemen, 'tis very well, I know you are of the laughters, the wits that take liberty to deride all things that are Magnificent and Solemn.' A little later in Act One, a gravedigger gave Mr. Sable a shroud and a cut off finger with a ring on it. These came from the body that was buried the night before.[86] Anyone seeing this comedy on stage or even reading it probably was left with the impression that undertakers were not only dishonest, but also immoral.

Robert Aubin elaborated on Steele's satire, which became a popular play at the turn of the eighteenth century. Focusing on the Preface and Act One, Scene One, Aubin listed eight unethical practices attributed to undertakers and upholders. They were: extravagant claims of the efficacy of embalming technique; providing lavish funerals for the unworthy; using cheap embalming materials; creating false heraldic devices; hiring of mourners to look sad; collusion with sextons and others to rob corpses; employing prostitutes as mourners; and using intelligence to learn of recent deaths. Aubin believed that these charges by Steele against upholders were true. He stated that upholders had 'trespassed' into the undertaking trade. By usurping the undertaking business from the trade's original founders, upholders took on a greedy persona.[87]

A pamphlet from 1725, *Funeral discipline: or, the character of Strip-Corps the dead-monger…* is a sarcastic essay, where Mr. Strip-Corps plays the role of The Great Undertaker. Strip-Corps and his assistant, Paul Meagre, perfunctorily prepare a body for burial and later lead the funeral procession. Like Mr. Sable from *grief a-la-mode*, Mr. Strip-Corps removes the shroud for reuse (for the twenty-ninth time!) and steals the deceased's ring.[88] Another play from about this time was *A Bickerstaff's burying; or work for the upholders*. The play was a farce and its foreword included a sarcastic dedication to the Magnificent Company of Upholders, an ironic reference to The Worshipful Company of Upholders. The author dedicated the play to upholders who were 'over fond of paper-credit, where there is no probability of recovering the debt'. The author wrote that the funerals furnished by upholders were a better spectacle than a puppet

[86] Sir Richard Steele, *The funeral: or, grief a-la-mode: A Comedy*, 1701, rev. ed. (London: J. Tonson, 1723), B, B3.

[87] Aubin, "Behind Steele's Satire on Undertakers," 1023–26.

[88] Anon., *Funeral discipline: or, the character of Strip-Corps the dead-monger. According to the instructions of Paul Meagre, once mourner in chief to the funeral undertaker.* (London: J. Roberts and A. Dodd, 1725), 7–8.

show and, should an admission fee be paid by the curious, it would better serve the State by garnering more money than from the candle tax.[89] This author implied that managed funerals were not decent. Indeed, it was commonly believed that managed funerals were sinful because they ran counter to the religious ideal against ostentatious displays of wealth. It may also be that these negative feelings arose from decreased control by family members in planning a loved one's funeral. The funeral undertaking trade offered the family choices in funeral goods and services, but they came at a cost. One of the social costs was that outsiders now performed what family members and servants once did. The family was now spending money for less personal involvement and control over a relative's funeral. Despite these negative opinions, the undertaking trade thrived.

Upholders Increase Advertising and Face Insolvency Risk

There was a noticeable change in the upholder business model after 1760. Newspaper advertising indicates that upholders were now more than upholsterers and cabinet-makers. Funeral undertaking became an established business for many of them by 1760. They also began advertising additional services that included appraising, brokering, and auctioneering, which will be discussed in the next chapter. Many upholders probably operated part-time in some of these additional business offerings as it does not seem possible to be competent in every one of them. The larger point here is that these advertisements were indicative of a growing consumer market and competitive economy in which upholders were looking to capture as much revenue as they could.

Analysing the volume of eighteenth-century upholders advertising undertaking in newspapers, rather than relying on trade cards, is another way of estimating the increase in upholder involvement in the undertaking and funeral furnishing trade. (Admittedly, there was growth in general newspaper advertising in the last half of the century.) Newspaper advertising shows that the commercial environment changed for upholders after 1760. There was a synergy between upholding and undertaking, which further supports suppositions that upholders dominated the funeral undertaking business. A search for the words upholder and undertaker in

[89] Susanna Centlivre, *A Bickerstaff's burying; or, work for the upholders. A farce; as it is acted at the theatres, with applause. By His Majesty's servants* (Dublin: S. Powell, 1724), 3–4.

the same advertisement from 1700 to 1750 yielded fifteen results. Nine of these results were death notices. Five results were various news items. Only one of the results was an advertisement, where Richard Annyson advertised himself as an upholder, sworn appraiser, and undertaker. (Sworn brokers and appraisers were licensed by the City of London and swore an oath to be fair and honest in their dealings.) In this instance, he announced he was auctioning some goods.[90] Except for this single advertisement, it can be concluded that upholders who also practised funeral undertaking rarely used newspaper advertising in the first half of the eighteenth century.

Surprisingly, no newspaper advertisements were found that included upholder and undertaker in the same advertisement during the period 1750 to 1759. There is no obvious reason for this, although during most of this period, the Seven Years' War was in progress, which may have dampened business activity and/or the amount of funeral undertaking advertising by upholders. Advertising by upholders for their undertaking goods and services increased after 1760. This same sort of increase was seen in the next chapter about sworn brokers and appraisers and auctioneers. In the decade 1760 to 1769, newspaper advertisements for upholding and undertaking increased to six. Advertising became more prevalent in the decades of the 1770s and 1780s; the 1770s had twenty-two advertisements and the 1780s, seventeen. The 1790s had a significant drop in upholding and undertaking advertisements. Only two were found (Table 2.1).

If one compares the number of upholder and undertaker advertisements by each eighteenth-century decade to the number of upholders admitted (licensed) as sworn brokers during the same time period, there appears to be a correlation for the period from 1760 through 1789. At the same time, the number of upholder bankruptcies reported in the newspapers trended upward for the period 1760 through 1789. This information is represented below (Table 2.2).

The information from Table 2.2 is graphically displayed (Graph 2.1). As can be seen from the graph, there is a strong correlation between advertising by upholders and undertakers and upholders and broker admission in the same time periods. There is a noticeable upward trend in both categories beginning around 1760, which continued until about 1780, when both categories began falling. The correlation between upholder and undertaking advertising and upholder and broker admission

[90] *London Daily Post and General Advertiser*, 17 January 1739.

Table 2.1 Upholder and undertaker together in same newspaper item by time period and reason

Period/item	*Advertisement*	*News*	*Death notice*
1700–1709	0	0	0
1710–1719	0	0	0
1720–1729	0	0	2
1730–1739	1	1	5
1740–1749	0	1	4
1750–1759	0	0	0
1760–1769	6	4	4
1770–1779	22	2	2
1780–1789	17	0	1
1790–1799	2	0	1

Source: Burney Newspaper Collection

Table 2.2 Upholder/undertaking advertisements, upholder/broker admittance, and upholder bankruptcy comparisons

Period/item	*Undertaking*	*Brokers admitted*	*Bankruptcies*
1700–1709	0	1	9
1710–1719	0	0	4
1720–1729	0	1	34
1730–1739	1	1	14
1740–1749	0	1	32
1750–1759	0	0	23
1760–1769	6	11	27
1770–1779	22	22	42
1780–1789	17	15	38
1790–1799	2	10	33

Advertisement Source: Burney Newspaper Collection. Broker Source: London Metropolitan Archives, City of London. Reference Code: COL/BR/02/074-075. Index to Brokers' Bonds A-H and I-Z and COL/BR05. Broker Sureties 1752–1813

is 0.93, a nearly perfect correlation. This high correlation means that upholders advertising undertaking services and upholders becoming sworn brokers increased in unison. With respect to bankruptcies, the correlation of upholder bankruptcies and upholder and undertaking advertising is 0.63. The correlation between upholder bankruptcies and upholder and broker admission is 0.69. This indicates that there was bankruptcy risk

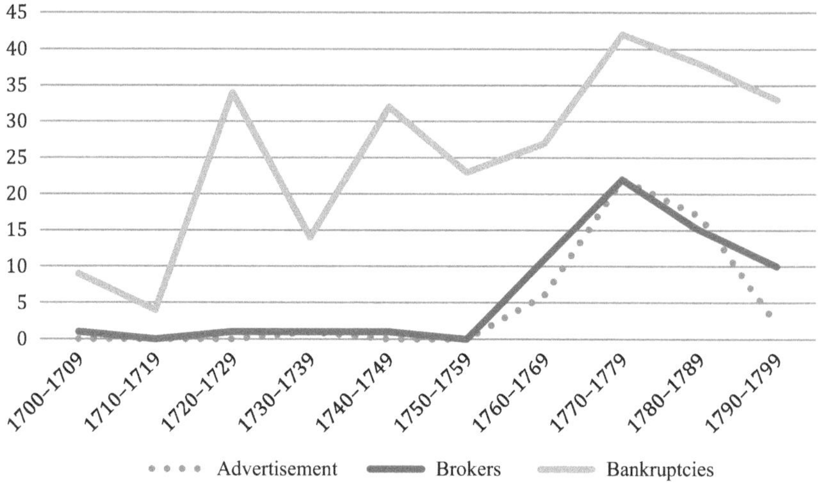

Graph 2.1 Frequency of Upholder/Undertaking Advertising, Broker Admission, and Bankruptcies by Decade. (Advertisement and Bankruptcy Source: Burney Newspaper Collection. Broker Sources: London Metropolitan Archives, City of London. Reference Code: COL/BR/02/074-075. Index to Brokers' Bonds A-H and I-Z and COL/BR05. Broker Sureties 1752–1813)

with upholders advertising undertaking services and becoming brokers, but it was not a foregone conclusion that such upholders would become bankrupt.

The simultaneous rise in upholder and undertaking advertising and upholder and broker admission in the period 1760 to 1780 is significant, and the large increase in upholder bankruptcies during this period is also significant, but less so. The primary reason for the rise in upholder undertaking and broker advertising in the 1770s was that these business owners were confident in economic growth. With the economy growing, these businesses expanded with the expectation of higher profits and used newspaper advertising to reach a wider audience. This expansion was fuelled by the use of private credit.

The overall increase in business advertising that began in the late 1760s was a result of increased business activity and increased competition in the aftermath of the Seven Years' War. Hoppit wrote that the economy grew at a steady pace during the last thirty years of the eighteenth century, but not in a straight line. Growth was interrupted by a financial crisis on an average of one every six years.[91] Even with the 1775 outbreak of hostilities in colonial America, it appears from the stable number of advertisements that consumer business confidence and activity remained high.

Analysing newspaper advertisements to determine the number of upholders furnishing the undertaking trade is imperfect. Newspaper advertising volumes, trade cards, and probates are indicators of upholder involvement in the trade, not a percentage estimate of their overall market share of the undertaking trade. Newspaper advertising was a way for upholders to promote their goods and services and generate more revenues. What the upholder advertisements after 1760 demonstrate is that the upholding trade was adapting to competition and offering new products and services.

Overall, it was the political, economic, and social changes by 1690 that allowed the funeral undertaking trade to become a commercial business opportunity. These changes evolved over the course of the seventeenth century. The loss of the College of Arms's control over elite funerals and the dilution of livery company influence helped create an unregulated funeral undertaking business environment. The middling sort had emerged and expanded in size. Their desire for 'decent' funerals worthy of the deceased's social standing grew. By the first quarter of the eighteenth century, funeral undertaking was considered a distinct business. Elite and common funerals relied on fabric, and because of their expertise in upholstery and cabinet-making, upholders dominated the business.

The economic growth that began in the 1760s gave Londoners choices, including in funerals. The upholding business model had changed by then. Along with cabinet-making and upholstery, many upholders expanded their business offerings, such as funeral undertaking, brokering, and auctioneering. This expansion was often financed by the use of private credit. Using private credit to expand and increase inventory, as Hoppit pointed out, was financially dangerous. An examination of newspaper advertising and announcements from 1760 to 1790 confirmed that many upholders entered these new business lines and that during this period of expansion, upholder bankruptcies rose. The ease of entry into the unregulated undertaking trade created competition. Pirohakul's probate research found that average family expenditure on a funeral fell during the last forty years of the eighteenth century, a result of competition.

[91] Hoppit, "Financial Crises in Eighteenth-Century England," *The Economic History Review* New Series, Vol. 39, No. 1 (Feb. 1986): 50.

Undertaking was a risky business line for upholders using private credit to purchase and hold large amounts of stock in trade, exacerbated by low pricing power in a competitive business environment in the later years of the eighteenth century. During the course of one hundred years, funeral undertaking had gone from being a profitable growth business to one with modest growth and low profitability. The business risks did not match the low investment returns. By the end of the eighteenth century, this risk/reward mismatch resulted in a consolidation of full-time funeral undertaking providers. Upholders offering undertaking goods and services were best served to practise the trade on an intermittent or part-time basis.

Besides funeral undertaking, there were other opportunities for upholders to earn extra money. Whereas funeral undertaking was a manufacturing and service business, the appraising, brokering, and auctioneering of used household goods were service businesses. The next chapter discusses the involvement upholders had in the secondary market for household goods.

CHAPTER 3

Upholders as Appraisers, Brokers, and Auctioneers

> You shall sincerely promise and swear, that you will truly and faithfully execute and perform the office and employment of a broker between party and party in all things appertaining to the duty of the said office or employment, without fraud or collusion, to the best of your skill and knowledge.[1]

Sworn appraisers used their expertise to value personal and household goods, and sworn brokers of household goods could either buy goods from clients and resell them at a profit or sell goods on a consignment basis. Upholders increasingly became sworn appraisers and brokers of household goods in the last forty years of the eighteenth century. As can be seen from the broker's oath quoted above, the sworn component implicitly implied honesty and fair business dealings as agents between the seller and buyer. At the same time, upholders became more involved in the auction business. Auctioneers were agents between sellers and buyers in a public setting and, although they did not swear an oath, honesty and fair dealing were expected of them, too. These three business lines represented a significant shift from the traditional upholding business model in that they were service-oriented in contrast to the manufacturing and assembly of household goods. Given that upholders sold new household goods,

[1] Eighteenth-century brokers oath required by Court of Mayor and Alderman. *The English Reports* (London: Stevens & Sons, Ltd., 1904), Vol. XXXV, 633. Joshua Montefiore, *A Commercial Dictionary: Containing the Present State of Mercantile Law, Practice, and Custom* (London: for the author, 1803), BRO. No page number; indexed by subject.

S. Sanders, *The Eighteenth-Century London Upholder*,
https://doi.org/10.1007/978-3-032-08660-0_3

they were in the position of knowing the values of second-hand goods, qualifying them to make appraisals and act as brokers and auctioneers. If upholders were motivated to enter these new business lines, there had to be consumer demand for them. Of course, a growing population would explain part of the increase in demand, but so would an increase in disposable consumer income. Upholders saw appraising, brokering, and auctioneering as a way to supplement their income, but why would a consumer be motivated to use their services? At the same time, why would consumers choose to purchase used goods over new goods?

Used Versus New Household Goods

The cost of 'new versus used' household goods was an important consideration for the middling sort of consumer. The Stuart Court after 1689 set a precedent by refurbishing and refashioning used furniture. The aim was to set an example of financial prudence, which was contrasted against French extravagance. Existing furniture was cared for through daily dusting and polishing by servants. When fabric and wooden furniture components needed replacement or repair, the Lord Chamberlain's office made the arrangements. This work was often contracted to outside tradesmen like John Trotter, a royal upholsterer in the 1750s. Out-of-fashion or broken furniture was often remade or altered.[2] The Stuart Court's financial prudence in re-fashioning and repairing the 'old' probably created a public perception that purchasing second-hand furniture was socially acceptable, at least in the first part of the eighteenth century.

By the time Chippendale published his famous *Director* in 1754, the emphasis on the new and fashionable was underway. Chippendale's furniture pattern book offered choices in styles that were then fashionable: gothic, Chinese, and modern taste (rococo). The *Director* was sold by subscription, mostly to the furniture trade. Chippendale-inspired furniture could now be produced in other workshops. Mahogany had become a fashionable wood by this time, replacing walnut. The replacement of walnut and older oak furniture by new and fashionable mahogany furniture, at some point, created a surplus of used furniture. The styles Chippendale promoted in 1754 were considered outmoded by the

[2] Olivia Fryman, "Recycling Furniture in the Late Stuart Court (1689–1714)," in *The Afterlife of Used Things Recycling in the Long Eighteenth Century*, ed. Ariane Fennetaux, Amélie Junqua, and Sophie Vasset. (New York: Routledge, 2015), 89–92.

mid-1760s, replaced by the neoclassical style.[3] Though the initial change in furniture style to the neoclassical probably only affected the upper end of the trade, this change, nonetheless, would have created an additional supply of second-hand furniture.

Jon Stobart and Illia Van Damme recognized that, later in the eighteenth century, consumer tastes placed a greater emphasis on the new and fashionable rather than on the old and worn. Because of industrial modernization and consumer interest in fashion during the last half of the eighteenth century, it is sometimes assumed that used goods were no longer in high demand. Stobart and Van Damme, however, disagreed with this assumption. They found that there were vibrant markets for used furniture and household goods.[4] If there was a supply of second-hand household goods, where was the demand? Why would consumers choose to purchase used goods rather than new goods?

Clive Edwards and Margaret Ponsonby gave explanations for the continued demand for second-hand furniture. Although their study was primarily concerned with nineteenth-century consumption, they also gave insight that applied to the eighteenth-century consumption of used furniture. Their opinion is that in the early modern period, it was the end product that mattered to a consumer, not whether it was new or used. Besides being more affordable, second-hand furniture appealed to middling consumers because it was often made of solid wood and well crafted. A piece of used furniture made from a fashionable wood like mahogany was considered a good investment because the prevailing thought was that it would hold its value. Finally, new furniture made with advanced manufacturing techniques and differing materials, though fashionable in appearance, was not always considered as having the quality of solidly made older furniture.[5]

Competition, at least in theory, should have led to lower prices, or at least to 'reasonable' prices. Although there was interest in inventing

[3] Michael Snodin and John Styles, *Design & the Decorative Arts: Georgian Britain 1714–1837* (London: V&A Publications, 2004), 44–53, 78–79, 145.

[4] Jon Stobart and Illia Van Damme, "Introduction," in *Modernity and the Second-Hand Trade: European Consumption Cultures and Practices, 1700–1900*, ed. Jon Stobart and Illia Van Damme (Basingstoke: Palgrave Macmillan, 2010), 4–6.

[5] Clive Edwards and Margaret Ponsonby, "Polarization of the Second-Hand Market for Furniture in the Nineteenth Century," in *Modernity and the Second-Hand Trade: European Consumption Cultures and Practices, 1700–1900*, ed. Jon Stobart and Ilia Van Damme, eds. (Basingstoke: Palgrave Macmillan, 2010), 93–95.

mechanical devices to make furniture production easier (and less costly) in the last half of the eighteenth century, inventions used in woodworking were not available until the nineteenth century. Even then, furniture production was mostly a handcraft. Eighteenth-century inventions like the mechanical circular saw and planer were for plank work by wood suppliers, not furniture-makers. The production of hand sawn and planed planks was costly from a labour standpoint. Reducing the labour costs in the production of raw materials did, nonetheless, help furniture makers lower their raw material costs. While raw material costs for upholders may have dropped, labour remained a significant part of the final product costs.[6]

The number of furniture-makers in the London area in the last half of the eighteenth century is unknown. J.L. Oliver estimated that there were sixty-six furniture manufacturers operating in the City and East End in 1801.[7] There were esteemed firms like Chippendale, Vile & Cobb, and Hepplewhite, but the middling sort most probably did not buy new and expensive furniture from these firms. The upper ranks, for that matter, probably did not exclusively purchase expensive furniture. For example, there was no need to 'fit out' servant quarters with fashionable furniture. There were many upholders who were furniture-makers and capable of supplying the middling marketplace. It was these firms, not the fashionable West End furniture-makers, who supplied much of the new furniture for the middling sort. As mentioned in Chap. 1, in 1753 George Seddon established the largest furniture-making firm in London. Located on Aldersgate Street, his firm employed at least three hundred employees and probably more.[8] (When his business premises were destroyed by fire in 1768, eighty journeymen lost their tool chests.[9]) Seddon supplied retailers with well-built, low-cost furniture, and his company was considered part of the 'honourable' furniture-making trade.

However, a growing 'dishonourable' East End furniture trade, in contrast to the West End makers, began using less costly materials in furniture construction. By 1830, this trade was fully developed. The dishonourable trade, according to Kirkham, sourced furniture components from a web of sub-contractors. These sub-contractors were sometimes called 'garret

[6] Pat Kirkham, *The London Furniture Trade 1700–1870* (Leeds: Furniture History Society, 1988), 109.

[7] J.L. Oliver, *The Development and Structure of the Furniture Industry* (Oxford: Pergamon Press, 1966), 4.

[8] Kirkham, *London Furniture Trade*, 6–8, 76–78.

[9] *Public Advisor*, 25 July 1768.

masters' because they often worked alone in attics. 'The dishonourable trade was characterized by low wages, very long hours, inferior materials, scamped workmanship, unskilled or child labour, and sub contracting', wrote Kirkham.[10]

Consumers, therefore, had purchasing choices for furniture. New and fashionable could be had from West End dealers. For the middling sort, purchasing from manufacturers like Seddon & Co. was a less costly choice. For consumers wanting new furniture at the lowest prices, purchasing from the dishonourable trade was another possibility. Along with these options, purchasing second-hand furniture was an alternative to new furniture.

The middling ranks may have strived to become wealthy, but they could be practical in their consumption. If a middling consumer needed a table, what mattered was that the table was available and affordable, not if it was new or used. It could have been a utility purchase, rather than a conspicuous or fashionable purchase. By purchasing second-hand furniture, a consumer could save money, obtain quality, and, sometimes, have an item that could be sold later for nearly the same price. A broker selling used household goods or an auction including second-hand furniture would have served the middling sort's needs very well.

Sworn Appraisers and Brokers

Both R. Campbell and Thomas Waller recognized appraising as a distinct trade in their apprenticeship advice books published in the mid-eighteenth century. Appraising, according to Campbell, was generally associated with upholding. He wrote that upholders sometimes carried on business as brokers of household goods and were also known as sworn appraisers.[11] Waller stated in 1747 that appraisers were best known as brokers of household goods, and that appraising was a service performed by upholsterers (upholders) or brokers with skills related to the commodities they valued. Because they took an oath to do justice between each party, they were called 'sworn' appraisers.[12] It can be concluded from Campbell and

[10] Kirkham, *London Furniture Trade*, 7–8.

[11] R. Campbell, *The London Tradesman* (London: T. Gardner, 1747), 175.

[12] Thomas Waller, *A general description of all trades, digested in alphabetical order: by which parents, guardians, and trustees, may make choice of trades agreeable to the capacity, education, inclination, strength, and fortune of the youth* (London: Printed at Crown and Mitre, 1747), 4–5.

Table 3.1 Number of upholders admitted as sworn brokers and appraisers by eighteenth-century decade

Decade	*Number*
1700–1709	1
1710–1719	0
1720–1729	1
1730–1739	1
1740–1749	1
1750–1759	0
1760–1769	11
1770–1779	22
1780–1789	15
1790–1799	10

Source: London Metropolitan Archives, City of London. Reference Code: COL/BR/02/074–075. Index to Brokers' Bonds A-H and I-Z and COL/BR05. Broker Sureties 1752–1813

Waller's statements that the occupations of sworn appraisers and brokers were closely related. Furthermore, the swearing of an oath implied that appraisers and brokers had legal standing.

The Index to Brokers' Bonds and the Broker Sureties held at the London Metropolitan Archives lists sixty-two upholders who posted broker bonds and/or broker sureties in the eighteenth century.[13] An analysis of these upholders demonstrates that the overwhelming majority of them were admitted as sworn brokers during the last four decades of the century (Table 3.1). Though no reason for this is known, one possible explanation is that a growing middling sort had more disposable income and savings to purchase used household goods. Also, the sworn appraisal component of the licence would have been useful for probate, insurance, and bankruptcy valuations.

Among the upholders in the Index to Brokers' Bonds was Robert Herring of No. 96, Fleet Street, who became a sworn broker in 1771. Herring became a freeman in the Upholders' Company in 1769 through 'redemption', a method by which an individual belonging to no company or having another company affiliation could purchase freedom in the

[13] London Metropolitan Archives, City of London. Reference Code: COL/BR/02/074–075. Index to Brokers' Bonds A–H and I–Z and COL/BR05. Broker Sureties 1752–1813.

Upholders' Company.[14] Herring may have taken out his freedom because livery company membership was a prerequisite to becoming a sworn broker.

Robert Herring advertised that he was a sworn broker. An example of this can be found in the 2 July 1772 *Gazetteer and New Daily Advertiser*. He announced he was auctioning the stock in trade of Mrs. Vaughan, a milliner and owner of a millinery and childbed warehouse in Fleet Street. Herring is listed as a sworn broker and upholsterer.[15] On 12 February 1783, Herring placed a notice in the *Daily Advertiser* that he moved from No. 96, Fleet Street to No.109, Fleet Street, on the opposite side of the street. His announcement also informed his friends and the public that he had opened a new warehouse with a complete assortment of upholstery and cabinet goods in the 'immediate taste'. He employed descriptive terms commonly used at this time, telling readers all branches of his work were 'executed with utmost dispatch in the genteelist taste and on the most reasonable terms'. He promoted his business as an upholder, cabinet-maker, undertaker, appraiser, and auctioneer. Finally, Herring ended this announcement with the statement that 'estates, stock in trade, household furniture, etc. [could be] bought and sold by commission'.[16] Combining phrases such as 'immediate taste', 'executed with utmost dispatch', and 'in the genteelist taste and on most reasonable terms' implied that his advertisement was meant to appeal to the middling sort of consumer. At the same time, he promoted his services of buying and selling estates and stock in trade, essentially the function of a broker. His business was comprehensive and served customer needs from birth to death and everything in between. Herring served the middling ranks by providing all sorts of new and used items available in his warehouse, and at death, whether it was physical or financial (bankruptcy), he facilitated the disposal of household goods.

Although not much is known about other upholders who became sworn brokers in the 1770s, it is clear that some of them experienced business failure. According to the Index of Brokers' Bonds, Samuel Martin of No. 19, Bucklersbury became a sworn broker in 1771. He became a freeman in the Upholders' Company in 1762 through servitude, meaning that he served an apprenticeship. Martin lived at No. 19, Bucklersbury

[14] Karin M. Walton, "The Worshipful Company of Upholders of the City of London," *Furniture History Society* Vol. 9 (1973): 43, 62.

[15] *Gazetteer and New Daily Advertiser*, 2 July 1772.

[16] *Daily Advertiser*, 12 February 1783.

until 1778, when he moved to Walbrook, followed by Snow Hill in 1786.[17] Martin's first known advertisement as a sworn broker was placed in the 11 July 1771 *Gazetteer and New Daily Advertiser*. He announced his role as auctioneer of freehold leases in Wiltshire, and at the bottom of the advertisement, he listed himself as an upholder and sworn broker.[18] By 26 February 1773, Martin was named as a co-auctioneer, along with Messrs. Merryman and Brown. This advertisement from the *Daily Advertiser* indicated that Martin had entered into a partnership with the other two auctioneers.[19] An advertisement in the 15 May 1773 *Morning Chronicle and London Advertiser* listed Joseph Merryman as an upholder and sworn broker.[20] Though Mr. Brown's first name was not given, he was perhaps William Brown of Duke Street, who became a freeman in the Upholders' Company in 1758.[21] He is possibly the same William Brown who became a sworn broker in 1765.[22] Because no partnership agreement or other advertisements of this co-auctioneer arrangement have been located, one can assume their partnership was short-lived.

Samuel Martin began promoting himself as an upholder, sworn broker, and auctioneer in the 4 May 1775 *Morning Post and Daily Advertiser*.[23] By 1 November 1775, Martin's business had failed, when the *Public Advertiser* announced he was to surrender himself as bankrupt to Guildhall on 7 and 14 November and 12 December.[24] The solicitors Gregg and Potts provided legal representation.[25] Martin was to be granted a 'certificate of bankruptcy' as of 20 February 1776, according to the 31 January 1776 *Public Advertiser*.[26] The 'certificate of conformity' referred to by Hoppit in the previous chapter was the same as the 'certificate of bankruptcy' Martin received on 20 February 1776. Bankruptcy, however, did not diminish Martin's aspirations to be an auctioneer. On 16 February

[17] Walton, "Company of Upholders," 66.

[18] *Gazetteer and New Daily Advertiser*, 11 July 1771.

[19] *Daily Advertiser*, 26 February 1773.

[20] *Morning Chronicle and London Advertiser*, 15 May 1773.

[21] Walton, "Company of Upholders," 54.

[22] London Metropolitan Archives, Index to Brokers' Bonds A–H and I–Z.

[23] *Morning Post and Daily Advertiser*, 4 May 1775.

[24] *Public Advertiser*, 1 November 1775.

[25] W. Bailey. *Bailey's List of Bankrupts, Dividends and Certificates from the Year 1772 to 1793, Both Included with the Names and Residence of the Different Solicitors Under Each.* (London: T. Williams, 1794), Vol. I, 64.

[26] *Public Advertiser*, 31 January 1776.

1776, he placed two separate auction notices in the *Daily Advertiser* and continued in that role for some time.[27]

The reason for Samuel Martin's business failure is unknown, and it is difficult for a modern researcher to find accurate information about any particular bankruptcy in the eighteenth century with so few surviving files.[28] Martin's financial problem was the result of him being the victim of a bad debt. The bad debt probably was connected to his upholding business, where a multitude of problems could occur. Too much stock that he could not sell, suppliers he could not pay, or clients unable to pay off credit he had extended to them are among the possible occurrences. The 1775 outbreak of war between Britain and the American colonies disrupted the credit markets, which was probably the overriding reason for Martin's financial difficulties.

In addition to newspaper advertising, which reached a wide audience, upholder trade cards sometimes advertised broker services. A 1784 trade card held in the British Museum's Heal Collection is a perfect example of this. 'Hunt' advertised that he was an upholsterer and an active buyer and seller of household goods in Long Acre. Since he listed upholstery work as a business line, it appears he operated as an upholder and furniture-maker, with significant side-line businesses in brokering, appraising, and auctioneering.[29] This is probably James Hunt, who became a member of the Joiners' Company in 1759.[30]

Eighteenth-century brokers were regulated by Parliamentary law. In 1697, Parliament passed a law regulating the activities of brokers in London (1 W. & M. ff.1.c.8.). This Act established the regulatory framework for the eighteenth century. The Lord Mayor and the Court of Alderman of the City of London were empowered to issue and regulate broker licences within the City and its liberties. (Liberties generally were the areas seven miles outside of the City.) The Act stated that the number of broker licences was not to exceed one hundred and the cost of the

[27] *Daily Advertiser*, 16 February 1776.

[28] Julian Hoppit, *Risk and failure in English business 1700–1800* (Cambridge: Cambridge University Press, 1987), 140.

[29] The British Museum, London. Heal Collection. Museum No. D, 2.811. Trade card of Hunt.

[30] Joiners' Company records, 1640–1783, in British and Irish Furniture Makers Online. https://bifmo.history.ac.uk/find-people?keywords=&name=Hunt%2C+James&active_from=1750&active_to=1800&place=&occupation=joiner&source=All (accessed 28 September 2021).

licence was not to exceed forty shillings. The Act authorized penalties for infractions, such as practising without a proper licence, not keeping accurate records, and charging excessive brokerage fees. Upon receiving a licence, each broker was required to swear the broker's oath.[31]

The 1697 Act was an attempt to regulate illegal and unscrupulous brokers within the City of London and its liberties. This Act was not the first time Parliament attempted to control the business activities of brokers. As early as 1603, Parliament attempted to regulate brokers in what was called An Act Against Brokers (10 Jacobi I. c. 21). The 1603 Act recognized that it was a tradition for the Mayor and Aldermen to appoint brokers who were freeman of the City of London. The appointment process required a committee of six City freemen to present broker candidates who were known for their honesty, integrity, and faithfulness. Once approved by the Lord Mayor and Court of Alderman, brokers were admitted and required to take an oath to conduct themselves uprightly and faithfully in their dealings. The 1603 Act further recognized that many hundreds of City citizens, freemen, and former tradesmen had illegally set up businesses as pawnbrokers and brokers of household goods. The central concern of the Act was that these illegal brokers were encouraging theft by trading in stolen property. The 1603 Act required all brokers, legally recognized and not, to disclose to requesting authorities how any item came into their possession, who was the seller or consigner, and who was the buyer. The penalty for dealing in stolen goods was compensation equal to twice the value of all illegally acquired items. The City of London, Westminster, and any location within two miles of the City were covered by this Act.[32]

Another law that was passed before the 1697 Act was intended to punish usury. In 1623, Parliament passed a usury law that set financial penalties for violators (21 Jacobi I. c. 17). Though not specific to only brokers, usury, evidently, was considered enough of a serious crime that brokers guilty of multiple violations of the 1623 Act were subject to a six-month prison sentence.[33]

The 1697 Act of Parliament regulating brokers was passed with a three-year expiration date, which Parliament extended in 1700. A new Act (6

[31] Danny Pickering, *The Statutes at Large from the Eighth Year of King William III to the Second Year of Queen Anne* (London: Joseph Benthan, 1864), Vol. X, 112.

[32] John Raithby, ed. *The Statues at Large of England and of Great–Britain: From Magna Carta to the Union of the Kingdoms of Great Britain and Ireland* (London: Eyre and Strahan, 1811), Vol. IV, 612–15.

[33] Raithby, *The Statues at Large of England and of Great–Britain*, Vol. IV, 755–56.

Anne, c.16 s.4 and officially known as the Admission of Brokers Act of 1707) reaffirmed the authority of the Lord Mayor and the Court of Alderman of the City of London over broker regulation and established a £25 fine for practicing the brokerage trade without a licence.[34] Prior to 1707, the Court of Alderman penalized unlicensed brokers with a fine of up to £500 and a sentence of three days in the pillory.[35] Upon receiving a licence, each broker was required to swear an oath to truly and faithfully perform their duties between parties without fraud or collusion, to the best of their skill and knowledge. (This required oath is quoted at the beginning of this chapter.)[36]

The 1697 Act limited the number of brokers to a maximum of one hundred, and the Court of Alderman at that time authorized twelve broker licences for Jewish traders and aliens unable to take up a City freedom. In 1708, the Court of Alderman authorized the issuance of twelve additional broker licences for French and Dutch Protestant refugees. To encourage good behaviour, the Court of Alderman established a rule that licensed brokers had to provide a £500 broker's bond, along with a £250 surety bond from a second party. The Court also allowed Quakers to affirm, rather than swear, their oath.[37]

That Quakers were allowed to affirm, rather than swear, their oath, was a sympathetic action by the Court of Alderman. Oaths were an important part of eighteenth-century British society. J.C.D. Clark characterized the period from the Restoration through the eighteenth century as 'polity defined by oaths'. He wrote about the difficulties encountered by those who refused to swear an oath of allegiance to the King, specifically Samuel Johnson. Whigs usually swore their loyalty oath, sometimes in good faith and often in bad faith. Those refusing to take the oath, as did Johnson, were called 'nonjurors', and their punishment, along with a fine, was public scorn. According to Clark, among those required to swear the oath of allegiance were the clergy, university and government officials, and military officers.[38] The broker's oath, however, was

[34] John Raithby, ed. *The Statues at Large of England and of Great–Britain: From Magna Carta to the Union of the Kingdoms of Great Britain and Ireland* (London: Eyre and Strahan, 1811), Vol. VI, 664–66.

[35] London Metropolitan Archives, *Sworn Broker Archives*. Leaflet No. 15.

[36] Montefiore, *A Commercial Dictionary*, BRO. No page number; indexed by subject.

[37] London Metropolitan Archives, *Sworn Broker Archives.*

[38] J.C.D. Clark, "Religion and Political Identity: Samuel Johnson as a Nonjuror," in *Samuel Johnson in Historical Context*, ed. Jonathan Clark and Howard Erskine-Hill (Cambridge: Cambridge University Press, 1994), 80–87.

essentially a statement to be honest and fair in business dealings and had nothing to do with allegiance to the King. The Court of Alderman apparently considered swearing and affirming to mean the same thing when it came to the Quakers.

A broker was issued a numbered medal with his (or her) name on it. This medal confirmed that the holder was a sworn and licensed broker and had to have been a status indicator. The medal could be sold and transferred. Broker medals were commonly sold for between £800 and £1500, according to Montefiore. If a broker medal-holder died before he sold or transferred it, the medal reverted to the Lord Mayor for reissue.[39] The fact that medals sold for a premium in the secondary market indicated that being a broker could potentially be a lucrative business. It may be that the noticeable increase in upholders becoming sworn brokers after 1760 was the result of existing medal holders leaving the broker and appraisal business and selling the medal to an upholder. Elderly, seriously ill, or financially distressed medal holders could quickly receive money by selling the medal. No clear explanation exists to explain why Parliament limited the number of licences, but it may have been encouraged to do so by the City of London. Legislation, with the force of Parliament behind it, would have helped the City protect the public from unscrupulous brokers. At the same time, fees paid by legitimate brokers and fines assessed upon unlicensed brokers would increase the City's revenue.

Although Campbell indicated that sworn appraisers and sworn brokers were essentially the same, there were differences.[40] Brokers were paid on a commission basis for their services. They sold goods on consignment or purchased the goods from a customer and sold them at a mark-up. Appraisers were paid a fee, rather than a commission. Upholders acting as appraisers were qualified to value household goods, both new and used. Probate and bankruptcy were primary reasons for requiring an appraisal, along with the purchase of fire and theft insurance. Their sworn duty was to give a fair value of stock in trade, production equipment, and business premises, usually stating it on a gross amount basis, rather than on an item-by-item basis. The fair valuations appraisers gave were often skewed

[39] Montefiore, *A Commercial Dictionary*, BRO. No page number; indexed by subject.
[40] Campbell, *The London Tradesman*, 175.

lower, however, because the appraiser could be compelled by the seller to purchase items at their appraised value.[41]

The initial capital outlay for a sworn appraiser and broker was the £500 broker bond, which was a sizeable amount. Operating an appraisal business would not have been difficult for an experienced upholder. After the initial capital outlay, ongoing costs would have been small. Thomas Mortimer estimated in 1819 that the capital required by a London-based appraiser and furniture broker was between £150 and £300. His estimate was a few decades after the period of study here and may or may not be indicative of the capital needed in, say, 1780. Mortimer also estimated that the capital costs for an auctioneer and appraiser were between £250 and £1000.[42] (Presumably, Mortimer deduced that adding auctioneering to an appraisal and broker business significantly increased capital costs because an auction room and staff were required.) The main business risk was that owners (sellers) might require the appraiser to purchase their household goods at their appraised values. As noted above, to mitigate the risk of financial loss from an owner 'putting back' household goods to the appraiser, valuations were lowered. As long as sworn brokers operated according to their oath (honesty and fair dealing), the business risks were not great, except, perhaps, if they had possession of the goods to be brokered and incurred a loss from theft or fire.

Just as other types of eighteenth-century brokers, such as East India Company and grain brokers, represented both the seller and the buyer, so did brokers of household goods. It would be naïve to think that unlicensed general upholders did not occasionally sell items on consignment and receive a commission or fee. Those upholders who provided appraisals and brokered on a large scale and consistent basis as an additional part of their upholding business, however, would have become sworn or faced financial penalties. All upholders had the practical knowledge to enter the household goods appraising and brokerage businesses, but in order to

[41] Montefiore, *A Commercial Dictionary*, APP. No page number; indexed by subject. 'When the appraisers have gone through the whole of the articles, they declare their respective estimates in the gross sum; and sometimes, although very rarely, of particulars.' '… and in some particular cases, they are compelled to take the goods at their own valuation if the parties think proper to relinquish them'. Mortimer, *A General Commercial Dictionary Comprehending Trade, Manufactures, and Navigation* (London: Longman, Hurst, et al., 1819), 2nd ed., APPRAISMENT, E3. 'If a sworn-appraiser value goods too high, he is obliged to take them at the price appraised. 13 Edw. I'.

[42] Mortimer, *A General Commercial Dictionary*, APPENDIX, No. II.

significantly participate in these businesses, they would have needed enough money to afford the sworn broker medal, performance bond, and associated costs.

Auctioneering

Nearly all eighteenth-century upholders who became auctioneers first became sworn appraisers and brokers. While becoming a sworn appraiser and broker was not an easy process, there were no similar prerequisites for becoming an auctioneer. It is probable that an auctioneer who was also a sworn broker was considered more trustworthy. Also, an upholder who became a sworn broker before becoming an auctioneer may have wanted a more comprehensive business. Whether or not these were the reasons for becoming a sworn broker before becoming an auctioneer, upholders generally became sworn brokers before they entered the auction business.

Christopher Cock is recognized as one of the pioneers of modern auctioneering in the eighteenth century.[43] He was not an upholder, and, for that matter, no information has been found that indicates he belonged to any livery company. His ascendancy in the auction business was unmatched by most, if not all, London auctioneers in the first half of the eighteenth century. He may not have been the first auctioneer to have an auction room or evening auctions, but the volume of his auctions was unparalleled. He frequently used newspaper advertisements to announce his auctions and was an early user of superlatives to promote sales. The breadth of what Cock auctioned was wide, from household goods to fine and decorative art to land, buildings, and leases. His business model quickly evolved from using the premises of the seller or a coffee house for auctions to having an auction room. Along with having a sales room, Cock's model included print advertising, catalogues that included cover page images for important auctions, conditions of sale stated in writing, and evening auctions.

Auction advertisements and catalogues started appearing in the late seventeenth century and, by the time Cock started his business, both were promotional methods. The first found advertisements by Mr. Cock were when he announced in the 31 January 1722 *Daily Courant* and the *Daily Post* that he would be auctioning 'a most excellent collection of pictures by the celebrated Italian and other famous masters'. He stated that the place

[43] Brian Learmount, *A History of the Auction* (London: Barnard & Learmount, 1985), 22.

and time of the sale would be announced later. His advertisement informed the reader that catalogues for the sale were available at his premises next to the Vine Tavern, Broad Street, Covent Garden.[44] Cock announced the sale's location in the 17 February 1722 *Daily Courant* and explained that the pictures would be sold every forenoon day until they were all sold. What is significant here is that Mr. Cock advertised his auction; used descriptions such as 'very curious', 'most excellent', 'most celebrated', and 'eminent'; and had catalogues available before the sale.[45] Apparently Cock estimated that the sale would take more than one day, which suggests there was a great number of sale items or that the auction went at a slow pace.

As the number of sale items increased, the time-consuming 'auction by candle' practice became impractical for a large auction. Eventually, because of its fast pace, the familiar modern 'ascending bid' method became the accepted method of auctioning household goods and personal effects, including fine art.[46] An indication of the sales pace (how quickly individual lots were sold) comes from the 27 February 1723 *Daily Post*, where an advertisement announced that the trustees of the South Sea Company were auctioning the property of several of the late directors of the South Sea Company. ('Late directors' refers to former South Sea Company directors whose assets were seized and sold under the South Sea Sufferers' Bill. This bill authorized restitution for losses incurred from the South Sea Bubble.[47]) The advertisement stated that there were a total of 360 lots comprising eminent Italian and other masters' pictures, a large lapis lazuli table, and various curiosities and rarities. The items were available for viewing at the place of sale, the South Sea Company's warehouse. Catalogues were available at South Sea House, Mr. Gouge's in the Piazza, Covent Garden, Mr. Cock's at Broad Street, St. James's, and at the place

[44] *Daily Courant* and the *Daily Post*, 31 January 1722.

[45] *Daily Courant*, 17 February 1722.

[46] Learmount, *A History of the Auction*, 17–20. In the sale by candle method, a candle is lit and written bids are made in increasing amounts. The last bid (and the highest) made before the candle burns out is the winning bid. The ascending bid method has a fast sales pace with the auctioneer verbally announcing the opening bid and receiving successive higher bids until there are no more bids.

[47] John Carswell, *The South Sea Bubble* (Dover: Alan Sutton, 1993) rev. ed., 219–34. Also: Malcolm Balen, *The Secret History of the South Sea Bubble: The World's First Great Financial Scandal* (New York: Fourth Estate, 2003), 214–231.

of sale. Starting at eleven each morning, sixty lots would be sold per day.[48] While there is no indication of how long a sale day was, if one item was sold every three minutes or twenty per hour, the sale would have lasted three hours each day. This sales pace, however, is speculation.

Cock's auction of the library owned by the late John Bridges gives better insight into the auctioneer's sales pace. The sale was spread over several intermittent days, beginning on 7 February 1726 and ending on 21 March. Held in Mr. Bridges's chambers at Lincoln Inn, over 4000 books and manuscripts were auctioned. Each sale day was divided into two sessions: 11 a.m. to 2 p.m. and 5 p.m. to 8 p.m. Eighty items were to be sold in the first session and eighty in the second. This indicates an expected sales pace of one item sold every 2.25 minutes. Cock used the ascending bid auction method, as it was not practical to use the candle auction method to sell 4000 books and manuscripts. Probably because of the importance of the sale, the catalogue's cover page had an image created by the printmaker A. Motte. This image alluded to a fallen learning tree being climbed by various men. Cock's catalogue also listed the basic rules of sale, which included the procedure for deciding who made the final accepted bid, challenges to an item's condition, minimum bid advances, and the commission rate of one shilling to the pound. The catalogue was a substantial 203 pages long.[49]

By 14 February 1732, Christopher Cock's auction business was apparently successful enough to require him to open an auction room. He promoted this in the *Daily Post* by stating, 'Mr. Cock's New Room in the Great Piazza, Covent Garden'. In this advertisement, Cock announced he was selling books, prints, and drawings belonging to Thomas Slater, deceased. Another interesting part of Cock's advertisement, outside the announcement of his new auction room, was that there were sale sessions beginning at five o'clock in the evening.[50] The previously mentioned John Bridges auction also had evening sales sessions. Evening auctions were, perhaps, a way to bring buyers to auctions after normal working hours. Cock used a one-page broadside to announce the February 1735 auction of works by Sir James Thornhill, late history painter to the King, including his work based on Raphael's cartoons at Hampton Court. Of interest in

[48] *Daily Post*, 27 February 1723.

[49] Christopher Cock, *Bibliothecæ Bridgesianæ catalogus: or, a catalogue of the entire library of John Bridges* (London: J. Tonson and J. Watts, 1726).

[50] *Daily Post*, 14 February 1732.

this auction broadside was the inclusion of an image of one of the works for sale.[51] Cock also used cover page images on other auction catalogues, including for the 13 April 1744 auction of the jewels of the late Duchess of Buckingham.[52] These cover page images would have been a way for potential buyers to visualize what was being sold.

By the time Cock died in 1749, he was the auctioneer whose business model was emulated by the major English auctioneers of the last half of the eighteenth century.[53] The first of the major English auction houses was Sotheby's, established by Samuel Baker, who began auctioning books as early as 1745. James Christie opened his auction business in 1766. Later in the eighteenth century, two other major auctioneers opened for business. William Charles Bonham opened for business in 1793, followed by Harry Phillips in 1796. These four men founded the major auction houses of the late-eighteenth century and are still in business today.

Learmount estimated there were about sixty auctioneers in London by the time Christie started his business.[54] The increase in the number of auctioneers during this time also coincided with an increase in the number of upholders becoming sworn brokers during the period from 1760–69, the decade in which Christie opened for business. In that decade, eleven upholders became sworn brokers, followed by twenty-two in the following decade. Previously mentioned Robert Herring and Samuel Martin became sworn brokers in 1771. Herring's first advertised auction was in 1770 and Martin's in 1771. Both of them had taken out their freedom in the Upholders' Company, Martin in 1762 and Herring in 1769.

One upholder who became a full-time auctioneer was Richard Winstanley. He became a freeman in the Upholders' Company in 1780 and is an example of an upholder who left the upholding business to become a full-time auctioneer.[55] The Brokers' Index lists him as becoming a sworn broker in 1779. The fact that he joined a livery company after becoming a sworn broker appears to violate the requirement that sworn

[51] Christopher Cock, *A catalogue of the intire collection belonging to Sir James Thornhill, late principal history painter to His Majesty, &c.* (London: For the Author, 1735).

[52] Christopher Cock, *A catalogue of Her Grace Kathrine Dutchess. of Buckingham's jewel's &c.* (London: For the Author, 1744).

[53] Learmount, *A History of the Auction*, 101–119. Learmount profiles the four main auction houses formed in the last half of the eighteenth century. These were: Sotheby's, Christie's, Phillips, and Bonhams.

[54] Learmount, *A History of the Auction*, 47–55.

[55] Walton, "Company of Upholders," 78.

brokers had to be livery members. There is no known reason for this discrepancy, but a recordkeeping delay or a recording error may have been responsible. Winstanley conducted auctions as early as 1780.[56] When he moved from Cheapside to Pater Noster Row, he promoted himself as an auctioneer, sworn exchange broker, upholder, appraiser, and undertaker.[57] After this advertisement, he only represented himself as an auctioneer, not as an upholder. He evidently decided that being a comprehensive upholder with expanded business services was not for him. One of his auctions was for the 25 September 1787 sale of ten pairs of double Dutch silk mills with associated equipment belonging to Thomas Kilner, a retiring silk thrower in Spital Square.[58] Not long after that, in the 23 January 1788 *World*, he was listed as an elected director and sworn appraiser for the Phoenix Fire Office.[59] Fire insurance developed in the late-seventeenth century in the aftermath of the Great Fire and gave businesses (and homeowners) a way to protect themselves from a fire causing financial ruin.[60] All the evidence indicates that Winstanley's successful business trajectory was from general upholder to sworn broker, auctioneer, and company director.

A significant difference in Winstanley's business model, when compared to other upholders who became auctioneers, was that he appeared to have left the upholding business and concentrated solely on auctioneering and insurance appraising. Because Winstanley did not have to maintain the inventory of an upholder, his risk of bankruptcy would have been reduced. His son, James, succeeded him in business. After multiple mergers and name changes, Winstanley's auction firm is known today as Jones Lang LaSalle (JLL), one of the world's premier commercial real estate services companies.[61]

[56] *London Evening Post*, 10 February 1780.

[57] *Morning Chronicle and London Advertiser*, 26 August 1780.

[58] Richard Winstanley, *Silk throwsters, &c. A catalogue of ten pair of double Dutch silk mills, with reels, spindles, and iron-work complete, in very good repair,* ... (London: For the Author, 1787).

[59] *World*, 23 January 1788.

[60] Peter Earle, *The Making of the Middle Class* (Berkeley: University of California Press, 1989), 78.

[61] https://www.lasalle.com/about/history/ (accessed 24 May 2025). https://www.funinguniverse.com/company-histories/jones-lang-lasalle-incorporated-history/ (accessed 24 May 2025). The Winstanley firm became known as Jones, Lang, Wootten (JLW) in 1939. In 1999, JLW merged with LaSalle Partners, becoming Jones Lang LaSalle (JLL). JLL's corporate headquarters is in Chicago.

In contrast to Winstanley, George Good was an upholder who also practised auctioneering but became bankrupt. Good joined the Upholders' Company in 1762.[62] His business model, when compared to Winstanley's from above, was comprehensive rather than specialized. By remaining in the upholding business, Good would have had a stock of goods. This fact, along with running multiple business endeavours, would have increased Good's risk of bankruptcy.

Good placed his first auction announcement for the sale of household furnishings in the 25 July 1764 *Gazetteer and New Daily Advertiser*, where he also promoted himself as an upholder and sworn appraiser in the Old Bailey near Ludgate Hill.[63] On 26 June 1765, he advertised the auction of a bankrupt surgeon's household furniture. In this instance, he listed himself as a sworn exchange broker in the Old Bailey.[64] Almost six months later, he advertised himself as an upholder and sworn broker.[65] In another of Good's auctions, he listed himself in the 12 April 1768 *Public Advertiser* as an upholder and auctioneer, No. 121, Fleet Street.[66] Because he continued to promote himself as an upholder, with the exception of the 1765 advertisement, it is apparent he continued to run an upholding business. Although he consistently identified himself as an upholder, Good used different names to describe his additional expertise, including those of a sworn appraiser, sworn exchange broker, sworn broker, and auctioneer. George Good went bankrupt for unknown reasons.[67] He died in 1787, and his probate stated his occupation as an auctioneer.[68]

Most of the upholders studied in this chapter who became auctioneers after first becoming sworn brokers appear to have continued running their upholding businesses. In a search of the Burney Newspaper Collection by auctioneer and upholder in the same advertisement for the years 1750 to 1800, it is apparent that there were many upholders who also practised auctioneering. For the time period from 1760 to 1769, there were 134 auction advertisements where the auctioneer also promoted himself as an upholder. This dropped to seventy-nine in the 1770s and rose to 144 in

[62] Walton, "Company of Upholders," 60.
[63] *Gazetteer and New Daily Advertiser*, 25 July 1764.
[64] *Gazetteer and New Daily Advertiser*, 2 June 1765.
[65] *Gazetteer and New Daily Advertiser*, 11 January 1766.
[66] *Public Advertiser*, 12 April 1768.
[67] *London Gazette*, 19–23 October 1779.
[68] The National Archives, Kew. PROB 11/1159/4. Will of George Good, Auctioneer of Racquet Court Fleet Street. 2 November 1787.

the 1780s. Although the research undertaken indicated few upholders in the eighteenth century became full-time auctioneers, many, nonetheless, participated in the auction process. This examination leads to the conclusion that the majority of upholders who advertised themselves as auctioneers practised auctioneering on a part-time basis, and seldom on a full-time basis. Some of these advertisements were for an upholder providing the details and catalogues for an upcoming auction, rather than acting in the role of auctioneer. This was the case with John Trotter, when he acted as an agent by providing sale particulars and catalogues for Mr. Pervil, who, in 1755, was the auctioneer of the personal effects of the late Lady Barbara Leigh, the daughter of the Earl of Scarborough.[69] General upholders who were not sworn brokers or auctioneers probably referred inquiries and business to sworn brokers and auctioneers. They were possibly paid a modest fee for referrals and for handing out auction catalogues and answering questions.

Upholders saw auctioneering as a way to supplement their income, but why would a consumer be motivated to use their services? Auctions were not only a method to transfer property between parties. As mentioned in Chap. 1, Cynthia Wall believed auctions also allowed people to project themselves as members of a higher social order.[70] This assertion by Wall may have applied to consumers who purchased used household goods from brokers as well. However, the purchase of previously owned fine art and household goods as a way to project one's self into a higher social order could not have been the reason for the majority of transactions in used goods. In his study of the auctions of used household goods from Northamptonshire country homes from about 1760 to 1830, Jon Stobart concluded that the luxury items that would connect a buyer with aristocracy were highly personal and included family portraits, silverware, clothes, and jewels. His study also concluded that these personal items were rarely sold at auction and usually were distributed to family members by bequest.[71] While it may be true that there were buyers of used luxury items who were not of the higher social classes, Stobart's work showed that there was little proof that consumers of these goods were primarily

[69] *Public Advertiser*, 27 February 1755.

[70] Cynthia Wall, "The English Auction: Narratives of Dismantlings," *Eighteenth-Century Studies* Vol. 31, No. 1 (Fall 1997): 1–15.

[71] Jon Stobart, "Luxury and Country House Sales in England, c. 1760–1830," in *The Afterlife of Used Things Recycling in the Long Eighteenth Century*, ed. Ariane Fennetaux, Amélie Junqua, and Sophie Vasset. (New York: Routledge, 2015), 31–32, 34.

motivated by a desire to project themselves into a higher social class, not only in the Northamptonshire area, but probably throughout England.

Stobart argued that buyers differentiated used luxury goods in three ways. First, a prospective buyer would consider the raw materials used to manufacture a particular item. For instance, a prospective buyer of silk curtains would be interested in how the fabric could be reconstituted into new curtains or seat coverings by resizing them. The reconstitution of raw materials from tables, looking glasses, and other furniture was also a possibility for potential bidders. A second consideration that differentiated used luxury goods from ordinary ones was exoticism. Previously owned imported porcelain from China, Japan, and France attracted buyers, especially usable items associated with coffee or tea. Finally, the complexity in the construction of a used luxury good attracted certain buyers, applying to furniture, silverware, and porcelain made by coveted manufacturers, which rarely became available for sale.[72]

The motivations of buyers at auctions were also varied. The opportunity to purchase a second-hand luxury item at a low price was always a motivator. Stobart estimated that curtains, which could be resized, sold for one-fifth of their original price. Another motivation was the opportunity to obtain an object without having to go through a middleman. Stobart used the example of a buyer purchasing a slab of marble at auction rather than sourcing it from Italy, saving time and money. Of course, the opportunity to purchase a luxury item that could not be bought elsewhere was a primary motivator for some buyers. Stobart points out that luxury auctions at country houses changed by 1815. In order to capture higher sales prices, the trend was for owners of luxury goods to consign them to London's large auction houses and specialist fine art and antique dealers.[73]

Although the demand for used luxury goods remained high during the period of this study, upholders who were auctioneers generally did not sell second-hand luxury goods. Instead, they auctioned used mundane items, which Stobart called necessities and decencies. This may be partially explained by the complexity and cost of purchasing new goods from the manufacturing and supply chain, which could be avoided by buying used items.[74]

[72] Stobart, "Luxury and Country House Sales in England," 27–28.

[73] Stobart, "Luxury and Country House Sales in England," 28–29, 32–34.

[74] Stobart, "Luxury and Country House Sales in England," 26, 28, 32.

Auctioneering had become a thriving London business in the second half of the eighteenth century. Neither Campbell nor Waller gave insight into the auction business in their apprenticeship advice books, probably because auctioneering was not associated with any particular livery company and had no apprenticeship scheme. It appears that the auction business was unregulated because no evidence has been found that indicates auctioneers had to be sworn or even licensed. Auctioneers came from a variety of backgrounds, including upholders, especially those who were also sworn appraisers and brokers. It may be that upholders who were sworn appraisers and brokers were signalling to the public that they were more trustworthy and honest than other auctioneers.

Because auctioneering became a popular means by which to exchange property, it seems unusual that auctioneers were not licensed and required to swear an oath. Being a sworn broker, after all, created the notion of trustworthiness that came from the expectations of honesty and fair dealing. One of the reasons for this lack of government oversight may be that Britain was transitioning from a moral economy to a political economy at this time.

E.P. Thompson wrote about the moral economy, and how the common folk in rural England often determined what was honest and fair with respect to the price of bread, including the prices and the quality of the raw and milled commodities needed for making it. The poorer masses considered it their right to conduct direct action (riot) if they believed the price for bread and its components were too expensive or if the quality was poor. The justification for direct action was rooted in Queen Elizabeth's *Book of Orders*, which gave magistrates emergency powers to intervene when grain shortages and, consequently, prices, were affecting the well-being of the poor. These emergency powers were essentially put into effect during the reign of Charles I.[75] When the government did not intervene to stop 'unjust' prices by enforcing the law during an emergency, the people would impose 'fairness' by either threatening or actually rioting against those responsible. According to Thompson this behaviour:

> … operated within a popular consensus as to what were legitimate and what were illegitimate practices in marketing, milling, baking, etc. This in its turn was grounded upon a consistent traditional view of social norms and obliga-

[75] E.P. Thompson, "The Moral Economy of the English Crowd in the Eighteenth Century," *Past & Present* No. 50 (Feb. 1971): 108–10.

tions, of the proper economic functions of several parties within the community, which, taken together, can be said to constitute the moral economy of the poor.[76]

Direct action in London occurred for a variety of reasons. Robert Bucholz and Joseph Ward summarized the causes of riots into five categories: riots over words and behaviour; economic riots; xenophobic riots; calendar riots; and political riots.[77] Of relevance here are economic riots, where direct action was based on a sense of fairness. Economic riots were more attuned to worker rights and pay. Silk looms, imported goods, and imported labour were among the flashpoints for journeymen in the trades. They wanted to maintain the status quo and petitioned their respective guilds to enforce the livery rules. If their demands were ignored, many times, they rioted. If teen-aged apprentices joined in, a riot could grow into a few thousand participants. The riot would eventually run its course and die out, or the City might use force to quell it and arrest the ringleaders. Nonetheless, a big riot got the attention of lawmakers. For instance, the Calico Act (1723) and Spitalfields Act (1773) were passed shortly after direct actions.[78] Thompson wrote that a new political economy was quickly developing to replace the moral economy. Adam Smith's *The Wealth of Nations* added weight to the argument for allowing the marketplace to set prices through the natural course of supply and demand.[79] It appears that auctions were not controversial and subject to the direct actions described above, probably because auctions were conducted in public. As long as the established rules were followed by the sellers and bidders, auctions followed the natural course of supply and demand.

Why were auctioneers not required to swear an oath similar to brokers, especially in a society so attuned to honesty and fairness? Part of the answer may be that by the 1760s, the decade when ten upholders became sworn brokers, Britain was already evolving into the political economy discussed above, and the moral economy was waning. J.R. Kellett argued that the population growth beyond the City walls made enforcing guild rules problematic and seriously weakened guild control of production. In addition, the City of London's Common Council was beginning to lose legal

[76] Thompson, "The Moral Economy," 78–79.

[77] Robert Bucholz and Joseph Ward, *London: A Social and Cultural History, 1550 – 1750* (Cambridge: Cambridge University Press, 2012), 274–81.

[78] Bucholz and Ward, *London*, 275–78.

[79] Thompson, "The Moral Economy," 129–31.

control over livery companies by the beginning of the seventeenth century. The Common Council, as previously mentioned, had lost five important legal cases by 1620, diluting the monopoly that livery companies enjoyed in their respective trades.[80] It was at the beginning of the eighteenth century that Parliament and the City passed broker laws and regulations. Auctioneers had no livery company that represented them, and if they had, Common Council laws may not have been effective in 1760.

It also may be that Parliament and the City of London Common Council did not pass laws requiring auctioneers to act honestly and fairly because the political economy was taking root and a laissez-faire attitude prevailed. However, a more practical answer to why auctioneers did not swear an oath to act honestly and fairly was because common law evolved as the auction business grew and, consequently, paternalistic oversight of auctioneers was not needed.

Disputes involving auctions were settled through the courts and common law. Case law and precedent, rather than a legal code, were used to resolve disputes. Montefiore's *Commercial Dictionary* addressed some of the auction rules that were part of settled law. Among them was *Payne* v *Cave*, 3 T.R. 148, where the court ruled that a bidder could retract a bid if done before the hammer dropped. The court decided in *Howard* v *Castle*, 6 T.R. 642, that if a seller of goods at auction used 'puffers' to bid up prices on his behalf without declaring it, the final purchaser would not be compelled to complete the contract. In another example, the court ruled in the case *Borough* v *Skinner*, 5 *Burr*. 2639, that it is always supposed that the seller has good title to the item, and if the title is found defective, the purchaser is entitled to his money back.[81]

Auctioneers who were sworn brokers may have operated under the expectation of fair and honest dealing, but rules were necessary for all auctioneers. The customs and practices of auctioneers evolved out of necessity. For instance, the ascending bid auction was the solution for efficiently selling a large number of items. Rules for minimum bids, determining the accepted final bid, defining an item's condition, commission rates, and purchase terms, including delivery versus payment, were also part of the evolution of auctioneering.

[80] J.R. Kellett, "The Breakdown of Gild and Corporation Control over the Handicraft and Retail Trade in London," *The Economic History Review* New Series, Vol. 10, No. 3 (1958): 381–85.

[81] Montefiore, *A Commercial Dictionary*, AUC. No page number; indexed by subject.

The growth in auctioneering accelerated after the Seven Years' War, which is probably why Parliament did not look to auctions as a source of revenue until the American War of Independence was underway. Parliament recognized by 1777 that auction sales would be a large source of tax revenue that could help finance the war with America. The 1777 and 1779 Acts of Parliament can be considered as the beginning of national government oversight of auctioneers.

In order to fund the American War of Independence, Parliament looked toward excise taxes.[82] The first Act of Parliament that regulated auctioneers was passed in 1777 and required auctioneers within London and Westminster to pay an annual licensing fee of twenty shillings. Nearly twenty years earlier, an Act was passed that required an annual licence fee of forty shillings 'for each person trading in, selling, or vending gold or silver plate'.[83] Prior to the passage of the 1777 Act, an anonymous editorial for the 6 January 1777 *Public Advertiser* argued for the passage of the Act. This editorial stated upholders and brokers were taking advantage of sellers of goods by offering below-market values for their goods. If a seller went to another upholder or broker for a competing bid, the editorial claimed that upholders entered into combinations that conspired to prevent the seller from receiving higher offers. (The author failed to mention that appraisers and brokers could be obligated to purchase goods at their valuation; to prevent the valuation from being 'put back' upon them, appraisers and brokers presented low valuations to prospective sellers.[84]) The editorial suggested it was the auction room that served to provide sellers with a fair sale price, and added '... the auction room may be considered as the Temple of Credit, and as such ought to be supported by the Pillars of the State'. The author argued that because the auction room dealt with ready cash on a commission basis, auctioneers could afford an

[82] Hoppit, *Risk and Failure*, 124–5.

[83] John Planner, *The Town and Country Auctioneer's Guide, Containing the Abstracts of All the Acts of Parliament Relating to the Management and Collection of the Auction Duties* (London: T. Burton, 1797), 9–12.

[84] Sara Pennell speculated that it was 'alcohol and tobacco fueled' auction bidders that drove prices above appraised values in smaller provincial towns. Although these stimulants may have created robust bidding, the 'put back' option that sellers had against appraisers must be considered. See: Sara Pennell, "'All but the Kitchen Sink': Household Sales and the Circulation of Second-Hand Goods in Early Modern England" in *Modernity and the Second-Hand Trade: European Consumption Cultures and Practices, 1700–1900*, ed. Jon Stobart and Ilia Van Damme (Basingstoke: Palgrave Macmillan, 2010), 49.

annual licence fee and excise taxes. In addition, the editorial presented possible rules to protect country market and fair day vendors, prevent the auctioning of contraband goods, and limit the number of days of shopkeepers selling bankrupt estates and the stock in trade of others to no more than five days per year.[85]

This anonymous author seemed to want it both ways when it came to the moral and political economies. On one hand, the author assigned blame to upholders and brokers for taking advantage of sellers by conspiring to keep offering prices low, which is a paternalistic argument. The author then opined that only in an auction would sellers receive a fair price, an argument that would support a political economy based on supply and demand. His support for protecting country markets and fairs, for preventing the sale of contraband goods, and limiting non-broker upholders to liquidating bankrupt estates to five days per year was a nod to a moral economy that provided something for everyone. However, the main intent of the editorial was to support a new Act that provided for the collection of excise taxes. Rather than the 'Pillars of State' supporting the auction business, the editorial was cleverly endorsing an increase in auction sales, which would support the 'Pillars of the State' through excise taxes.

The Act for licensing auctioneers was enacted into law on 29 September 1777 (17 George III Cap. 50). An excise tax of six pence for every twenty shillings was imposed for the sale of household goods and personal goods, and auctioneers were required to post a £200 security bond ensuring the excise tax would be paid to the Commissioner of Excise within fourteen days after a sale. This 1777 Act was replaced on 5 July 1779 by a new Act (19 George III Cap. 56).[86] The payment of duties from auction sales must not have been meeting expectations. The general thrust of the 1779 Act was to strengthen compliance with the law. One of the main requirements under the 1779 Act was that, two days before any auction, the auctioneer had to deliver to the Office of Excise a written notice of the auction date along with a catalogue of the items to be sold and their respective sales price estimates. Within six weeks of the sale, the auctioneer was required

[85] *Public Advertiser*, 6 January 1777.

[86] Officially called: *An Act for granting to his Majesty certain duties on licenses to be taken by all persons acting as auctioneers, and certain rates and duties on all lands, houses, goods, and other things, sold by auction, and upon indentures, leases, bonds, deeds, and other instruments.* See: Planner, *The Town and Country Auctioneer's Guide*, 13–27.

to deliver to the Excise Office an accounting of the sale. Though the 1779 Act covered other facets, including bankruptcy sales, Parliament put the onus of collecting taxes on auctioneers by requiring them to swear under oath that sales proceeds and tax calculations were correctly reported and the taxes paid.[87]

By 1760, upholders recognized that auctioneering was a growth business in which they could specialize as an extension of their upholding businesses, but it should not be assumed that auctions seldom occurred in the first half of the eighteenth century. Auctions were common, and there were auctioneers who advertised through broadsheets and newspapers in the first half of the century, just not at the volume seen after 1760. By 1770, newspapers were replete with auction advertisements.

While this section is primarily focused on London auctioneering in the second half of the eighteenth century, Sara Pennell's research found that provincial auctions were a common event in the first half of the eighteenth century. Small town auctions occurred for a variety of reasons, death and debt being the primary reasons. Auctioneering in the smaller towns was not a specialized occupation as it was in London and, perhaps, the large provincial cities. The small-town auctioneer often worked in another trade and called auctions on an ad hoc basis.[88] The upholders studied for this chapter viewed auctioneering as a way to supplement their upholding revenue. Richard Winstanley was one upholder who left the upholding trade and became successful as a full-time auctioneer. There may be a few other upholders who were also successful as full-time auctioneers, but the evidence indicates that, for the most part, upholders practised auctioneering on either a part-time or peripheral basis and remained in the upholding trade on a full-time basis.

In summary, because the number of upholders becoming sworn brokers increased greatly from the 1760s and through the 1780s, it is apparent they were looking to grow their revenues through adding new business lines. The synergy between upholding and appraising, brokering, and auctioneering was high, and upholders must have been keen to enter what they perceived as profitable businesses with low risk. They apparently viewed appraising, brokering, and auctioneering of household goods as steady businesses. All three were service businesses, rather than the

[87] Montefiore, *A Commercial Dictionary*, AUC. No page number; indexed by subject.
[88] Pennell, "'All but the Kitchen Sink'", 40–4.

business of assembling, manufacturing, and selling of household furnishings that upholders were known for.

Along with providing new household goods, upholders looked to selling second-hand goods as a way to increase revenue. Dealing in second-hand household goods was nothing new to the upholder trade, but by 1760, some upholders made it a distinct business line by becoming sworn brokers and appraisers. Brokers were regulated by law and swore an oath to act honestly and fairly. Death, debt, and fashion obsolescence were the main contributors to the supply of used (and sometimes new) furniture. The main reasons for appraisals were death (probate), debt (bankruptcy), and household and business insurance. Broker services were provided for a commission and appraisals were done for a fee.

The barriers to entry for sworn brokers and appraisers in London were high. Becoming a sworn appraiser and broker required not only money for the broker's bond, but also required peer sponsorship and approval by the City to obtain a broker medal, making entry difficult. The ongoing business costs and risks would have been low. Appraising and brokering were static business lines with slow growth potential beyond death and debt. Nonetheless, it must have been a profitable business because a broker medal could be sold for between £800 and £1500 in the secondary market. Regulation of the number of licences should have eliminated competition, but unlicensed brokers and appraisers were allowed to practise on a smaller scale.

Many upholders also provided auction services, mostly on a part-time or ad hoc basis. No matter how an upholder participated in the auction business, auctions became a popular way to exchange personal property, land, buildings, and leases in the last half of the eighteenth century. In contrast to brokers, auctioneers were not regulated by Parliament, but through common law, which evolved throughout the late-seventeenth and early-eighteenth centuries. Upholders who conducted auctions were often sworn appraisers and brokers, conveying a sense of honesty and trustworthiness.

There were no substantial legal barriers as to who could become an auctioneer and no regulations as to their numbers. The lack of regulatory oversight allowed nearly anyone with enough money to enter the auction business. Although upholders entering the auctioneering business had lower barriers to entry than sworn brokers and appraisers, their ongoing expenses were higher, especially if they maintained sales rooms. The ease of entry into auctioneering created more competition, which is why most upholders were unable to become full-time auctioneers and remained anchored to the upholding business.

Some upholders examined in this work failed not because they entered the appraising, brokering, and/or auctioning business, but because they remained in the upholding business, where maintaining stock was expensive and the risk of becoming a victim of bad debt was higher. Richard Winstanley, upholder-turned-auctioneer, left the upholding business early on and built a successful auction business. It appears most upholders were unable to establish a substantial business in brokering and auctioneering. If they had, they most probably would have left upholding as Winstanley did. These other upholders were unable to enter the 'opportunities' phase of the business trajectory, where savings were often used to enter unrelated businesses. It is concluded in Chaps. 4 and 5 that Robert Williams and John Trotter, helped by their gentry backgrounds, were able to accumulate wealth because they entered niche businesses that were difficult to break into. Upholders specializing as appraisers, brokers, and auctioneers were unable to accumulate much wealth because these businesses either had static growth (appraising and brokering) or were not difficult to break into (auctioneering). In other words, they tried to accumulate wealth in businesses with limited growth potential or considerable competition.

The research into upholders acting as appraisers, brokers, and auctioneers shows mixed financial success. With the exception of Richard Winstanley, most of those studied for this chapter remained in the upholding business. The bankruptcy risk was higher for those remaining in the upholding business, which would have been exacerbated by maintaining a large stock of goods that consumers were unwilling to purchase. This research leads to the conclusion that the supplemental revenues from the appraising, brokering, and auctioneering business lines were not significant enough to offset potential upholding losses.

So far, this work has examined upholders' involvement in funeral undertaking, appraising, brokering, and auctioneering as ways to earn extra money. There were a handful of upholders who found niche business lines or special clientele that allowed them to become wealthy. The next two chapters examine the business trajectories of two upholders, Robert Williams and John Trotter, both of whom found niche business lines and became financially successful.

CHAPTER 4

Case Study of Robert Williams

One item in the London Metropolitan Archives collection is an account book of Robert Williams (Illustration 4.1) that details his upholding business from 1763 to 1772. This account book provides information including descriptions and prices of the goods and services he provided to clients during this time period. The archival administrative history entry states that he was an upholsterer and cabinet-maker of Bow Street, Covent Garden.[1] Examination of the ledger's entries found that Williams was more than an upholsterer and a cabinet-maker. As we will see in this case study, Robert Williams was an upholder, and as such, sold everything needed to furnish or 'fit out' a residential interior, including furniture, upholstery goods, rugs, curtains, blankets, and glass. He frequently sold various household goods to ship captains and provided funeral undertaking and appraisals on a limited basis. While upholders were primarily known for 'fitting out' residences, it is evident from Williams's account book that he did a substantial amount of business with East India Company ship officers as well. What is argued here is that because of the breadth of the goods and services he provided, Robert Williams must be considered an upholder with a specialty niche business in furnishing East India Company officer quarters and selling goods to ship officers engaged in private trading in India and Asia.

[1] London Metropolitan Archives, City of London. Reference Code: ACC/0426. Account Book of Robert Williams.

S. Sanders, *The Eighteenth-Century London Upholder*,
https://doi.org/10.1007/978-3-032-08660-0_4

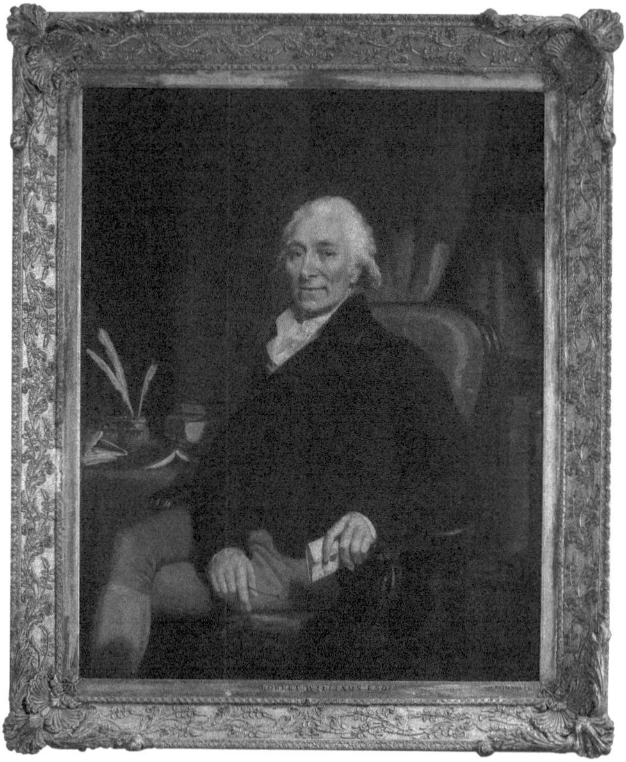

Illustration 4.1 Portrait of Robert Williams (1735–1814). Ramsay Reinagle, RA. c. 1810. (Photograph by Sue Macpherson, ARPS. ©Williams Family Collection, Bridehead, Dorset, by permission of Sir Philip Williams)

While surviving account ledgers from the eighteenth century may be common, Robert Williams's account book is interesting because it contextualizes one part of the story of an upholder who began his working life as an apprentice upholder and later became the general partner of a bank, the controlling owner of several East India ships, an East India Company director, a member of Parliament, and the owner of two large estates. His wealth was estimated at well over £600,000 (more than £740 million in today's value[2]) when he died in 1814.[3] Williams's accomplishments in terms of wealth accumulation and business activities placed him in the upper commercial class. Stephen Farrell in *The History of Parliament* described Williams as a 'self-made' man, though he was born into a minor landed gentry family.[4] Coming from even a minor gentry family was important to Williams's business success; nonetheless, his accomplishments cannot be attributed to class status alone.

Family Connections

Robert Williams was one of five sons of Robert and Anne Williams and was baptized at Charminster, Dorset, on 23 April 1735.[5] Of significance, and to be explained later, are that his oldest brother, John, and his younger brother, Stephen, were important in Robert's business success. Robert also had three sisters, including Honour, whose significance will be discussed shortly.[6] Robert followed his father when he moved the family from Dorset to London.[7] This move is supported in *Moor Park, with a biographical sketch of its principal proprietors…*, where Robert Bayne points out that Robert's father was allegedly disinherited for marrying a woman of inferior rank, although she was of great worth and respectability.[8] The

[2] This calculation is based on the relative income or economic status of wealth method from MeasuringWorth.com (accessed 29 June 2025). Measuring Worth is a not-for-profit organization that provides historical price measures and comparisons for the United Kingdom, the United States, and Australia. Economic historians from around the world use the site for teaching and research. The online currency converter at The National Archives refers users to the Measuring Worth website.

[3] For a brief biography of Robert Williams, see: Lawrence Taylor, *The History of Parliament: the House of Commons 1790–1820*, ed. R. Thorne (London: The History of Parliament Trust, 1986), Ref. Vols. 1790–1820.

[4] Stephen Farrell, *The History of Parliament: the House of Commons 1820–1830*, ed. D.R. Fisher (London: Cambridge University Press, The History of Parliament Trust, 2009), Ref. Vols. 1820–1832.

[5] Ancestry.com. *England & Wales Christening Records, 1530–1906* [database on-line] (accessed 7 November 2014, Newberry Library). *Charminster, Dorset, England*; Date Range: *1721–1832*; Film Number: *1279491*.

[6] John Burke, *A Genealogical and Heraldic History of the Commoners of Great Britain and Ireland* (London: Henry Colburn, 1836), Vol. 1, 618–19.

[7] Sir Robert Philip Williams Bt., of Bridehead, Dorset (great-great-great-great grandson of Robert Williams), e-mail message to author, 11 December 2014.

[8] Robert Bayne, *Moor Park with a biographical sketch of its principal proprietors…* (London: Longmans, Green and Co., 1871), 104.

Williams brothers had to 'earn their living'.[9] At the age of fourteen, Robert was apprenticed as either an upholsterer or a cabinet-maker in Bow Street, Covent Garden.[10]

Pat Kirkham's research supports the probability that Williams's father paid an apprenticeship premium of between £34 and £49, and that he completed it in seven years or less.[11] There is no reason to believe that he did not live with his master at Bow Street. Also, there is no evidence that Williams became a livery company freeman at the end of his apprenticeship, but such a practice was not unusual among journeymen.[12] The enforcements of freedom admissions and apprenticeship licensing remained sources of conflict between craftsmen and livery companies during much of the eighteenth century. Perhaps Robert Williams believed that he was financially secure enough to not need the protection and benefits offered by livery company membership.

Given that Robert Williams was born in 1735 and was bound to a cabinet-maker or upholsterer at age fourteen, it can be assumed he began laying the foundation of his independent upholding career between 1749 and 1750. There are no known documents relating to his work before that of the account ledger, beginning in 1763. Holden, however, tells two stories about Williams during this time. The first concerns furniture that Williams made during his apprenticeship, when Sir Lawrence Dundas ordered furnishings for his home. Dundas was the owner of the Moor Park estate in Hertfordshire. When Robert Williams bought Moor Park in 1801, it is said that he also bought the bedstead and other items he had made himself. The second story is from an 1861 letter written to Lord Ebury from William Cotton. Cotton wrote to Lord Ebury, then owner of Moor Park, detailing his conversations with Jane Williams, Robert's widow. She told Cotton that her husband was a bound apprentice to an

[9] Kenneth Holden et al., *Williams Deacon's 1771–1970* (Manchester: McCorquodale & Co. Ltd., 1971), 4–5. Many parts of this work are from anonymous contributors. Supporting footnotes are, therefore, lacking in many areas.

[10] There are no known documents confirming the Williams family's move to London and no known records confirming Robert Williams's apprenticeship and his master's name. Bayne wrote that he was an apprentice upholsterer at age fourteen. Other sources, including Holden's *Williams Deacon's 1771–1970*, speak of his apprenticeship as a cabinet-maker at age fourteen.

[11] Pat Kirkham, *The London Furniture Trade 1700–1870* (Leeds: Furniture History Society, 1988), 136, 177, TABLE 11.

[12] For an explanation of journeymen and masters not joining a livery company see: Kirkham, *London Furniture Trade*, 136–144.

upholsterer and that she used to work in the shop with her needle.[13] It is noteworthy that Jane Williams referred to her husband as an upholsterer's apprentice rather than a cabinet-maker's. There is the possibility that the shop was that of an upholder and that Cotton confused the term with upholsterer. Regardless of whether or not the master was an upholder, an upholsterer, or a cabinet-maker, it is plausible that Williams's master operated much like an upholder, furnishing residential interiors. The freedoms admissions list of the Upholders' Company includes no upholder named Robert Williams.[14] Furthermore, record searches yield no evidence of a master paying the apprenticeship tax for Robert Williams. However, a master not registering an apprentice was not unusual.[15] There was a master joiner and cabinet-maker at this time named Henry Williams, but no family connections between Henry and Robert Williams have been found.[16]

Following the account book that begins in 1763, the next documented mention of Robert Williams is the recording of his 27 October 1764 marriage to Jane Chassereau at St. Paul's, Covent Garden.[17] On 4 April 1768, Williams paid two guineas to have sole use of pew No. 1B, on the north side of the middle aisle at St. Paul's, Covent Garden. The purchase required that Robert and Jane remain householders, live in the parish, and pay and discharge all parochial duties.[18]

Robert's wife, Jane Chassereau (Illustration 4.2), was born in 1739 to Anne and Francis Chassereau and was the youngest of six children of Huguenot heritage. Francis, her father, was born in Niort, Deux-Sèvres, France, in 1698. The family left France and was 'received into the French Church, Leicester Fields, London, on 2nd May 1714'.[19] Robert and Jane Williams were doubly related; Jane's oldest sibling, Francis Chassereau,

[13] Holden, *Williams Deacon's*, 6–7. The authors offer no supporting footnotes for these two stories, though the document and letter must exist.

[14] Karin M. Walton, "The Worshipful Company of Upholders of the City of London," *Furniture History Society* Vol. 9 (1973): 50–79.

[15] Kirkham, *London Furniture Trade*, 48.

[16] Henry Phillips, *Annals of the Worshipful Company of Joiners of the City of London* (London: Privately Printed, 1915), 127.

[17] Ancestry.com. *England, Select Marriages, 1538–1973* [database on-line] (accessed 8 October 2014, Newberry Library). FHL Film Number: 942 B4HA V. 35.

[18] Dorset Record Office, Dorset. D289/F1. Robert Williams Warrant for the Pew No. 1B, St. Paul, Covent Garden.

[19] David C.A. Agnew, *Protestant Exiles from France, Chiefly in the Reign of Louis XIV* (For Private Circulation, 1886), 3rd Ed., Vol. 2, 501.

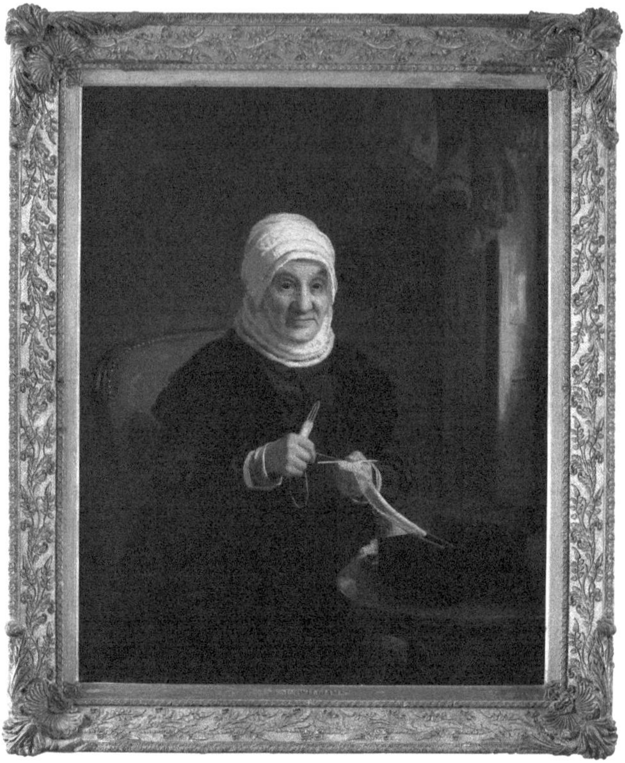

Illustration 4.2 Portrait of Jane Chassereau Williams (1739–1841). Ramsay Reinagle, RA. c. 1810. (Photograph by Sue Macpherson, ARPS. ©Williams Family Collection, Bridehead, Dorset, by permission of Sir Philip Williams)

Jr., married Robert's sister, Honour Williams.[20] The Chassereau family were fan makers and stationers, a business that Francis, Jr. and Honour also entered.

Francis Chassereau, Sr., father of Jane Williams, died in 1788 and named his sons-in-law, Robert Williams and Hugh Burgess, as executors and left them £1000 each in Old South Sea Annuities for the benefit of his grandchildren. Other bequests to his children and grandchildren were Old

[20] Though early records indicate the spelling of her first name as Honor, after her marriage she adopted the spelling of Honour. Francis's first name was originally recorded as Francois, but was later reported as Francis. The first names Honour and Francis are used in this work.

South Seas annuities between £700–1300 and three per cent East India annuities. Household items were left to his wife, Anne.[21] It can be seen from his will that Francis Chassereau, Sr. was a successful business owner and managed to save enough money to invest in annuities.

Francis Chassereau, Jr. was not financially successful, probably because he died in 1767 at the age of thirty-eight. His will made no bequests, indicating that he was not financially successful beyond the norm for an ordinary owner of a fan-making and stationery business. His assets, after paying debts, were left to Honour. He stipulated that she could keep the stock-in-trade and associated items if she wished to continue in the business. Robert Williams's brother, Captain John Williams, and Francis Chassereau, Sr. were named executors.[22] Honour continued the business, and Robert privately lent her money. After Honour's death, Robert commented upon her business skills during an 1804 legally required audit of her business debts, writing that, 'I was at that time (1767) continually transacting business for my Sister, she having so recently lost her Husband & being totally ignorant of any business herself.'[23] This audit, dated back to 1763, examined revenues, funeral expenses, and partnership dividends, an audit which was undoubtedly expensive in terms of time and money.

Family and Business at Bow Street, Covent Garden, and Beyond

Williams lived at Bow Street when he began running his own upholding business. Whether or not he took over his master's premises when he started his business is unknown, although Holden says he did. According to the 42nd edition of *Kent's Directory*, for the years 1751–1775, Williams practised his trade at Bow Street, Covent Garden, his occupations being listed as upholder and cabinet-maker.[24] The 46th edition of *Kent's Directory* lists Williams's place of business at No. 28 King Street, Covent

[21] The National Archives, Kew. PROB 11/1166/325. Will of Francis Chassereau, Gentleman of Saint Marylebone, Middlesex, 21 June 1788.

[22] The National Archives, Kew. PROB 11/927/291. Will of Francis Chassereau (the Younger), Fan Maker and Stationer of St. Martin in the Fields, Middlesex, 13 April 1767.

[23] Hertfordshire Archives and Local Studies, Hertford. GH 723. Williams and Chassereau Accounting.

[24] Henry Kent. *Kent's Directory* (London: Richard and Henry Causton, 1774, 42nd ed. Ancestry.com. *U.K. and U.S. Directories, 1680–1830* [database on-line] (accessed 8 October 2014, Newberry Library).

Garden, from 1776–1800. Again, his occupations were listed as upholder and cabinet-maker.[25]

There is no information about the number of employees in Robert Williams's upholding business. He did, however, work closely with Thomas Williams, one of his brothers. Thomas's exact role in the business cannot be discerned, but he occasionally signed for the delivery of goods and for payment. Thomas was not an ordinary employee, however. The Heal trade card collection at The British Museum possesses the trade card of Thomas Williams of Bow Street, Covent Garden, which advertises his cabinet, upholstery, and carpet warehouse. The product line included making and selling cabinet work, chairs, upholstery goods, and carpets. Significantly, the card also advertises looking glasses and lanterns for exportation.[26] Thomas and Robert probably had some sort of a familial partnership agreement with the upholding business.

Some information about Robert's employees was found in a long news article in the 14 October 1773 *Public Ledger*. The article reported on thefts from his Bow Street upholding shop by his porter, Edward Wilson, whom Robert originally considered to be a remarkably honest employee. Williams first dismissed two journeywomen on the suspicion that they were the culprits stealing from his shop, but a journeyman employee had observed Wilson removing a piece of carpet and informed Williams. Wilson was questioned and confessed to stealing the carpet and other items, including looking glasses intended for shipment to America. Wilson and three other men, including a journeyman upholder from another firm, were committed for trial. From this news report, it can be seen that Williams's business was substantial enough to employ a porter, a journeyman, and two journeywomen, although he most certainly had more employees. The news item also points out that Williams was involved in exporting looking glasses to America.[27]

There is one piece of information about Williams residing at Bow Street. Shops were usually located at street level for easy customer access, and the owner's family often occupied the first floor. Servants, apprentices,

[25] Henry Kent. *Kent's Directory* (London: Richard and Henry Causton, 1778, 46th ed.) Ancestry.com. *U.K. and U.S. Directories, 1680–1830* [database on-line] (accessed 8 October 2014, Newberry Library).

[26] Ambrose Heal. *The London Furniture Makers from the Restoration to the Victorian Era 1660–1840.* (London: B.T. Batsford Ltd., 1953), 202, 204. The British Museum, London. Heal Collection. Museum No. Heal,28.236. Trade card of T. Williams.

[27] *Public Ledger*, 14 October 1773.

and renters lodged on the floors above the family quarters. If the shop took up multiple floors, the family might live next door.[28] There is one indication that the Williams family lived above his shop, from a news item in the 13 June 1777 *Gazetteer and New Daily Advertiser*. This news item reported that:

> Wednesday afternoon a fine girl, only seven years of age, daughter of Mr. Williams, Upholder, in Bow Street, Covent Garden, fell from a two pair of stairs window into the street, by which accident she had an arm and thigh broke, and was otherwise much bruised.[29]

The young girl was probably Anne Williams, born on 30 July 1770. She recovered well enough to marry and later died in 1846. *Kent's Directory*, 46th edition, reported Williams's business address at this time as 28 King Street, not Bow Street, where young Anne was injured. The reason for these different addresses may be that Williams had moved his business to King Street and kept his residence at Bow Street. Also, the timeframe for this *Kent's Directory* is 1776–1800, allowing ample time for Williams to move his business to another address.

Jane and Robert Williams had five children: Robert, Jr., William, Anne, Harriett, and Sophia. They all lived into adulthood and each married. Presuming the Williams's household was typical when compared to other tradesmen, Jane, along with the servants, looked after the children, and, according to Earle, the children would have attended school for eight to ten years, beginning at age six.[30] Whether or not the children were involved in helping with the family upholding business is unknown, but Robert, Jr. later worked with his father and learned the banking and East India Company businesses.

At some point, the Williams family moved from Covent Garden to Leytonstone, seven miles to the north-east, near Epping Forest.[31] The 11 April 1810 election list of The Honourable Court of Directors of the United East India Company gave a different address for Robert Williams,

[28] Peter Earle, *The Making of the Middle Class* (Berkeley: University of California Press, 1989), 209–11.

[29] *Gazetteer and New Daily Advertiser*, 13 June 1777.

[30] Earle, *Making of the Middle Class*, 237–39.

[31] Holden, *Williams Deacon's*, 7.

recording his residence at Mill Hill, Hendon, Middlesex.[32] In addition to the home in Hendon, Williams bought the Bridehead estate near his Dorset ancestral home in 1797 and the Hertfordshire Moor Park estate in 1801.

Williams possibly moved his upholding business to 28 King Street, Covent Garden sometime around 1776. How long he continued in business is unknown, but it is certain that he provided some goods to East Indiamen after that date. As his wealth accumulated from his banking and East India businesses, devoting substantial time to the upholding business would have become economically unattractive. He possibly turned the upholding business over to his brother, Thomas. However, his upholding experience surely served him well in his 'ship husbandry' role, where 'fitting out' an entire ship for an ocean voyage was complicated and expensive.

The Account Book

According to Holden, Robert stayed on with his master after completing his apprenticeship and saved enough money to purchase his master's business.[33] There is no evidence to support this, but it was common for a master to sell his business premises, including stock in trade, to an employee. An announcement was often placed in one or more of the London newspapers about the new ownership of a business, but in this case, a search of newspapers yielded no announcement of Williams acquiring his master's business.

Williams's index of upholding clients is located in the first pages of the account book. He divided each index page into four columns and created nine rows. In these large boxes, he wrote the name of the client and recorded the page number of each client's transactions. Other than technical competence in a trade, the ability to read, write, and perform basic mathematical calculations was not only required for success, it was expected of successful merchants and tradesmen.[34] Looking at Williams's

[32] Charles Hardy, *A Register of Ships, Employed in the Service of the Honorable the United East India Company, from the Year 1760 to 1810.* (London: Black, Parry, and Kingsbury, 1811, as revised by Horatio Charles Hardy). Reprint. Memphis: General Books LLC, 2012. APPENDIX, 2.

[33] Holden, *Williams Deacon's*, 5.

[34] David Cressy, "Literacy in context: meaning and measurement in early modern England," in *Consumption and the World of Goods*, ed. John Brewer and Roy Porter (London: Routledge, 1993), 315–316.

account book, he clearly could read, write, and perform addition and subtraction. These skills having been taught by his parents or developed as an apprentice. There is, of course, the possibility that clerks were responsible for recording the accounting information rather than Williams himself; however, his portrait is staged with books, letters, and writing quills, items that imply he was an educated and successful businessman.

While the account book recorded sales revenue, no recording of the cost of goods sold was made. Without this, gross profit (sale price minus unit cost) cannot be calculated. Given the business success he later had, it seems fair to assume that Williams was certainly aware of his profits and losses and must have used another ledger to account for them.

The role of London women in eighteenth-century business must not be overlooked. The wives, daughters, and female domestic staff of shop owners often worked in the front of the shop, while the men performed the heavier aspects of the work. This could include sales, staff management, and overseeing inventories of raw materials. It was not unusual for a wife to keep the shop's books.[35] Given William Cotton's letter recalling how Jane Williams told him that she worked 'with her needle' in the shop where Robert apprenticed, it may well be that she had at least a role in the upholstery aspect of the business.

Williams had a diverse clientele. Among the occupations listed in his ledger entries are: players (actors), a glass scolloper, an apothecary, carvers, a hairdresser, a lace man, tailors, dancers, a stay maker, an attorney, doctors, a coach maker, a joiner, a barber, a cheese monger, an engraver, a tin man, a shoemaker, and ship officers. Excluding the work for ship captains that will be discussed shortly, Williams worked with residential clients, which can be discerned by charges for porters to transport goods sold and for workmen to install curtains, blinds, and other goods.

An example of a residential client was Mr. Richards, an attorney, billed by Williams for household furnishings on 6 August 1764. Included in these furnishings was a goose feather bed and bolster at £6.15.0, and two down pillows for £1.1.0. Counterpanes, blankets, and a good flock mattress were other soft goods purchased by Mr. Richards. Williams charged £1.16.0 for making a mahogany Pembrook table with a drawer and shelf. Also included in the bill were two stained beech elbow chairs for £1.1.0 and a night table for £2.0.0. Two stuffed French armchairs with castors cost £3.10.0. A chest of drawers with a serpentine front and a mahogany

[35] Earle, *Making of the Middle Class*, 163.

commode were provided for £7.0.0. It is possible that the white stone pan Williams provided for three shillings was for the commode. One item stands out as being unrelated to household goods. Mr. Richards purchased six pounds of tea at a cost of £3.12.0.

While the list of goods sold to Mr. Richards was large, many of Williams's client transactions were only for a few items. Sales transactions included not only new goods but often used items too. Repairing and refurbishing a client's worn household goods was commonplace for upholders, and Williams's business was no different in that regard. Robert provided repair services to Captain Quick on 6 April 1763, which included charges for repairing the dining room carpet for £0.4.6, mending a stool for £0.2.0, putting a new flap and part new frame on a large table for £2.2.0, and resizing and repainting a sideboard for £0.4.0. Captain George Willison used Williams on 28 July 1763 to restuff chair seats for £1.4.0. This work was done at Robert's upholding shop, and Willison was charged £0.1.6 for a porter to cart the chairs 'backwards and forwards'. On 8 June 1763, among the charges to Captain Lessell were repairing and bracing the corners of chairs and adding new feet for £0.2.0, repairing and repainting a glass frame for £0.3.6, new silvering of glass for £0.7.0, repairing a desk and a bookcase for £0.1.6, and mending a corner table and adding a new leg for £0.6.6. Most of these repairs and refurbishments were carried out in Williams's shop, as indicated by the charges for porters and transportation carts.

One sales entry also demonstrated that Williams sold stock to another cabinet-maker. He recorded the 9 March 1766 receipt of ten guineas from the sale to Mr. Langlois of a mahogany bookcase with wire doors and the inside full of partitions. The sale also included a large mahogany top in one piece. Mr. Langlois was probably the famed cabinet-maker Pierre Langlois (active 1759–1767). Langlois was noted for making French-style commodes with marquetry inlay. He ran his business in Tottenham Court Road, and, given his expertise, he may have been trained in France.[36] Presuming that Mr. Langlois was the eminent cabinet-maker, it appears that when he needed a rather ordinary piece of furniture, he purchased it from Williams rather than making it himself, and, at the same time, he had need of a large piece of mahogany stock. Here we see Williams acting as a

[36] *The British and Irish Furniture Makers Online*, https://bifmo.furniturehistorysociety.org/entry/langlois-pierre-1718-1767 (accessed 11 June 2025).

supplier to the cabinet trade, and it may be that his marriage into a Huguenot family led Langlois to his shop.

Upholders often served as undertakers and provided the accoutrements for funerals, but the account book gives no evidence that Williams practised this aspect of the upholding trade. There is, however, one notable exception. In 1765, he provided funeral undertaking goods and services that were billed to his father-in-law, Francis Chassereau, Sr. (Table 4.1). There is no information about for whom the services were required. The entry details the items provided for a funeral, the most expensive being the accessorized elm coffin at £3.3.0 and the hearse and a coach at £1.1.0. The total expense came to £7.6.8. The costs for this funeral were not extravagant, and the deceased was most likely of the lower middling rank. Williams also charged for two crepe hatbands, six cloaks, and four pairs of ribbon-bound gloves, which, taken together, indicates that the funeral attendance was small. The interment was in Paddington, but in which graveyard is unknown. It appears that Williams provided the funeral goods and services as an accommodation to his father-in-law, and, in this instance, he probably purchased the accessorized coffin and shroud from a funeral

Table 4.1 1765 Funeral expenses billed to Francis Chassereau, Sr.

Goods and services	*Cost (£)*
Elm coffin covered with fine flannel, burnished buttons (brass nails), plate (deceased's name), three pair of handles, lined and ruffled, and a shroud and ruffled pillow	3.3.0
Best pall	0.10.0
6 Cloaks	0.6.0
2 Crape hatbands	0.7.6
4 Pair men's and women's ribbon bound black gloves	0.6.0
Dues at Paddington (graveyard) and grave digger	0.17.8
4 Bearers to Paddington	0.8.0
Hearse and one coach to Paddington	1.1.0
Drinks for coachmen and bearers, making affidavit (buried in wool), and turnpikes	0.4.0
Taking of ground at Paddington, tending the funeral, and bran for the coffin (bran kept the body from shifting and absorbed body fluids)	0.3.6
Total funeral costs billed to Mr. Chassereau, Sr.	£7.6.8

Source: London Metropolitan Archives, City of London. Reference Code: ACC/0426. Account Book of Robert Williams. 1765 account entry for undertaking expenses charged to Mr. Chassereau, Sr. by Robert Williams

supplier. The other goods, including the pall, hatbands, cloaks, and gloves, would have been rented. From a business standpoint, this ledger entry proves Williams had the ability to provide funeral undertaking, but the account ledger entries suggest undertaking was not a regular business line for him.

The account ledger has three entries for appraisal services. Two of these are dated 1763 and include written inventories. Williams charged £10 for the first appraisal. In the second appraisal, he set the values with John Trotter and wrote up the inventory, charging £5.5.0. Similar to the funeral undertaking business, Williams did not pursue appraising as a regular business line.

A peculiar transaction occurred in August 1765. Williams sold several household items amounting to £143.6.4. In this instance, Williams accepted chinaware as payment rather than cash. This is the only barter transaction found in the account book. Another transaction that stands out, this one unrelated to household goods, is from the 1763 sale to Mr. Levi, a tailor, of 186 pairs of handkerchiefs for £234.16.0 and sixty-eight pairs of neck cloths for £102.0.0. Levi also bought over eighteen yards of yellow silk damask. Though an upholder's sale of silk damask may not be unusual, the sale of expensive handkerchiefs and neck cloths was. Williams may have been acting as a wholesaler to Mr. Levi.

It is not known where Williams purchased his stock in silk goods and if the silk was from domestic or imported production. However, there were business risks with selling imported silk goods that came not long after the Mr. Levi transaction. Importation of foreign silk goods was considered by Parliament as damaging to England's wrought silk producers, and a 1766 Act of Parliament made it illegal to sell foreign wrought silks or velvets. The Weavers Company published an abstract of the new law in the 9 July 1766 *Gazetteer and New Daily Advertiser*. The abstract warned mercers, haberdashers, upholders, milliners, tailors, and others that stocking and selling foreign wrought silk and velvet was illegal as of 14 June 1766. The law applied to any article that used foreign wrought silk or velvet, such as chair coverings. The onus of proving that any suspected goods were imported before the law became effective was placed on the owner, not the prosecutor. If not exempt from the law, the items were seized and the owner fined £100 plus court costs.[37] Textile protectionism was not new to Britain. Earlier in the century, a similar act was passed to prevent the

[37] *Gazetteer and New Daily Advertiser*, 9 July 1766.

wearing of and selling of calicoes. Anyone wearing calico was subject to a £5 fine. Upholders, mercers, and other sellers of calico were subject to a £20 fine, unless the calicoes were for exportation.[38] As previously noted, prior to the eighteenth century, the 1678 Act for Burying in Woollen assessed a £5 fine for using shrouds and associated funeral goods made of non-woollen or imported material.[39]

It is clear from over seventy-five of the entries in the account book that Robert Williams had a substantial niche upholding business with East India Company ship officers. Two of Robert's brothers, John and Stephen, were East India ship captains, which probably accounts for how he got into this business. East India ship captains ensured that their quarters were 'fitted out' for comfort at their own expense with furniture, rugs, curtains, looking glasses, lanterns, and other items for voyages to India and China. The lesser ship officers purchased more modestly.

The majority of the account book entries are not for a complete 'fitting out' of captains' cabins. For instance, on 13 April 1765, Williams billed Captain Pearce £30.14.6 for several chairs, over twenty-nine yards of Wilton carpet, a large screen covered with India paper, and lesser items. Noteworthy is the entry of £2 for a second-hand easy chair, indicating that Williams dealt in used furniture. Captain Pearce was likely the captain of the *Earl of Ashburnham* East Indiaman, which would begin its second voyage on 24 December 1765.[40]

Lesser ship officers, including chief, first, and second mates, were also clients of Williams's upholding business. On 11 December 1763, a chief mate by the name of Mr. Leton (or Seton) purchased two 48″ × 26″ looking glasses and three 36″ × 24″ looking glasses, all in rich carved and burnished gold frames, for £26 and £54, respectively. The total bill for the looking glasses and packing, paid for by a ninety-day draft, equalled £84.17.0, a large sum for a chief mate. He probably was purchasing the looking glasses as a wholesaler to foreign purchasers, because it is doubtful he would have needed them for his personal use aboard the ship. For Williams, this looking glass transaction shows the breadth of his product line, further supporting the argument that he was an upholder.

[38] *Weekly Journal or British Gazetteer*, 8 April 1721.

[39] "Charles II, 1677 & 1678: An Act for burying in Woollen," in *Statutes of the Realm: Volume 5, 1628–80*, ed. John Raithby (s.l: Great Britain Record Commission, 1819), 885–886.

[40] Hardy, *A Register of Ships*, 21.

Another entry shows Robert Williams selling a large amount of crown glass and plate glass to Captain Sandys. This was probably the Captain John Sandys who sailed the *Norfolk* Indiaman on 20 February 1764.[41] Several charges for packing the glass in strong cases are also noted. Though there are relatively small charges for painting ten Windsor chairs and for purchasing a pair of chair seats with elbows, the total cost of the glass and packaging was £327.14.6. This glass was not part of the ship's expenses because the ship's main owner, called the 'ship husband', would have paid this expense. It appears here that Captain Sandys purchased glass on his own account for resale in a foreign port. This sale demonstrates that Williams was able to obtain large amounts of glass, likely directly from a glass manufacturer.

Similarly, on 2 February 1768, Robert Williams sold Captain Jones looking glasses worth £271.13.5, many of them framed in carved and burnished gold frames. This cost included packing all the items in cases wrapped in blankets. As in the prior examples, these would have been for resale in a foreign port. Engagement in private trade explains the large sales of framed looking glasses Robert Williams made to ship captains. In 1766, a ledger entry details his brother's purchases of looking glasses and lanterns. The entry's heading is 'Captain John Williams Bill of Trade'. The transaction total was £1196.7.0, which included delivery to East India House. A similarly worded 'Bill of Trade' transaction for £336.9.6 was recorded in 1766 for Captain Smith. Later transactions do not state 'Bill of Trade', but resale goods to the export market are identifiable by Williams's charges for wrapping the items in blankets and packing them in crates. His business had expanded from providing upholding services for captains' quarters to also providing ship officers with goods for their private trade.

The account book of Robert Williams reveals a lot of information about his business practices. He kept detailed records about his clients and their purchases. Williams must have had a large number of suppliers because the goods he offered were so varied, among them furniture, carpets, fabrics, lanterns, and glass. Small charges to clients for hanging curtains, installing blinds, painting chairs, making repairs, and similar tasks indicate his willingness to take on more mundane work for his customers as well. Williams most likely had sub-contracting or wholesaling arrangements. Carving and gilding frames required special expertise, but unless he had a

[41] Hardy, *A Register of Ships*, 12.

substantial business in finished frames, he would have purchased finished frames on a wholesale basis, perhaps attaching the looking glasses to the frames in his shop.[42] Williams most likely purchased glass from a manufacturer or wholesaler.[43] He was also practical in his offerings, selling a used easy chair to Captain Pearce. On at least one occasion, he acted as a wholesaler by selling a bookcase and tabletop to Mr. Langlois. He at least once took payment on a barter basis. Finally, Williams knew how to be an appraiser and funeral undertaker. Whether or not Robert Williams made all the goods on his premises is not of great importance. What is important is that he operated his business as an all-inclusive provider of everything needed to furnish a residence and a captain's quarters. This all-inclusiveness of products and services clearly demonstrates he was an upholder.

The upholding business was profitable for Williams, enough that he was able to take advantage of business opportunities unrelated to upholding. The next section details the two opportunities presented to Robert Williams and his subsequent investment in them. He first invested in the lucrative banking business, followed shortly by ownership of East India Company ships.

[42] Kirkham, *London Furniture Trade*, 29.

[43] No documents have been found that indicate where Williams sourced framed looking glass. There were mirror glass manufacturers and wholesalers in London early in the eighteenth century, including Glass House at Vauxhall and Bear Garden Glass House on Bankside. John Gumley established a manufacturing facility in Lambeth in 1705. Other examples are John Minshall's Looking Glass Store of Hanover Square and Luke Young's Looking Glass Manufactory of Covent Garden. Later in the century, when Williams was selling framed looking glass to ship captains, there were several manufacturers and wholesalers. A search of the British and Irish Furniture Makers Online database using the keyword 'looking glass' for the period 1760 to 1800 yielded seventy-seven results. Among the descriptions were manufacturers, wholesalers, carvers, and gilders. See: Adam Bowett, *Early Georgian Furniture 1715–1740* (Woodbridge: Antique Collectors' Club, 2009), 266. Clive Edwards, *Turning Houses into Homes: A History of the Retailing and Consumption of Domestic Furnishings* (London: Routledge, 2017), 49. *The British and Irish Furniture Makers Online*, https://bifmo.furniturehistorysociety.org/find-people?keywords=looking+glass&captcha_sid=1104040&captcha_token=owweiNYRC5JddbH_mtgbjVbVPyuFhlAl7Tbk0-J9Y9k&captcha_response=3&name=&active_from=1760&active_to=1800&place=London&occupation=&source=All (accessed 15 July 2025).

Beyond Upholding: Banking and East Indiamen

An opportunity arose for Robert Williams to invest the profits from his upholding business in the financially lucrative banking business.[44] When his brother, John Williams, died in 1774, Robert took over his brother's banking partnership.[45] One needed more than money to enter the banking business; it required personal connections. Charles Raymond was the connection he needed. Raymond became a ship captain at age twenty-one and made four journeys. He married Sarah Webster in 1743 and bought the Ilford Valentines estate in 1756.[46] One of his Ilford neighbours, also a ship captain, was John Williams, the brother of Robert. John married Ann Guy, a stepsister of Raymond's wife.[47] The maritime and marital connections between Charles and John were strong enough that they entered the banking business together in 1771.

Charles Raymond, John Williams, and three others founded the bank Raymond, Williams, Vere, Lowe & Fletcher in 1771. The founding partners each invested £5000 in capital to establish the bank.[48] On 31 December 1774, the year in which John Williams died, the bank's asset balance sheet was £380,678, of which £338,156 was in deposits.[49] This is a remarkable growth of assets in less than four years, though from an accounting standpoint, assets are always matched with liabilities plus owner's capital and retained earnings. In this case, most of the liabilities were client deposits, which would have been loaned out. John Williams's £5000 initial partnership contribution was certainly worth more at the time of his death. John's will provided no directive about the disposition of his bank investment. The partnership agreement would have spelled out what happened in the event of a partner's death, but this has not been found. Therefore, it is not possible to know the terms under which Robert entered the banking partnership, but it is conceivable that he was named John's heir and successor in the partnership agreement.[50] Raymond, Vere,

[44] Holden, *Williams Deacon's*, 10.

[45] Holden, *Williams Deacon's*, 4–5.

[46] Holden, *Williams Deacon's*, 1–2.

[47] Georgina Green "Valentines, the Raymonds and Company Material Culture," in *East India Company at Home, 1757–1857*, ed. Margot Finn and Kate Smith (London: UCL Press, 2018), 237.

[48] Holden, *Williams Deacon's*, 32.

[49] Holden, *Williams Deacon's*, 37.

[50] Holden, *Williams Deacon's*, 5, 9–10.

Lowe, and Fletcher were profitable businessmen, and they may have demanded a premium beyond John's original £5000 investment. If he did not inherit the banking position, then Robert's upholding business must have been profitable enough that he had the significant savings needed to pay the initial £5000, plus any premium for John's banking partnership. From 1774 to 1789, the bank went through five name and partnership changes, including Raymond's resignation in 1777. Robert Williams became the managing partner in 1790, and the bank became known as Williams, Son, Wilkinson & Drury, the Son being Robert Williams, Jr. The bank was located at 20 Birchin Lane in the City, and each partner now had a £10,000 initial capital position.[51]

Three years after entering the banking business, another opportunity arose for Williams. He had, apparently, developed an overall understanding of the East India Company from his niche business in selling household goods to East India ship officers. He purchased controlling interest in two East India ships, the *Lord Holland* and the *Nassau*, in 1777, the latter bought from Charles Raymond. From 1777 to 1810, Robert Williams was the managing owner of fourteen ships that made a total of forty-nine voyages.[52] Four ships husbanded by Williams were lost in mid-voyage. Presumably, insurance would have helped mitigate the financial loss, though when the *Hindostan* was lost during a severe storm in 1803, there were several deaths.[53]

The East India Company (EIC) chartered ships rather than building, fitting out, and manning them themselves, creating business opportunities for a select few.[54] Similar to the banking business, it took more than money to invest in East India Company ships; one also needed a personal introduction to the shipping community. Williams's brother and Charles Raymond undoubtedly played key roles in his introduction to the shipping community and the establishment of his niche upholding business with EIC ship officers.

[51] Holden, *Williams Deacon's*, 38.

[52] Hardy, *A Register of Ships*, 77, 89, 94, 119, 106, 110, 112, 121, 134, 138, 143, 154, 159, 165, 178, 181, 184, 203, 207, 209, 246, 262, 292, 310. The *Princess Amelia* burned on her 4th voyage. A new *Princess Amelia* was built and made her maiden voyage in 1809. Therefore, Williams husbanded fourteen ships under thirteen different names.

[53] Hardy, *A Register of Ships*, 223.

[54] Holden, *Williams Deacon's*, 8.

Among the syndicate of investors owning a ship was the managing owner, often called the 'ship husband'.[55] Ship husbandry of East India ships carried several responsibilities. The most important responsibility was the maintenance of a capable crew for a round-trip voyage lasting more than a year. Other responsibilities included paying wages, providing supplies, and protecting the crew as much as possible from pirates and Crown warship commanders looking to impress EIC crewmembers into the Royal Navy during a voyage.[56] Finally, engaging the services of an able captain was crucial in maintaining the seaworthiness of the ship, navigating the trade route, and protecting the cargo and crew.

Williams's ship expense account books detail the costs of 'fitting out' a ship. These included everything needed for a long voyage, including food, beer, sails, nails, and so on, paid by the owners. The cost of preparing a ship for her first voyage was especially high. Preparing the *Sulivan* for her first voyage on 16 March 1783 cost the owners £27,892.16.8.[57] When the *Hindostan* made her maiden voyage on 17 January 1790, fitting her out cost the partnership £31,894.15.9.[58] (By tradition, ships were female gendered as 'her' and 'she'.) The responsibility for recording the expenses for the *Sulivan's* first voyage (to Bombay) fell upon Captain Stephen Williams, Robert's brother.[59] Robert presented two bills for providing glass to the *Sulivan*. For the first voyage, he billed £13.5.8 for store glass.[60] On 3 October 1788, he billed to the *Sulivan*'s third voyage £14.16.0 for glass.[61] These entries are evidence that Robert Williams still practised the upholding trade (most likely at 28, King Street, Covent Garden) or at least knew from prior experience how to obtain glass.

East India Company required ships to be surveyed for seaworthiness, and in 1773, restricted the total number of voyages to four. This restriction was relaxed after 1780 when it became common to install copper sheathing over the hulls to protect against damage from woodworm and

[55] East India ship ownership was divided into one-sixteenth shares, and the 'ship husband' presumably owned at least two-sixteenth shares, while fourteen other investors owned one-sixteenth share each. In practice, 'ship husbands' often owned more than two-sixteenth shares and the total number of minority investors was fewer than fourteen.

[56] Holden, *Williams Deacon's*, 14.

[57] The British Library, London. Mss Eur D1051. Account Book for the *Sulivan*.

[58] The British Library, London. Mss Eur D1051/7. Account Book for the *Hindostan*.

[59] Hardy, *A Register of Ships*, 100.

[60] The British Library, London. Mss Eur D1051, 120. Account Book for the *Sulivan*.

[61] The British Library, London. Mss Eur D1051/3, 49. Account Book for the *Sulivan*.

barnacles. The new EIC rules permitted an additional six voyages if the ship continued to pass an annual survey after the third voyage.[62] Thus, the ship surveyor was important to ship owners. When Thomas Massett, a ship surveyor from Deptford, was murdered, Williams offered a £50 reward for information leading to the perpetrator's capture in an announcement he placed in the 3 November 1786 *Public Advertiser*. This announcement further stated that Thomas Massett's job was that of Overseer for Managing Owners of East India Ships.[63]

The owners of East Indiamen profited by transporting trade goods to and from foreign ports, mostly in India and China. Woollens represented over one half of the freight EIC ships carried from England, followed by raw metals and general merchandise.[64] Silk from India and tea and porcelain from Asia were typical goods imported into England on return voyages. EIC paid between £22 and £47 a ton for freight from 1773 to 1795.[65] East Indiamen were often used to transport military personnel and materials. The East India Company reimbursed ship owners at distinctly different rates for transporting civilian freight and military supplies. In 1803, at the beginning of the Napoleonic War, Williams's ship *Airly Castle* was contracted for two years to carry civilian freight at £21 per ton and war supplies at £17 per ton.[66] *Airly Castle* was an 813-ton ship, and a cargo of fifty per cent civilian freight and fifty per cent military supplies could have yielded single voyage revenue of £15,447 (average rate of £19 per ton × 813).[67]

[62] Holden, *Williams Deacon's*, 15–16; J. R. Harris, "Copper and Shipping in the Eighteenth Century," *The Economic History Review* New Series, Vol.19, No. 3 (1996): 563–68.

[63] *Public Advertiser*, 3 November 1786.

[64] H.V. Bowen, "Sinews of Trade and Empire: The Supply of Commodity Exports to the East India Company during the late Eighteenth Century," *The Economic History Review* Vol. 55, No. 3 (Aug. 2002): 471.

[65] Holden, *Williams Deacon's*, 8.

[66] Hardy, *A Register of Ships*, APPENDIX, 28.

[67] During the Napoleonic War, a serious concern was the impressing of East Indiamen sailors and officers by His Majesty's ships. On 19 March 1810, the Directors of the East India Company filed a complaint with the Admiralty that the illegal impressing of their best sailors and petty officers was harming the Company. Furthermore, the Company requested that the Admiralty inform the commanders and officers of His Majesty's ships that they must certify that they conformed to the laws regulating the impressing of any East India Company ship crew. See: Hardy, *A Register of Ships*, APPENDIX, 50–52.

Another source of income to the managing owner came from what was known as 'selling the ship'. It was customary that when a new ship was built, her command was sold to a suitable captain for up to £10,000. Though the practice of 'selling the ship' was prohibited by the East India Company in 1796, ship owners still had the right to name the captain, meaning some sort of financial consideration was still paid.[68]

There were two advantages to having a captaincy. First, the position was transferrable to the captain's heirs. Second, the East India Company permitted ship captains and lesser officers to engage in private trade. It was not unusual for a captain to make up to £10,000 in private trading. In special circumstances, a captain could make as much as £20,000 in private trading.[69] The EIC had established regulations for private trading by captains and junior officers, and violations could be financially costly.[70] Being a ship captain could be financially rewarding, but appointing a captain did not always go smoothly.

The importance of a captaincy was illustrated in 1791 when Capt. John Walsby wrote a long narrative addressed to all involved with the East India Company. He asserted that Robert Williams had broken his promise to appoint him (Walsby) as captain for one of his ships. Walsby had served as a chief mate on an East India ship and believed he was qualified to be an EIC captain. He promoted his qualifications within the EIC community and finally met with Robert Williams. According to Walsby, Robert promised him the captaincy of the *Princess Amelia*, provided that the current captain, his brother, Captain Stephen Williams, resigned his captaincy of the *Amelia*. Should that not happen, Walsby claimed Robert promised him a captaincy on one of his other ships if an opening occurred or if he could convince a current captain to retire. Among the allegations made by Walsby was that Williams originally agreed to sell him a ship captaincy for £5000, but as the negotiations dragged on, the price was raised to an astonishing £20,000. It appears that this price increase was a signal that Robert wanted nothing more to do with Walsby. Furthermore, when Stephen Williams resigned his captaincy, Robert hired his nephew as captain. Walsby continued to press Williams to honour their alleged verbal

[68] Holden, *Williams Deacon's*, 10.

[69] Holden, *Williams Deacon's*, 10.

[70] Elaborating on the regulation of private trade is beyond the scope of this work. Extracts of the rules and regulations can be found in: Hardy, *A Register of Ships*, APPENDIX, 54–62, 66–75, 114–115.

agreement. He met with and wrote to influential EIC members about the dishonour and dishonesty Robert exhibited. Williams remained steadfast in denying he promised Walsby a captaincy. The situation apparently came to a head when Walsby filed a lawsuit against Williams for reputational and financial harm. Just how the dispute was resolved is unknown, but Walsby (as author of the narrative) designated himself as 'Capt. (Captain) John Walsby', meaning sometime between suing Williams in late 1789 and publishing this narrative in 1791, Walsby became a captain, perhaps a self-appointed one. One must remember that there are many sides to a complicated situation like this. Walsby's long narrative certainly does not cast Williams in a positive light. At the same time, it appears that Walsby's bitterness prevented him from 'moving on' to look for other opportunities.[71]

If Robert Williams escaped a financial judgement against him in the John Walsby lawsuit, he was not so fortunate in a claim brought against him by Captain William Farington. The painter and diarist Joseph Farington, brother of Captain Farington, wrote in his diary in 1813 that his brother brought legal action against Robert Williams. The lawsuit concerned the *General Coote*, which was husbanded by Williams and made her first voyage in September 1782. The original captain, Daniel Griffith Hoare, died during the voyage, and William Farington, as chief mate, assumed the captaincy of the *General Coote* for the remainder of the voyage. Evidently, Robert did not like the amount of private trade acting Captain Farington claimed was his. Captain Farington sued. The lawsuit was protracted, lasting twenty-three years. According to the diarist, '... Williams was cast on every point with costs and everlasting disgrace in the minds of those who were acquainted with His proceedings'.[72] It is not surprising *General Coote* sailed her second voyage in the 1784–1785 sailing season under Captain James Baldwin, not Captain William Farington.[73]

It appears that Robert Williams employed legal strategies to 'out last' plaintiffs. In the Walsby case, for instance, Robert delayed the trial by

[71] Capt. John Walsby, *The ship's husband; a narrative; being a state of facts; addressed to the honorable Court of Directors of the East India Company; the ships' husbands, and commanders and others in that service.* (London: Sold by T. Richardson, T. and J. Egerton, J. Ridgway, and H.D. Symonds, 1791).

[72] Joseph Farington, *The Farington Diary*. Vol. VII, ed. James Greig, 1927. (London: Hutchinson & Co., 1813), 195–96.

[73] Hardy, *A Register of Ships*, No page number. See: Sailing Season 1781–1782 and Sailing Season 1784–1785.

calling as a witness a captain who he knew was at sea. That the Farington case lasted twenty-three years indicates that his defence lawyers used extensive delaying tactics. Whether or not delaying tactics were commonly used by the commercial aristocracy is not known, but Robert Williams apparently used these tactics with the hope that legal disputes would fizzle out. This was an intransigent way of conducting business. These disputes aside, Robert's wealth accumulated.

Williams's business trajectory was remarkable. It was finding and developing a niche business that differentiated Williams from other upholders. It stands that he had moved from the role of a general upholder providing residential household goods and services to being a niche provider to East India Company ship captains and officers. There were undoubtedly other general upholders who could have provided ship officers with household goods for their private trade, but this niche business was difficult to break into. Williams's gentry background and family connections gave him the social and business introductions he needed. Using the accumulated savings from his upholding business, he was able to invest in opportunities unrelated to upholding, namely banking and EIC ship ownership.

At this stage in his life, he must have been concentrating more and more time on the banking and East India businesses rather than his upholding business. However, Williams was still listed in *Kent's Directory* as an upholder in King Street, Covent Garden, which gives evidence of him retaining some involvement in the upholding trade. The fact that Robert Williams became managing owner of East India ships not long after entering the banking business demonstrated a high level of ambition and financial and social mobility. He was in the opportunities phase of his business trajectory, where the profits from his upholding business allowed him to invest his extra money in ventures unrelated to the upholding trade. These ventures were financially successful, and Williams entered a new phase: wealth accumulation.

The Later Years

At the turn of the century, Robert turned his attention to his estates outside of London, Bridehead in Dorset (Illustration 4.3) and Moor Park in Hertfordshire. He remained involved with his bank and became an East India Company director. That Robert Williams fully retired from the upholding business and resided at his country estates was not unheard of. Kirkham gives examples of wealthy tradesmen who retired from their trade

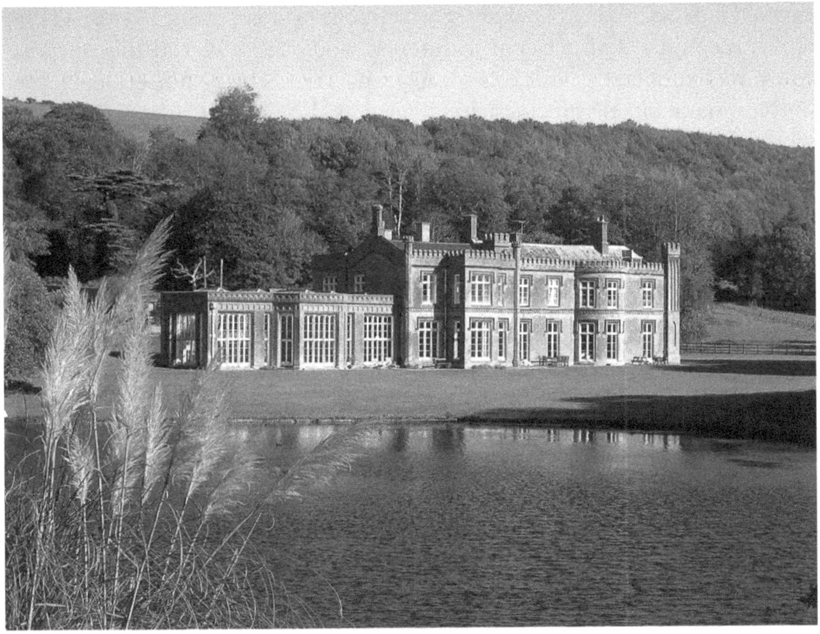

Illustration 4.3 Bridehead. (Country Home of Robert Williams. 2009. ©Williams Family Collection, Bridehead, Dorset, by permission of Sir Philip Williams)

to live as country gentlemen, among them William Hallett and William Bradshaw.[74] John Trotter, the upholder studied in the following chapter, also accumulated enough wealth to buy a country estate. It would be wrong to conclude that all wealthy upholders aspired to be country gentlemen, but it was apparently a goal for some of them.

Williams and those mentioned above were entrepreneurs who accumulated wealth in an evolving business environment. Rather than depending on commercial profits later in life, these retired businessmen lived off their investments in government bonds, companies like the East India Company, and property rents from their estates. Gordon Mingay argued that entering even the middling gentry rank required an investment of £30,000 to

[74] Kirkham, *London Furniture Trade*, 90–2.

earn £1000 per year.[75] Owning government bonds paying between three and three and a half per cent in interest would have served this purpose. Martin Wiener states that this money was 'rentier' and not connected to entrepreneurship or productivity. This was the way the aristocracy lived. The British idealized the country and, according to Wiener, wealthy merchants aspired to own country estates in emulation of the aristocracy. Though not immediately accepted as members of the local gentry, acceptance would happen over time.[76] Wiener's study concerns the period 1850–1980 and speaks to a decline in the British industrial spirit. This decline was characterized by high taxes and low entrepreneurial investment. The genesis of this decline began late in the eighteenth century when men like Robert Williams moved to country estates.

After serving as High Sheriff of Dorset from 1804 to 1805, Robert was elected to Parliament from the Borough within Dorset in 1807. He was generally in favour of the Tory administration but made no known speeches. He retired from Parliament in 1812 in favour of his son, Robert, Jr. Before their elections to Parliament, he and his son, in 1795, declared their loyalty to William Pitt the Younger by signing the London Declaration. Williams donated £20,000 to the Pitt cause, and his bank pledged £80,000 in 1797.[77]

While generous with his time and money to business and politics, Williams was also generous to his family. This is apparent in the marriage settlements he provided for his daughters. For instance, the settlement for his daughter, Anne, to Rev. Edward Aubery, dated 14 December 1810, included the release of uses of freehold farmlands and woods in the Parish of Hambledon in the County of Berks, £3333.6.8 in South Sea Annuities,

[75] Gordon Mingay, *English Landed Society in the Eighteenth Century* (London: Routledge and Kegan, 1963), 93.

[76] Martin Wiener, *English Culture and the Decline of the Industrial Spirit, 1850 – 1980* (Cambridge: Cambridge University Press, 2004), 8, 47.

[77] Farrell, *The History of Parliament: the House of Commons 1820–1832*, Ref. Vol. 1820–1832. The Pitt administration faced growing financial demands for conducting the war with France. The national debt was at nearly £400 million, and bankers advised him (Pitt) that selling additional government bonds would be unsuccessful. Pitt and his supporters developed a scheme to privately borrow £18 million on behalf of the government. Because these loans were risky, Pitt presented the borrowing as an opportunity to express one's patriotism, hence they were known by the term 'loyalty loan'. See: Earl Stanhope, *Life of The Right Honourable William Pitt* (London: John Murray, 1879) New Edition, Vol. II, 162–63.

£17,021 in the three per cent Consolidated Bank Annuities (British government bonds known as Consols), and £1000 of East India stock.[78]

Rather than succeeding his father in the upholding trade, Robert, Jr. followed his father into the banking and East India Company businesses and, eventually, Parliament. He married Frances 'Fanny' Turner of Putney in 1794, who was a friend of Princess Amelia.[79] Just how this friendship started is unknown, but a bundle of letters from Amelia to Fanny survives.[80] Princess Amelia sometimes sent money to Fanny to pay for lottery tickets. Evidently, playing the lottery was a secret indulgence of Princess Amelia, and Fanny was an abetting party in this. In another letter, Princess Amelia wrote about how the King enjoyed pears from Fanny's father-in-law's (Robert, Sr.) Moor Park estate. In addition to the letters from Princess Amelia, often signed 'A', Fanny received letters from Princess Elizabeth and Princess Mary. In a letter to Fanny, Princess Mary wrote that her mother, the Queen, wanted an India shawl for her brother and hoped that Robert, Jr. could arrange it.[81]

Fanny Williams's friendship with King George's daughters is interesting because it brings up the fact that, somehow, the Williams family was known at the Royal Court. Princess Mary obviously knew that Fanny's husband's family owned ships that travelled to India, which explains why Mary asked Fanny about obtaining an India shawl. The Royal family also knew that the Williams family owned two ships named *Princess Amelia*.[82] Robert, Sr. would have been known because his business successes made him very wealthy, much the case for his successor, Robert, Jr., as well. Also, Robert, Jr. had been an Alderman and Sheriff of London. Being commercially successful, however, was not the same as being a member of the aristocracy. Nonetheless, Robert Williams, Sr. did ascend from an

[78] Hertfordshire Archives and Local Studies, Hertford. GH 851. Marriage Settlement between Robert Williams and Rev. Edward Aubery.

[79] Farrell, *The History of Parliament: the House of Commons 1820–1832*, Ref. Vol. 1820–1832.

[80] Dorset History Centre, Dorset. Williams of Bridehead, Littlebredy, Archive fonds. D-WIB 1737–1924 Fanny Williams sub-series. D-WIB/C/1-6 1802-1817.

[81] Dorset History Centre, Dorset. Williams of Bridehead, Littlebredy, Archive fonds | D-WIB 1737-1924 Fanny Williams sub-series. D-WIB/C/1-6 1802-1817.

[82] Holden, *Williams Deacon's*, 16.

upholder's apprentice to a member of the gentry, and a very wealthy one at that.[83]

Robert Williams died on 17 January 1814 at Moor Park in Hertfordshire at the age of seventy-nine. He was buried in Rickmansworth Church in Hertfordshire rather than at his ancestral estate in Dorset.[84] *The Gentleman's Magazine* for 1814 stated that he 'possessed freehold and personal property to the amount of considerably above half a million sterling'.[85] This amount is generally verified in a document held at Hertfordshire Archives and Local Studies.

The Stamp Office Legacy Duty on Residues of Personal Estates for Williams was filed on 13 August 1824, ten years after his death. There is a calculation detailing the exclusion from the residue of £300,000 of Robert's assets on which tax was already paid. The final residue reported to the Stamp Office was £318,382.19.9, of which one per cent (£3183.0.7) was paid as duty. These two amounts together put Robert's wealth at over £600,000. At the time of his death, the amount of 'cash at bankers' was £156,857.10.6, an amount indicative of great liquidity. Finally, his funeral expenses were recorded as £466.10.8.[86]

Robert Williams's will was written by his attorney and friend, Thomas Lane of Goldsmiths' Hall, and is replete with recitations of how a male heir would be established, including even his daughters' sons who were yet to be born. Robert Williams, Jr. inherited the bulk of his father's estate. Robert's wife, Jane, inherited a £100,000 annuity, £10,000 in his bank stock, £10,000 in East India stock, and all the silver, jewels, books, and household goods. She was also given living rights at either Moor Park or Bridehead, whichever she chose. His son, William, was bequeathed £70,000, and his three daughters received £10,000 each.[87] Jane Williams chose to live at Moor Park with Robert, Jr. and his family. When an 1825 economic crisis put pressure on his banking assets, Robert, Jr. sold Moor Park in 1828 to the Grosvenor family. The Williams family moved to their

[83] For a review of the attitudes of the aristocracy toward wealthy cabinet-makers and tradesmen, See: Kirkham, *London Furniture Trade*, 90–93.

[84] Bayne, *Moor Park*, 105.

[85] *The Gentleman's Magazine: AND Historical Chronicle.* From January to June, 1814. VOLUME LXXXIV.

[86] Hertfordshire Archives and Local Studies, Hertford. GH 1729. Stamp Office Legacy Duty on Residues of Personal Estates for Robert Williams.

[87] The National Archives, Kew. PROB 11/1552/502. Will of Robert Williams, Banker of Moor Park, Hertfordshire. 25 February 1814.

Dorset estate, where Jane died in 1841 at the age of nearly 102.[88] Robert staged his portrait as a successful businessman, but Jane staged hers, not as a wealthy woman dressed in expensive clothing, but as a contented older woman quietly needlepointing. Jane Chassereau Williams is Britain's first documented centenarian with matching baptism and death records.[89]

Even though there is little published material specific to the life of Robert Williams, there is enough information to allow for the building of a profile about where the upholding trade took him. This allows for making conclusions about the reasons for his financial success. It is also possible to contrast his business experiences against those of Thomas Chippendale.

Williams started out as an apprentice at about the same time that Thomas Chippendale began his famous business. However, unlike Chippendale, Williams became financially successful by building upon his apprenticeship and becoming a general upholder with a niche business in 'fitting out' East India Company ships. Much of this success can be attributed to his brothers' maritime connections. Williams was astute enough to understand that the living space of a ship captain was no different than the living space of a residential home, only smaller. Ship captains needed furniture, curtains, rugs, and so on, just as homes of substance did. What Robert Williams did was to apply residential upholding needs to the commercial maritime industry and build a niche business within the upholding trade.

Whereas Chippendale was burdened by partnership debt for much of his career after his partner died, Robert Williams was not involved in such a partnership.[90] Chippendale, most often referred to as a cabinet-maker, was an upholder whose business model mostly served the wealthy residential marketplace.[91] In contrast, Williams's business model did not rely on aristocratic and gentry wealth. He had a diverse clientele, which spread credit default risk among several customers. The account ledger shows he was meticulous in tracking the amounts outstanding. Extending large amounts of credit to ship officers to purchase goods for their private trade

[88] Bayne, *Moor Park*, 106.

[89] John Withington, *Secrets of Centenarian: What it is Like to Live a Century and Which of Us Will Survive to Find Out?* (London: Reaktion Books, 2017), 25–26.

[90] Christopher Gilbert, *The Life & Work of Thomas Chippendale* (New York: Tabard Press, 1978), 11–15, 30–33.

[91] Valerie Hope, Clive Birch, Gilbert Torry, *The Freedom: The Past and Present of the Livery, Guilds and City of London* (Buckingham: Barracuda Books, Ltd., 1982), 198.

was potentially risky. However, the account ledger indicates he experienced no problems with being paid.

It would be unfair to say that Thomas Chippendale did not have aspirations to become wealthy. His vision was to achieve this goal by growing his furniture business through appealing to a variety of consumer tastes. His *Director* presented furniture in the rococo, Chinese, and gothic styles, giving the customer style options. However, Chippendale's skill, experience, knowledge, and judgement were in a craft, not in managing a business. Williams's apprenticeship likely included learning the business management part of the trade. He understood that to be successful, learning a craft skill was not enough. The ability to honestly assess competition, supply and demand, how quickly product imitators could enter the business, accounting, and the dangers of extending credit and taking on debt was critical for success.

Williams saved, and maybe borrowed from his family, enough money to buy his master's upholding business, including the customer base. Chippendale acquired capital through a partnership arrangement. His firm was mostly a start-up business without the advantage of an existing customer base. Because he lacked business management skill and personal financial resources, it is not surprising to find that Thomas Chippendale had financial problems throughout most of his productive life. He would not retire to a grand country estate like Williams. And, it would be his successor and son, Thomas, Jr., who would eventually suffer the indignation of bankruptcy.

It is not exactly clear how Williams funded his £5000 stake in the bank, but savings from his upholding business appear the most plausible source. It was through the relationships that his two brothers, John and Stephen, had established in the East India Company ship business that Robert met Charles Raymond. Raymond knew Robert as a competent business owner and invited him to take over his deceased brother's partnership interest in the bank. The bank partnership was lucrative for him, and, in a case of money begetting more money, Robert Williams became a ship husband to two ships in 1777.

Ship ownership was a profitable business for Robert. Knowing the financial risks of losing a ship and its cargo, he would have insured his investment against these risks, and he continued to invest in more ships. His upholding account book goes through only 1772, but even without account books for subsequent years, there is no reason to believe that he ended his upholding business for East India ship officers, perhaps even to the officers of ships he owned, until at least 1790. At the same time, his brother, Thomas, was an important part of Robert's upholding business.

In his sixties at the turn of the century, Robert spent most of his time at Moor Park, though he obviously had strong feelings for Bridehead, his Dorset ancestral home. His wealth placed him within the upper commercial class, but there is no evidence to suggest that Robert and Jane Williams participated in lavish entertaining and parties, even though their daughter-in-law, Fanny, had friendships with three of the King's daughters. The marriage settlements for his daughters and his will provide evidence of his generosity to his wife and children, although Robert, Jr. was named the primogeniture heir to the bulk of his wealth. The detail in his upholding account book, his accounting reconciliations of Honour's business, and his ship expense books show that Robert was a methodical and meticulous man. The number of contingencies built into his will attest to his attention to detail, and these also show that he was a planner for the future and a man not wanting to leave anything to chance.

The evidence presented here seemingly points to Robert Williams being a self-made man. However, being born into a minor gentry family did give him advantages. His parents provided him with at least a basic education, and he was placed in an upholding apprenticeship that prepared him for business success. He worked hard at learning the upholding trade and its attendant business lines, including funeral undertaking. However, it was the familial and social connections that made it possible for Williams to accumulate great wealth.

This case study is not intended to be a biography of Robert Williams. Rather, it is intended to tell the story of how a young apprentice upholder became wealthy through hard work, intelligent decision making, and capitalizing on opportunity. Most of all, Williams was a visionary, a man who could see beyond the traditional role of residential upholding to find profitability in new business opportunities. This was the trajectory that led to Williams becoming a wealthy man.

CHAPTER 5

Case Study of John Trotter

This chapter discusses another financially successful London upholder, John Trotter. The previous chapter detailed how Robert Williams began his working career as an apprentice upholder and then established a niche upholding business in 'fitting out' the quarters of East India Company ship officers and providing them with goods for private trade. John Trotter also began his career as an apprentice and built a niche upholding business by providing upholstery goods and services to the royal household. He later found opportunity in supplying camp equipment to the British army, which brought him wealth. This chapter will end with an examination of the business similarities and differences between these two upholders.

Business Beginnings

John Trotter was born in Scotland in 1713 to Alexander and Jean Trotter. He grew up in the family home in Cattleshield in the Shire of Barwick.[1] No information about John has been found before his apprenticeship began in 1726. Trotter, like Robert Williams, came from a landed gentry background; the Trotter family history notes that John's grandfather

[1] The location of the family home is taken from John Trotter's Apprenticeship Indenture dated 21 March 1726. There are spelling variations of Cattleshield but the spelling used here is from this indenture. London Metropolitan Archives, City of London. Reference Number: COL/CHD/FR/02/0689-0-696. Apprenticeship Indenture of John Trotter.

S. Sanders, *The Eighteenth-Century London Upholder*,
https://doi.org/10.1007/978-3-032-08660-0_5

purchased the estate of Cattleshield (spelled Kettisheill in the family history) in 1671.[2] John Trotter's apprentice indenture lists his father as a 'Gent', or gentleman, which also indicates that he was from a gentry background. He began his upholding career as an apprentice joiner on 21 March 1726, with his master being Henry Williams of London. His apprenticeship premium cost £30.10 and was for a seven-year term.[3] Trotter's master, Henry Williams, was the royal joiner and must have been considered honest and of good reputation and wanted the same of his apprentices. Kirkham estimates that in the period from 1712 to 1741, eight per cent of apprentice furniture-makers were the sons of gentlemen, while twenty-two per cent of apprentice upholsterers were the sons of gentlemen.[4] John Trotter was admitted free of The Worshipful Company of Joiners of the City of London on 4 February 1745. He joined the Joiners' Company livery on 29 October 1751, presumably after working several years as a journeyman.[5]

According to *Kent's Directory*, John Trotter established his business at Frith Street in Soho in 1751, where his occupation was listed as an upholder, even though he was a freeman in the Joiners' Company, not the Upholders' Company.[6] Kirkham wrote that in the eighteenth century, a tradesman was not obligated to join a company that matched their trade, but one that suited their needs. It was not unusual for cabinet-makers to be members of companies such as the Goldsmiths and Drapers through the patronage system of their father's company. The Joiners' Company lost a legal challenge in 1725 against a Merchant Taylors' Company member, who was practicing as a joiner. Later legal challenges were unable to stop individuals from practicing a trade by being freemen in another company.[7] In addition, Trotter subscribed to Thomas Chippendale's 1754 *Director* and was listed as a cabinet-maker, which is another illustration of

[2] Trotter family history, Alexander Trotter of Kettilsheill, Berwickshire. http://powys.org/pl_tree/ps05/ps05_361.html (accessed 19 November 2020). Timothy Powys-Lybbe is the heir general of John Trotter. He is the John Trotter family historian and maintains the website.

[3] Apprenticeship Indenture of John Trotter.

[4] Pat Kirkham, *The London Furniture Trade 1700–1870* (Leeds: Furniture History Society, 1988), 172.

[5] Henry Phillips, *Annals of the Worshipful Company of Joiners of the City of London* (London: Privately Printed, 1915), 127. *British History Online*, John Trotter, https://www.british-history.ac.uk/no-series/dict-english-furniture-makers/t (accessed 26 June 2025).

[6] Henry Kent. *Kent's Directory* (London: Richard and Henry Causton, 1774, 42nd ed.

[7] Kirkham, *London Furniture Trade*, 137, 142.

the interchangeability of occupational terms.[8] Although there is no explicit evidence of Trotter's transition from joiner to upholsterer, he was clearly beginning to run part of his business as an upholsterer. His knowledge of the furniture and upholstery crafts placed him in the upholding trade, regardless of which livery company he belonged to.

Trotter received a royal warrant in 1756, naming him the royal upholsterer, not joiner, cabinet-maker, or upholder.[9] His former master, Henry Williams, also a royal warrant holder, was denoted as a joiner in His Majesty's Great Wardrobe account books. (The Great Wardrobe was the part of the Royal household that was responsible for furniture and textiles.[10]) The trade transactions associated with Henry Williams in the Great Wardrobe were furniture-related, thus fitting into his background as a joiner. Trotter's transactions associated with the Great Wardrobe, however, were all of upholstery, not furniture. It is apparent that after accepting his livery membership in 1751, Trotter's business aspirations went beyond those of a joiner and cabinet-maker.

John Trotter married in 1752, but there is some confusion about his wife's maiden name. Burke's *A Genealogical and Heraldic History of the Landed Gentry of Great Britain & Ireland, Volume 2* states that John Trotter married Ann Locke.[11] However, the 23–25 June 1752 *London Evening Post* reported the following:

> … married at Morden College, Black-Heath, Mr. John Trotter, an eminent Cabinet-Maker and Upholder, in Frith-Street, St. Ann's, Soho, to Miss Betts, an agreeable young Lady with a Fortune of £5,000.[12]

Interestingly, a Samuel Betts was bound to Trotter as an apprentice in 1754, adding credence to the likelihood that Trotter married Anne Betts, not Anne Locke.[13] However, both surnames are correct because Ann

[8] Thomas Chippendale, *The gentleman and cabinet-maker's director…* (London: Thomas Chippendale, 1754), ix.

[9] The National Archives, Kew. Lord Chamberlain's Appointment Books–Series II, 1755–1760, Reference: LC3/66. Royal appointment of John Trotter, 7 January 1756.

[10] Geoffrey Beard, *Uphosterers and Interior Furnishing England 1530–1840* (New Haven: Yale University Press, 1997), 322.

[11] Bernard Burke, *A Genealogical and Heraldic History of the Landed Gentry of Great Britain & Ireland* (London: Harrison, 1871), Vol. II, 1413.

[12] *London Evening Post*, 23–25 June 1752.

[13] The National Archives, Kew. Series IR 1. Register of Duties Paid for Apprentices' Indentures, 1710–1811. Board of Stamps: Apprenticeship Books.

Locke and Ann Betts are the same person. She was apparently the illegitimate daughter of Mrs. Betts and James Locke. Locke was a member of the Turkey Company and a trustee of Morden College.[14] Apparently, Locke felt obligated enough to arrange for his illegitimate daughter's marriage ceremony at Morden College and provide a £5000 marriage settlement. Anne Trotter died in October 1759 and was buried in St. Ann's Church, Soho.[15] The Trotters had three children who lived into adulthood: James, John, and Ann.[16]

An important fact is that Trotter's wife brought £5000 to the marriage, a significant amount of money, but it is not known if this money was used in his business. In that regard, the National Library of Scotland holds letters confirming that his mother loaned him money to begin his upholding business, which he repaid.[17] Also of importance is that Trotter was recognized as an 'eminent cabinet-maker and upholder' in the newspaper announcement. The use of the word 'eminent' in describing Trotter implied that he was of good financial and social repute for a tradesman. R. Campbell wrote this about upholders in the 1747 *London Tradesman* stating that, 'This Tradesman's Genius must be universal in every branch of furniture…' He added further, 'The Upholder… must be no Fool; and have a considerable Stock to set up with…'[18] In other words, to become an eminent cabinet-maker and upholder, Trotter had to have had strong skills in all aspects of furnishing a residential interior and the capital necessary to set up business. There is uncertainty as to exactly when Trotter set up his own business, but his seven-year apprenticeship ended sometime around 1733. As noted above, *Kent's Directory* states he owned his own business by at least 1751. He may have worked as a journeyman for some time before starting his own business, and it is likely that he had begun it before he became a liveryman in the Joiners' Company in 1751.

[14] Timothy Powys-Lybbe (heir general of John Trotter) et al., e-mail messages to author, 14 August to 17 August 2015. And: Trustees from the Turkey Company. http://www.british-history.ac.uk/survey-london/bk10/pp36-51 (accessed 23 November 2015). Morden College was founded in 1695 by Sir John Morden as a home for traders having fallen on hard times. https://mordencollege.org.uk/history/ (accessed 8 February 2021).

[15] Burke, *A Genealogical and Heraldic History of the Landed Gentry*, 1413.

[16] The National Archives, Kew. PROB 11/1194. Will of John Trotter, Soho Square, Middlesex, 24 July 1790.

[17] *British History Online*, John Trotter, https://www.british-history.ac.uk/no-series/dict-english-furniture-makers/t (accessed 26 June 2025).

[18] R. Campbell, *The London Tradesman* (London: T. Gardner, 1747), 170.

Nonetheless, Trotter evidently had a thriving business when he married Miss Betts in 1752, and the £5000 marriage settlement could have provided him with extra capital if he wanted to expand his business.

Upholders were often associated with and involved in the appraisal and auction businesses. There is little evidence to suggest that Trotter was involved in the appraising side of the upholding business. Robert Williams's account ledger from the previous chapter listed a 1763 appraisal done for John Remant, Esq., where Williams added, 'For self appraising your goods and fixing the value with Mr. Trotter'.[19] There is not enough information from the ledger transaction to determine the relationship between Trotter and Williams other than for some unknown reason they collaborated on Mr. Remant's appraisal. This is the only mention of Trotter being associated with appraising.

Trotter, however, did have involvement in auctioneering. A short time before his royal upholsterer appointment in 1756, Trotter was involved in the auction of the personal effects of Lady Barbara Leigh, the daughter of the Earl of Scarborough. The sale included furniture, plates, dishes, jewellery, and a light town coach. The 27 February 1755 newspaper advertisement for the auction stated that a free catalogue could be obtained at Mr. Trotter's, upholder, Frith Street.[20] On 2 June 1755, Trotter had catalogues available for another sale, this time for the auction by Mr. Pervil of the household goods belonging to a gentlewoman gone abroad.[21] In a 25 June 1755 newspaper announcement, where Trotter again supplied catalogues for an auction by Mr. Pervil, the following sentence was added, 'Not one article in this sale but was the property of the above gentleman'.[22] Some auctioneers must have been allowing items from multiple owners into a single auction, evidently considered an unethical practice by estate executors. In their statement, Pervil and Trotter made it clear that this auction was solely for the benefit of the deceased's estate, implying they adhered to ethical business practices. Trotter was not only involved in the auction of household goods and personal effects. The house owned by Lady Barbara Leigh in Great Brook Street, Grosvenor Square, was

[19] London Metropolitan Archives, City of London. Reference Code: ACC/0426. Account Book of Robert Williams.

[20] *Public Advertiser*, 27 February 1755.

[21] *Public Advertiser*, 2 June 1755.

[22] *Public Advertiser*, 25 June 1755.

advertised for auction on 14 April 1756, and the announcement stated that the sale particulars could be obtained from Mr. Trotter.[23]

According to the advertisements mentioned above, Trotter did not act as the auctioneer. Rather, his role seemed to have been one of a provider of information about the sales. He likely had intimate knowledge of the personal and real property being sold by having seen the items and knowing the values. He, presumably, received a fee or commission for his work. The absence of his name in newspaper advertisements after the auction of Lady Leigh's home goods and personal effects indicates that he did not pursue a role in the auction business after April 1756. By that time, Trotter had been named the royal upholsterer.

Royal Upholsterer

Just how and why John Trotter became the royal upholsterer is unknown. It is fair to speculate that his former master and royal joiner, Henry Williams, had a large role in the process. He would have vouched that Trotter was of good character and had the ability to perform the duties of royal upholsterer in an honest and timely way.

The royal warrant that appointed John Trotter as upholsterer to His Majesty's Great Wardrobe was recorded on 7 January 1756 in the Lord Chamberlain's appointment book (Illustration 5.1).[24] Along with the prestige and profits that came from this appointment, it carried privileges and advantages such as exemption from jury duty and serving as sheriff.[25] Trotter was paid for one Great Wardrobe transaction before this date. On

[23] *Public Advertiser*, 29 March 1756.

[24] The National Archives, Kew. Lord Chamberlain's Appointment Books–Series II, 1755–1760, Reference: LC3/66.

[25] I am grateful to Dr. Robert Bucholz for providing the following information. The National Archives, Kew, LC 5/202, pp. 145–46, 8 May 1703, Order in Council excepting Household Officers from serving in local office, in response to petitions from the yeomen of the guard, grooms of the Chamber, Messengers in ordinary, citing an order in Council of 16 May 1692, '…that Her Majesty doth not take it well That any of her servants in Ordinary with fee should be Enjoyned to bear any Publick Offices in the Parishes where they Inhabit, or elsewhere; or be Summoned, or serve on Jurys, or to Watch or Ward, And it is her Majesty's Express Pleasure, that her Servants have and Enjoy all ye s[d] Ancient Libertys, Rights & Priviledges; And that hence forward none of her Servants in Ordinary with fee be enforce'd or any way oblidged to bear any Publick Offices, Serve on Jurys or Inquests; or Watch and Ward in any Place where they Dwell, or elsewhere, Nor Subjected to any Mulct or Fine for not submitting thereto.' This order stipulates that the lord chamberlain, lord

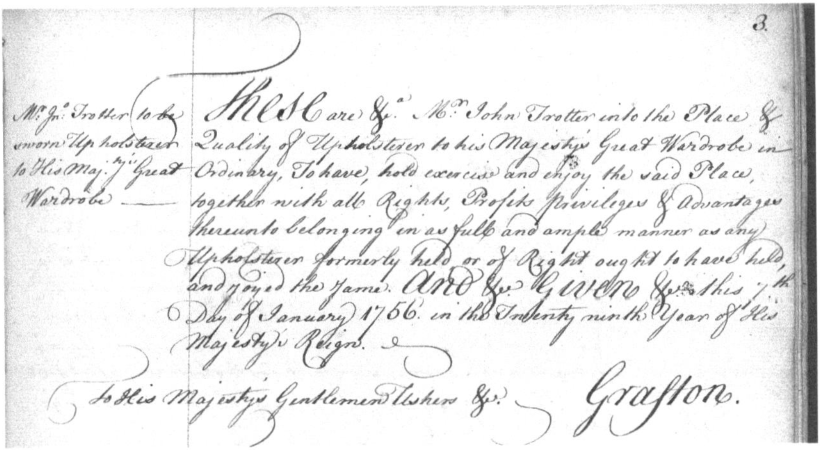
3.

Mr. Jno. Trotter to be sworn Upholsterer to His Maj.ty's Great Wardrobe —

These are &c.a Mr. John Trotter into the Place & Quality of Upholsterer to his Majesty's Great Wardrobe in Ordinary, To have, hold exercise and enjoy the said Place, together with all Rights, Profits Privileges & Advantages thereunto belonging in as full and ample manner as any Upholsterer formerly held or of Right ought to have held, and joyed the same. And &c. Given &c. this 7th Day of January 1756. in the Twenty ninth Year of His Majesty's Reign.

To His Majesty's Gentlemen Ushers &c. Grafton.

Illustration 5.1 The National Archives, Kew. Lord Chamberlain's Appointment Books–Series II, 1755–1760, Reference: LC3/66. Royal appointment of John Trotter, 7 January 1756. (With permission from The National Archives, Kew)

15 November 1755, Trotter signed for receipt of £35.1.0, representing work done for the King at St. James, the House of Lords, the Prince of Wales at Leicester House, and other residences. The Great Wardrobe account book lists six transactions for Trotter in the fiscal year ending 10 October 1756. Among those he provided upholstery services for were the King and his daughters, Princesses Caroline and Amelia. Along with the residences at St. James, Kensington, and Kew, he also made goods for the royal tent and tennis court at Whitehall and chapels royal in Virginia and Barbados. The upholstery goods he provided were varied, including such items as curtains, mattresses and other bedding items, carpets, and large brass cloak pins. He also billed for various repairs and reinstallations of carpets, window curtains, hangings, bed canopies, and umbrellos. (Cloak pins were threaded pins to attach the draw lines of window curtains. Umbrellos were sunshades above a window.[26]) His total billings for the

steward and master of the horse submit lists of household servants to the lord mayor of London, J.P.s of Westminster or any place necessary.

[26] Beard, *Upholsterers and Interior Furnishing*, 319, 327.

fiscal year 1755–56 amounted to £1480.5.1, which was fifteen per cent of the total Great Wardrobe tradesmen expenses of £9719.14.1.[27]

In the following fiscal year, 1756–1757, Trotter provided materials and services amounting to £1407, or over thirteen per cent of the tradesmen's bills of £10,356. Noteworthy at this time was his work on the *Fubbs*, the Royal Yacht, billing £3.10.0 for the following material and work:

> For making a Crimson Damask Furniture to a standing Bedstead with in & outside Vallens and Bases bound & flat Laced and Covering a set of outside Cornices finished in the neatest manner with Lace and Covering a set of Base mouldings finished with Lace and making a neat Counterpain lined with Karateen bound & flat Laced and finished in the neatest manner and for all materials used in making.[28]

To illustrate the typical upholstery work Trotter provided to the Great Wardrobe, the following entry, also from fiscal year 1756–1757, details the materials and services he provided for His Majesty's Private Bed Chamber in St. James's Palace for a cost of £7.10.0:

> For Making a Crimson Silk Damask Furniture to a new four post Bedstead Studded with in & out side Vallens & Bases lined with Crimson Lustring the Head Cloth & Teaster lined with red Linnen, Making Damask Cases for the Feet Pillars & Foot Board & a Counterpain lined with fine Crimson Shalloon & Covering a Set of Vauzes to the whole finished in the neatest manner and fixing up.[29]

Trotter's work was similar in subsequent years. In 1758, he provided finished upholstery goods, some with gilt nails and gold fringes, to the Earl of Bristol, Ambassador to the King of Spain.[30] Trotter provided comparable upholstery goods to the Earl of Kinnoul, Ambassador to the King

[27] The National Archives, Kew. Lord Chamberlain's Department, Great Wardrobe, Bill books: series II: tradesmen's bills etc. 10/10/1755–10/10/1756. Reference: LC 9/301.

[28] The National Archives, Kew. Lord Chamberlain's Department, Great Wardrobe, Bill books: series II: tradesmen's bills etc. 10/10/1756–10/10/1757. Reference: LC 9/302. No. 14.

[29] The National Archives, Kew. Lord Chamberlain's Department, Great Wardrobe, Bill books: series II: tradesmen's bills etc. 10/10/1756–10/10/1757. Reference: LC 9/302. No. 38.

[30] The National Archives, Kew. Lord Chamberlain's Department, Great Wardrobe, Bill books: series II: tradesmen's bills etc. 10/10/1757–10/10/1758. Reference: LC 9/303.

of Portugal, in 1760.[31] Probably one of the more unusual items received into the Great Wardrobe from Trotter was the King's travelling bed with a white leather folding mattress and a pair of swanskin blankets.[32]

The Great Wardrobe Day Book from November 1758 to November 1760, which recorded the goods delivered to the Great Wardrobe by the various tradesmen, has some entries of note for John Trotter. Along with curtains, carpets, bedding, and other upholstery goods, in September 1759 he delivered sixteen upholstered walnut chairs on behalf of himself and Henry Williams, his former master. In November 1759, the Great Wardrobe received bedding, six beech chairs, and a walnut night chair from John Trotter and Catherine Naish, who was the daughter of Henry Williams and assumed her father's position as royal joiner.[33] The fact that Trotter was involved with Henry Williams and his daughter does not prove that a partnership existed between them, but it does indicate that they collaborated. This working relationship could have been as simple as Williams sourcing chairs and delivering them to Trotter for upholstering, who in turn delivered the finished chairs to the Great Wardrobe.

Not all of Trotter's work as the royal upholsterer involved interior spaces. In the fiscal year 1756, Trotter completed work for His Majesty's tent. Included in this work was over 154 yards of hair cloth to cover the floor of the tent, consisting of five apartments, at a cost of £13.10.4. He charged £159.4.0 for providing 398 yards of Wilton carpeting to cover the floors of the tent's five apartments and passages. Included were canvas bags for packing the carpets, thirty-six camp chairs, and three large armchairs. He stuffed the chair seats with curled hair inside canvas and covered the seats with Wilton carpet, attaching them using burnished brass nails. Including these items and lesser items, Trotter's total bill for provisioning His Majesty's tent was £293.10.6.[34]

Even though the royal tent might be called a temporary interior living space, Trotter's work on His Majesty's tennis court at Whitehall was not for a living space. It may be best characterized as a recreational space. In

[31] The National Archives, Kew. Lord Chamberlain's Department, Great Wardrobe, Bill books: series II: tradesmen's bills etc. 10/10/1759–10/25/1760. Reference: LC 9/305.

[32] The National Archives, Kew. Lord Chamberlain's Department, Great Wardrobe, Day Book, 17/11/1758–17/11/1760. Reference: LC 9/212.

[33] Great Wardrobe, Day Book. Reference: LC 9/212.

[34] The National Archives, Kew. Lord Chamberlain's Department, Great Wardrobe, Bill books: series II: tradesmen's bills etc. 10/10/1756–10/10/1757. Reference: LC 9/302. No. 44.

this instance, Trotter's work included taking down existing curtains, valances, and nets. He used 471 yards of strong sailcloth to make and install twenty-six new curtains and valances at a cost of £35.6.6. New netting, costing £24.0.0, was installed. His £118.6.4 bill also included heavy rods and rings for the curtains and valances, leather curtain straps, and ropes and blocks for moving the curtains.[35]

In addition to providing the needs for the royal residences, the tradesmen holding royal warrants provided the necessities for special events, including coronations, weddings, and funerals. These events were recorded in the Lord Chamberlain's records of special events. These detailed records list the goods and services provided by Trotter and the other tradesmen.

The first special event that John Trotter was involved in was the funeral of Princess Caroline, the third daughter of George II, who died on 28 December 1757. Her embalmed body was sealed in a lead coffin, and her bowels were placed in an urn, which was delivered in her coach to Westminster the evening of 4 January 1758. A hearse carried her body to the Abbey early in the afternoon on 5 January. The casket was covered with black velvet and white feathers. She was interred in the King Henry VII Chapel at 11:00 that evening.[36]

John Trotter did the upholstery work for the coffin, which included a lining and a pillow of white satin and two black palls. He made a black velvet state canopy that was carried over the body on poles. The canopy was lined with black silk and had silk fringes. He provided the upholstery goods to dress the hearse and horses, including seventeen white ostrich feathers. For the coachman and postilion, he provided mourning cloaks, gloves, and hatbands (Illustration 5.2). His work included black window and door hangings in the princes' chamber, and inside the Abbey, Trotter covered areas of the chapel and vault in black cloth. Trotter's charges for these funeral services were £127.9.0, just over ten per cent of the total tradesmen's bills of £1213.7.3.[37]

When Princess Elizabeth, the second daughter of the late Frederick, the Prince of Wales, died on 4 September 1759, Trotter was again involved in

[35] The National Archives, Kew. Lord Chamberlain's Department, Great Wardrobe, Bill books: series II: tradesmen's bills etc. 10/10/1756–10/10/1757. Reference: LC 9/302. No. 44.

[36] The National Archives, Kew. Lord Chamberlain's Department, Records of Special Events, Funeral of Princess Caroline, Daughter of George II. Reference: LC 2/27.

[37] Lord Chamberlain's Department, Records of Special Events, Funeral of Princess Caroline. Reference: LC 2/27.

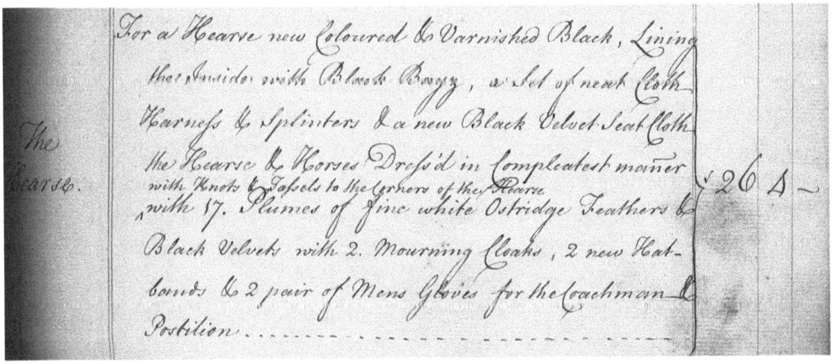

The Hearse.

For a Hearse new Coloured & Varnished Black, Lining the Inside with Black Bayz, a Set of neat Cloth Harness & Splinters & a new Black Velvet Seat Cloth the Hearse & Horses Dress'd in Compleatest manner with Knots & Tassels to the Corners of the Hearse with 17. Plumes of fine white Ostridge Feathers & Black Velvets with 2. Mourning Cloaks, 2 new Hat-bands & 2 pair of Mens Gloves for the Coachman & Postilion .... 26 4 –

Illustration 5.2 The National Archives, Kew. Lord Chamberlain's Department, Records of Special Events, Funeral of Princess Caroline, Daughter of George II. Reference: LC 2/27. (With permission from The National Archives, Kew)

providing goods and services for her funeral. He 'dressed' the coffin using silk, velvet, and satin materials. Along with making her coffin canopy, he also provided the hangings for the princes' chamber. He made the arrangements for the hearse to bring her body (noted as not embalmed) from Kew to Westminster. The hearse was done up similar to Princess Caroline's, including horses with seventeen ostrich feathers. He also provided coverings for the chapel and vault, as he had done for Princess Caroline. Because Princess Elizabeth died in Kew, Trotter made the arrangements for Mr. Ely to provide an outside coffin and material for £27.17. Trotter added a seven and one-half per cent fee to Ely's bill and charged the Great Wardrobe £30.3.0, indicating that when he sourced finished materials from suppliers, he marked up the cost to the Great Wardrobe.[38] It cannot be discerned if Mr. Ely's charges were for a fully 'dressed' coffin or if Trotter had his own employees 'dress' it. Seven and one-half per cent was probably the mark-up that he used in his business, perhaps aimed at a four per cent premium over the average eighteenth-century interest rate of three and a half per cent.[39] His total charges for Princess Elizabeth's funeral were £175.3.0.

[38] Lord Chamberlain's Department, Records of Special Events, Funeral of Princess Elizabeth Caroline. Reference: LC 2/27.

[39] Paul Schmelzing, "Eight centuries of global real interest rates, R–G, and the 'suprasecular' decline, 1311–2018," *Bank of England*, Staff Working Paper No. 845 (Jan. 2020): 40.

King George II died on 25 October 1760, and the Great Wardrobe engaged John Trotter's services for the funeral and burial. As with the funerals of Princesses Caroline and Elizabeth, Trotter supplied the satin lining and pillow for the coffin and the velvet outside coverings. He made two palls of purple velvet and a state canopy covered with velvet and silk. Absent from his bill was a charge for the hearse to the Abbey, implying that the Great Wardrobe made other arrangements in that regard. Trotter's total charges for the King's funeral were £212.13.6, just over seven per cent of the total tradesmen's cost of £2946.7.[40]

John Trotter left the royal upholstery business in 1761. The coronation of King George III and Queen Charlotte occurred on 22 September 1761, and William Vile and John Cobb, not John Trotter, provided the upholstery work.[41] The last Great Wardrobe entries for Trotter are routine, with the last one on 6 March 1761 being a payment to him for £454.10.7. As an example of the interchangeability of the terms upholsterer and upholder, this same entry lists his occupation as an upholder, rather than as an upholsterer. For this fiscal year, total payments to Trotter equalled £908.15.10 (over three and one-half per cent of all the trade bills totalling £24,888.16.5). Vile and Cobb received £3720.13.3, or nearly fifteen per cent, of the total bills.[42]

It is unknown why John Trotter stopped his upholstery work for the Great Wardrobe. It may be that King George III issued new royal warrants. The work he did for the royal residences was steady and, presumably, profitable and prestigious (Table 5.1). Nonetheless, the number of upholstery items for a particular commission could be large and the price per item relatively small, possibly creating a high volume, low profit situation. The work was probably time-consuming. Completing an order would have involved taking measurements in the palace spaces, finding the right materials and having them delivered, and, finally, making up the items, all of which was time-consuming. Moreover, working with materials such as satin, velvet, and gold and silver thread meant that any mistake was costly. It is probable that mistakes were avoided by employing only experienced and, therefore, expensive workers. It is not known whether

[40] Lord Chamberlain's Department, Records of Special Events, Funeral of King George II. Reference: LC 2/27.

[41] The National Archives, Kew. Lord Chamberlain's Department, Records of Special Events, Coronation: George III and Queen Charlotte. Reference: LC 2/30.

[42] The National Archives, Kew. Lord Chamberlain's Department, Great Wardrobe, Bill books: series II: tradesmen's bills etc. 10/10/1760–10/10/1761. Reference: LC 9/306.

Table 5.1 Great Wardrobe revenues for John Trotter in £'s rounded down

Fiscal year	*All tradesmen*	*John Trotter*	*Trotter's % of total*
1755–1756	9719	1480	15.2
1756–1757	10,358	1407	13.6
1757–1758	12,412	1132	9.1
1758–1759	14,009	3018	21.5
1759–1760	12,130	2277	18.8
1760–1761	24,888	908	3.6
Total	£83,516	£10,222	12.2%

Sources: The National Archives, Kew. Lord Chamberlain's Department, Great Wardrobe, Bill books: series II: tradesmen's bills etc. 10/10/1755-10/10/1761. References: LC 9/301-306

Trotter sourced or sub-contracted some of his Great Wardrobe work, but it is possible he did. All in all, being the royal upholsterer was demanding in time, capital, and skill.

Just what happened to the specific palace interior goods Trotter worked on is unknown, but some may still survive. Upon the death of the monarch, a tradition of perquisites over royal household furnishings had been established. The tradition was that the Lord Chamberlain was entitled to take possession of the monarch's furnishings from the royal bedroom and associated rooms. Except for tapestries, sculptures, and paintings, the Lord Chamberlain would often claim the royal beds and associated furnishings, including fabrics. In the case of George II, the Lord Chamberlain was William Cavendish, the Duke of Devonshire, who succeeded the Duke of Grafton (Charles FitzRoy) in 1757. (It was Grafton who issued Trotter's warrant that named him the royal upholsterer.) The Duke of Devonshire claimed George II's deathbed as a perquisite, and it is now part of Chatsworth House. It is possible that John Trotter furnished the luxurious upholstery for the royal bed. Other furnishings and fabric goods Trotter provided for the royal bedchamber and associated rooms may have been claimed by Cavendish or by a subsequent Lord Chamberlain. There are records, but not always complete ones, at the National Archives that can help trace what happened to furnishings that are no longer in the royal household inventory. Complicating this tracing is the fact that the Lord Chamberlain could gift royal furniture to those subservient to him. In one instance, royal furniture was consigned to a London upholsterer and art dealer for sale in the secondary market.[43] Without the proper documentation to confirm provenance, attributing secondary market furnishings to the royal household, let alone John Trotter, is difficult at best.

If Trotter had been having thoughts of leaving the Great Wardrobe behind him, it is possible that the death of King George II in 1760 helped him make the decision. King George III and Queen Charlotte moved into the king's quarters, and with that, there would have come changes in interior furnishings. Great Wardrobe orders could be extensive, as evidenced by the one from 10 September 1759, which consisted of eleven pages of items for the Leicester Fields home of Princes William and Henry. On 2 February 1760, another extensive five-page order of items came from the Great Wardrobe for the Prince of Wales and Prince Edward at Savile House.[44] Along with his upholstery work for the royal residences, John Trotter had built a business providing camp equipment to the army. Sometime in 1760, he chose between these two endeavours in which to invest his time, capital, and expertise. The endeavour that Trotter chose to concentrate on was supplying camp equipment to the British army, discontinuing his work for the royal residences in 1761.

Army Camp Equipment Contracting

John Trotter may have lost his royal patronage, but he made up for it by becoming a military contractor. According to Gordon Bannerman, Trotter was a very successful supplier of army camp equipment.[45] Trotter's career in supplying army camp equipment began during the Seven Years' War (1756–1762) and continued beyond the American Revolution (1775–1783). Bannerman stated that among the items Trotter provided to the military were tents, marquees, knapsacks, and gaiters. Furthermore, Trotter supplied items to troops in North America, Germany, and, of course, Britain.[46] At a later point, Trotter's nephew (also named John Trotter but not his son, as is sometimes reported) learned the military contracting business, which he carried on after Trotter's death in 1790. It

[43] Olivia Freyman, "Rich Pickings: The Royal Bed as a Perquisite 1660–1760," *Furniture History*, 2014, Vol. 50 (2014): 119–136.

[44] Great Wardrobe, Day Book. Reference: LC 9/212.

[45] Gordon Bannerman, *Merchants and the Military in Eighteenth-Century Britain* (London: Pickering & Chatto, 2008), 69.

[46] Bannerman, *Merchants and the Military*, 69. Gaiters are protective coverings for the lower legs and boots.

was Trotter's nephew who started a factory in Soho Square (which would later become the Soho Bazaar) where he warehoused surplus blankets, tents, and knapsacks, which he typically purchased in peacetime and had ready for shipment when the army requested them. Having these items ready for immediate delivery cut out other contractors, allowing him to fix his own prices and earn a ten per cent commission. There were, naturally, objections to Trotter's nephew having what was essentially a monopoly over military camp supplies, but these were alleviated when the government created the post of Store Keeper General's Department.[47]

The Admiralty had a large and efficient supply organization during the eighteenth century as part of Britain's maritime strategy, but the army had no official supply organization. Bannerman related that the basic reason for not having an army supply system was because Article VI of the 1689 Bill of Rights stated that there could be no standing peacetime army in Britain without the approval of Parliament. This legislation was a reaction to King James II's domestic use of troops. While having a standing army was discussed by Parliament from time to time, no action was taken because it was feared that a standing army could be used for personal and political gain and would increase taxes.[48] Thus, when an increase in army strength was required, the need for supplying equipment to the additional troops was also required. Without a formal supply organization, the army relied on private contractors to supply horses, hay, straw, wagons, food, camp equipment, and other necessities.

It was the Seven Years' War that created global opportunities for military contractors to supply British army troops. Troops fighting in North America, Europe, Africa, and India needed supplies on a regular basis, and as the British army had no formal supply organization, the military had to rely on contractors who could reliably deliver what was needed. It was an expensive war, during which the British public debt grew by nearly eighty per cent.[49] The government strived to avoid raising land taxes to pay for the war. Consequently, custom duties and excise taxes were raised.[50] At the same time, the government attempted to control contracting costs through a competitive bidding process.

[47] Bannerman, *Merchants and the Military*, 86.

[48] Bannerman, *Merchants and the Military*, 16.

[49] William Gibson, *A Brief History of Britain 1660–1851* (London: Constable & Robinson, Ltd., 2010), 151–52.

[50] Bannerman, *Merchants and the Military*, 19.

Bidding for military contracts was generally open to the public, but the bidders were required to demonstrate business competence.[51] The Treasury, not the Admiralty, accepted and considered proposals for army equipment and supplies, with army and navy armament (guns and ammunition) contracts issued through the Ordnance Board. On 10 July 1758, the Treasury Board met, and the contracting process was deliberated. After discussing the Duke of Marlborough's thoughts on 'practicing a better economy' with contractors, the Board considered advertising for bread, bread wagons, and forage contracts. The Duke of Marlborough and Lord Barrington 'agreed in remonstrating strenuously against advertising contracts because it would bind the Board to accept the lowest offer from whosoever it shall come…' The minutes further stated, 'Subsistence of the troops must depend upon the exactness and punctuality of the contractor, the character of the person contracting is a consideration no less essential to be regarded than the cheapness of the contract.' The Board directed staff to invite proposals from as many persons of good credit and character as they could.[52] There were three elements to a contract: offer, acceptance, and performance. Before any contractor was awarded a contract, his ability to perform or deliver the supplies was examined. Would he be able to deliver the exact supplies ordered, deliver them on time, and deliver them to the right place? Another part of the government's due diligence was an examination of contractors' character and substance.[53] Since Trotter held a royal warrant with the Great Wardrobe, his business dealings would have been easy to verify. Presumably, his ability to deliver upholstery goods at the right time and place demonstrated that he had the organizational skills needed to produce camp equipment and deliver it to the army. In other words, Trotter convinced the government and the military that he could perform according to the terms of an army camp supply contract.

The Treasury considered the overall price of each proposal, not wanting to split the contract among different suppliers on an article-by-article basis. Proposals that were comprehensive for all articles, rather than those proposing a few of the items at a lower price, were considered more secure

[51] Bannerman, *Merchants and the Military*, 41–42.

[52] The National Archives, Kew. Treasury Board Minutes. 1/12/1757–30/11/1760. Reference: T 29/33.

[53] Bannerman, *Merchants and the Military*, 48.

from failure.[54] Contractors providing food and forage had to have a network of foreign supply agents capable of procuring these items locally. Trotter, however, did not need to use agents in other countries to act on his behalf since the camp equipment he supplied was produced domestically. Still, he needed to organize a group of sub-contractors and suppliers to manufacture the ordered items and then manage them to ensure quality and timeliness. The last part of Trotter's supply chain would have been consolidating all the items in one place and, for instance, delivering them by coastal ship or wagon to the Portsmouth shipyard. Once delivery was made on board a ship, Trotter would have completed his part of the supply contract.[55]

It is not surprising that there were some in Parliament who groused that there was not enough competitive bidding in the awarding of military contracts. There were reasons why the contracting group was small.[56] Besides proving a demonstrated ability to perform the terms of a contract, the other reasons for contracting being a small group were financial. Contractors, including Trotter, were required to post a surety as a test of credit worthiness and as an incentive to ensure contract performance. Many contractors were required to post a surety of twice the amount of any government advances that lowered prices through encouraging bulk purchasing. The surety requirement, therefore, had to have eliminated bidders that were qualified to carry out the work but did not have the financial means to perform. Another reason that bid winners were typically wealthy businessmen is that anyone with the required expertise for military supply contracts had to have already run a financially successful business. In addition, properly performing the terms of a contract did not mean that the government promptly paid what was owed a contractor. Contractor payments were often delayed until the following fiscal year when Parliament voted to increase the national debt. The average time for a contractor's final payment being settled was about nine months after performance.[57] Trotter likely had saved enough money from his upholding business to get into military camp supply contracting by 1759, and the

[54] Bannerman, *Merchants and the Military*, 59–62.

[55] The National Archives, Kew. Treasury Papers. NORTH AMERICA: Provisioning: T 1/396. And: 28 June 1759 Memorial of John Trotter to Right Honourable Vicount Barrington, His Majesty's Secretary of War. Provisioning: Memorial of John Trotter asking payment for provisions supplied to America.

[56] Bannerman, *Merchants and the Military*, 41–42.

[57] Bannerman, *Merchants and the Military*, 32–33, 62–63.

1752 £5000 marriage settlement was surely important in improving his capital position and financial wherewithal to weather late government payments.

The National Archives at Kew possesses a letter from John Trotter to Viscount Barrington, Secretary of War, dated 28 June 1759. In the letter, Trotter requests Barrington's help in collecting £5050 due to him for supplying camp necessaries for ten regiments in America. He also told Barrington that he had performed as required, including packing and delivering the supplies on board a ship in Portsmouth. Furthermore, he wrote that he had paid various tradesmen ready cash out of his own pocket so that he could fulfil the order on short notice. For four months, Trotter tried to get payment from the Treasury before finally being told there was no money for his work. Trotter ended the letter by stating that he had several creditors 'extremely impatient' with him. There was no indication of when he was actually paid, but a handwritten notation on the letter's back stated, 'Ordered to be issued'.[58]

Trotter's letter reveals some facts about his military contracting business. Trotter was given short notice to supply ten army regiments in America during the Seven Years' War. Because this was a large order and with Barrington's direct involvement in placing it, one must conclude that Trotter was a capable contractor. Specific to Trotter's business was his statement that he paid other tradesmen ready money, which indicates he sourced the supplies and used sub-contractors. He also wrote of extremely impatient creditors, indicating that he did not always pay his sub-contractors in advance or before he was paid. This letter is an example of Bannerman's point that the government did not pay contractors on time. Trotter was, in a sense, extending credit to the government. This dilatory payment had a cascading effect since, because without payment from the Treasury, Trotter could not pay tradesmen who had, in the same sense, extended credit to him.

Though Trotter's army contracts were not examined, there is information about his business dealings in this regard. This information comes from the bank account that Trotter opened in 1758 with an initial cash

[58] Treasury Papers. NORTH AMERICA: Provisioning: T 1/396. 28 June 1759 Memorial of John Trotter to Right Honourable Vicount Barrington, His Majesty's Secretary of War. Provisioning: Memorial of John Trotter asking payment for provisions supplied to America.

deposit of £119.[59] It appears that this was initially a business operating account through which he paid for goods and services. In 1759, Trotter issued fifty-one notes payable to various tradesmen amounting to £1178. Most of these payments were less than £50, but two amounted to over £100 each. Trotter paid James Standerwick, a cloth haberdasher and commercial merchant in Cornhill, £112 in January 1759. He paid Thomas Chamberlain, a commercial merchant in Soho, £200 that July. Trotter made eleven deposits, all in cash, totalling £1979 throughout 1759. Given that he supplied equipment for ten army regiments in America in 1759, his bank account does not indicate that he paid out large sums for the equipment in that year.

However, the bank account for 1760 does indicate that he owed large sums to various creditors as outlined in his letter to Viscount Barrington. He issued sixty-six notes payable amounting to £5443 in 1760, including £50 to his mother-in-law, Mrs. Betts. Thomas Palin, a rope maker and textile manufacturer in Old Street, London, was paid £205. Mr. Burgess, a clothing manufacturer from Southwark, was paid £302. Trotter took in receipts of £5238, of which £5138 was received in cash.

There was no single account deposit of £5050, which Trotter wrote about to Barrington in 1759. It is possible the Treasury gave him multiple payments. It is also possible that Trotter did not deposit the money he received from the Treasury into his bank account in one lump sum and only deposited enough to cover the banking drafts as he issued them. Nonetheless, it is apparent that Trotter paid his suppliers more than a year after he delivered the army equipment to Barrington.

In subsequent years, there were a growing number of tradesmen that Trotter paid through his banking account. Among the London-area suppliers were: William Innes, commercial merchant; John Hawkins, commercial merchant; Greenwollers & Co., linen drapers and textile sellers; Grubb & Jeffery, linen drapers and textile sellers; Abraham Chambers, commercial merchant; Ferdinand Gillard, feather merchant and textile seller; Matthew Winter, lace and fringe maker and textile and clothing manufacturer; and Wagstaff Shuttleworth & Co., warehousemen. Although there had to be a shipper among the multitude of payments, it cannot be discerned who this was.

[59] Trotter's bank account was opened in 1758. Permission kindly granted by Coutts & Co. and Timothy Powys-Lybbe to examine the account. Photographs not allowed. Trotter's bank account ledgers are chronologically organized by year.

John Trotter also withdrew cash from his account for no discernible reason. Many of his cash withdrawals were £1000 or less. Since he wrote to Barrington that he had paid some tradesmen in ready cash, some of these cash withdrawals were likely for paying these suppliers. On 12 August 1768, he withdrew £12,000, a significant amount of money. The best explanation for this large withdrawal is that Trotter bought Horton Manor, a country estate, that year, and the money was used for the purchase.

At the beginning of Britain's war with the American colonists, Trotter's account activity significantly increased in the period from June 1775 to June 1776. During this period, he made over 360 payments from the account as compared to just over ninety in the prior year. Some of these were personal, such as payments to himself, his children, or investments. By January 1776, the number of transactions with his suppliers had increased. Names familiar from 1760, like Standerwick, Jeffery & Son, and Greenwollers & Co., were among the suppliers paid hundreds and, sometimes, thousands of pounds. Britain was at war, and Trotter's bank account shows that he was involved with a large army equipment contract. On 14 June 1776, Trotter's account balance was over £16,200.

The bank account provides information about John Trotter's wealth accumulation. Between March 1763 and June 1764, he bought 17,000 four per cent Consolidated Annuity Bonds. He bought 500 shares of the East India Company in 1766 and owned East India Company bonds. These transactions indicate that, rather than maintaining large cash balances that earned no money for him, he invested the money to earn additional income.

Bannerman believed that military contracts were not fortune makers. Rather, military contracts were a safe way to invest extra money. It was thought at the time that military contractors became wealthy from fulfilling contracts. Bannerman, however, argued that contractors were not necessarily seeking contracts to become wealthy. Rather, he argued that most contractors were already rich or modestly wealthy before they entered the contracting business. Why would already rich businessmen seek government contracts? It is here that Bannerman maintains that these contracts were generally low risk because of the government guarantee of payment. These contracts were, therefore, seen as a way of maximizing profits while minimizing risk.[60] Though the payment risk may have been low, contractors

[60] Bannerman, *Merchants and the Military*, 123–25.

like Trotter needed enough liquidity to maintain business while awaiting government payment.

Though army supply contracts may have been a means of preserving wealth, risks had to be managed. Among the most common risks were bad weather, enemy seizure, and inventory shrinkage.[61] Insurance for maritime shipping losses was sometimes used, but a more cost-effective way of minimizing losses was to use ship convoys.[62] It is likely that the goods Trotter wrote about in his letter to Barrington were shipped to America by convoy from Portsmouth, thus mitigating the risks associated with enemy seizure or shipwreck. In addition, Trotter's letter indicated that he was only responsible for delivering the camp equipment to the ship, not to an American destination. There were two other risks he had to manage. The main one was failure of a sub-contractor to provide items of the right quality, on time, and to the right place. It is here that Trotter would have had to spend time managing the sub-contractor's delivery process and quality control. Inventory shrinkage or theft would have always been a possibility, and to lessen this risk, Trotter would have likely dealt with suppliers, warehouses, and sub-contractors of good reputation, partially explaining why the same supplier names in his bank account frequently occurred. At the same time, these trusted suppliers must have had confidence that Trotter would pay them.

The Later Years

It was not unusual for wealthy merchants to purchase country estates in the eighteenth century. Like Robert Williams, John Trotter also purchased a country estate. Trotter purchased an Epsom home known as Horton Manor in 1768.[63] Many businessmen like Trotter continued residing in town and conducted their business activities from there. They looked at their country estates as places to enjoy country living on a part-time basis.[64]

John Trotter died in July 1790, and his will requested a decent but not expensive burial inside the vault beside his wife at St. Ann's Church, Soho. His will included many bequests of £300 or less to distant relatives and

[61] Bannerman, *Merchants and the Military*, 150.

[62] Bannerman, *Merchants and the Military*, 54–55.

[63] Surrey History Centre, Woking. Properties of John in Epsom and Elsewhere: Deeds and Papers. SHC Ref. No. 186.

[64] Bannerman, *Merchants and the Military*, 131–33.

household staff. The main beneficiaries were his three children. His eldest son, James, inherited the Horton Manor estate and £25,000, less £5000 given to him at marriage. The second son, John, was a military officer and received £25,000 and an additional £2000 to purchase a major or lieutenant colonel commission in the army. Because his daughter, Ann, received a large amount of money upon her marriage to Robert Trotter (her first cousin), Trotter's will stipulated she was to receive only £200.[65] It is apparent that John Trotter was financially successful enough in his business dealings to bequeath large amounts of money. There is no information about the values of his land, buildings, and leases, but it seems reasonable to presume that he was worth at least £100,000 when he died. This places John Trotter in the financially successful category.

This chapter about John Trotter and the previous one about Robert Williams present the facts about their lives and their paths to financial success. While both men had the training and skills required of all upholders, there were certain commonalities between them that were crucial to their success. The most important commonality was their respective networks of familial, social, and business connections.

Both Trotter and Williams had family connections that helped them throughout their business careers. John Trotter's apprenticeship with Henry Williams underscores the importance of securing an apprenticeship with an elite master. It had to be Trotter's former master who gave him the introduction to the Great Wardrobe. His connection with his distant relative, Thomas Coutts, is unclear, but it was strong enough for the banker to be listed in his will as an executor. This connection could have given him borrowing access to working capital when needed. While it is not known who Robert Williams's master was, he was able to buy his business, a benefit of the apprenticeship system. His familial connection was more transparent in its importance than Trotter's. His brother, John Williams, was a neighbour of and a business partner with the banker and East India Company investor Charles Raymond. It was because of these connections that Robert was able to specialize in supplying household goods to East India Company ship officers, and, upon his brother's death, enter the banking and East India Company businesses.

Trotter and Williams, even with their familial, business, and social connections, did not become wealthy by being general upholders. They, along

[65] The National Archives, Kew. PROB 11/1194/170. Will of John Trotter of Soho Square, Middlesex. 24 July 1790.

with using Thomas Chippendale for the sake of comparison, began their careers by serving apprenticeships, though Chippendale did not serve his in London. These three men established their own businesses in London's fashionable West End and were by all accounts considered capable men in 'fitting out' residential interiors. From a career standpoint, all three went from their trained trade, i.e. joiner, upholsterer, or cabinet-maker, to become generalist upholders in furnishing homes. Chippendale stayed in the generalist role and continued to promote himself as a cabinet-maker. Trotter and Williams, in contrast, had business trajectories that took them well beyond general upholding. They became specialist upholders in that they each found a niche business within the upholding trade. These niche business lines were not easy to get into. Along with needing money, one also needed introductions from influential individuals. Williams, along with 'fitting out' ship officer quarters, provided goods for EIC ship officers engaged in overseas private trade. Trotter became the royal upholsterer. These specialized upholding roles must have been financially rewarding because both men soon moved into roles unrelated to furnishing private spaces. Williams made a fortune by owning East Indiamen and a bank; Trotter became wealthy and best known as a supplier of army camp equipment.

Specialization is where there was a distinct difference between Trotter and Williams and Thomas Chippendale. While Trotter and Williams found specialties, Chippendale's career did not go beyond that of a general upholder. There is no doubt that he had social and business connections, including a working relationship with the great architect Robert Adam. Rather than finding an upholding niche, Chippendale sought to increase his general upholding business through marketing. Initially, his main marketing strategy was to expand his cabinet-making business through publishing the *Director*. The publication was successful in terms of being fully subscribed. However, its reliance on current styles of the time, especially the rococo, made the *Director* hostage to changes in style and taste.[66] This certainly would have been the case when neoclassicism came into vogue in the late 1750s.[67] The *Director* also had a business weakness for Chippendale in that furniture-makers could copy his designs and sell Chippendale-

[66] Christopher Gilbert, *The Life and Work of Thomas Chippendale* (New York: Tabard Press, 1978), 26–27, 74.

[67] Michael Snodin and John Styles, *Design & the Decorative Arts: Georgian Britain 1714–1837* (London: V&A Publications, 2004), 83–86.

inspired products at lower prices. The *Director* enhanced Chippendale's reputation among architects, designers, and patrons as a most capable cabinet-maker.[68] This likely explains why he increased his production capacity (and fixed costs).

It would be unfair to say that Thomas Chippendale was not an entrepreneur and unwilling to move into new areas of business. His production of the *Director* was an entrepreneurial undertaking. The fatal blow to Chippendale's business aspirations was the death of his partner and main financial backer, James Rannie.[69] While he may have been presented with new business opportunities, Chippendale had no ready cash to invest in new endeavours, with Rannie's heirs demanding back capital. Accepting Rannie's capital allowed him to expand his production capabilities, but it was ultimately a bad business risk to take. He had to remain in what he knew best, which was general upholding.

A commonality shared by Trotter and Williams, but not by Chippendale, was that they came from gentry backgrounds. This fact must be acknowledged before ascribing Chippendale's lack of wealth accumulation entirely to the misfortune of his financial backer dying. One can speculate if Chippendale would have become wealthy had his financial backer not died, but he lacked one advantage that Trotter and Williams had, namely, the familial and social connections that came from being a younger gentry son. Though Trotter's and Williams's business trajectories were similar, there was a major difference between them. Williams took a more societal role later in his life and joined Parliament, whereas Trotter, it seems, was comfortable merely being wealthy.

Overall, the key aspect of financial success for Trotter and Williams was finding a niche business that allowed them to break out of the general upholding role. While there was no sure-fire formula that resulted in financial success in the upholding trade, there were commonalities that existed between Williams and Trotter that led to their financial success. Both were younger gentry sons who completed apprenticeships with reputable masters. They became successful general upholders and used their familial, social, and business connections to become specialized upholders in niche businesses. Finally, they were entrepreneurs with the financial means to invest in new opportunities beyond upholding.

[68] Gilbert, *Thomas Chippendale*, 94–98.
[69] Gilbert, *Thomas Chippendale*, 3–33.

CHAPTER 6

Conclusions

London's eighteenth-century upholders were key figures in fashionably and stylishly furnishing homes, increasingly so for those of the middling ranks. The upholding trade adapted to changes throughout the eighteenth century. At the beginning of the century, upholders were primarily manufacturers, assemblers, and sellers of household goods. By mid-century, about the time Thomas Chippendale opened for business, they had also become primary providers of funeral undertaking goods and services. Their business model continued to evolve and, by 1760, upholders became measurably more active as brokers and appraisers of household goods. Also growing was their involvement in the auction business. One important conclusion in this book is that the desire for more profits motivated upholders to change their business model to include these other business lines.

Consumer demand increased for household goods during the mid-eighteenth century. To meet this demand, upholders increased their stock in trade through their own production or by purchasing goods from wholesalers. Circumventing the shortage of coin money at this time, many upholders used private credit in the form of promissory notes. They received these notes from their customers and issued them to their suppliers. These paper instruments were often sold at discounts to others or endorsed over to suppliers, creating chains of responsible parties. Although upholder bankruptcies surged between 1760 and 1780, this should not be

S. Sanders, *The Eighteenth-Century London Upholder*,
https://doi.org/10.1007/978-3-032-08660-0_6

taken to mean that upholders were taking unnecessary business risks. Running a successful upholding business could be complicated by events outside of the owner's control. This was especially true with the uncertainties created by war. The volume of upholder bankruptcies increased after 1760, and it seems reasonable to conclude that the use of private credit was responsible for the majority of these bankruptcies.

Upholding evolved into a more diversified business by the middle of the century. The core business of making and selling household furniture and upholstered goods remained, but upholders also found other sources of income. An important conclusion is that these business changes were evolutionary, not revolutionary. These changes did not happen suddenly; rather, the changes evolved as the century progressed. Upholders were not particularly inventive in the services and goods they offered. However, they quickly adopted marketplace innovations.

Understanding the evolution of the upholding trade necessitated exploring the social, political, and economic changes that emerged in the seventeenth century. This was a period in which the middling sort expanded in size and developed its own sense of taste and fashion. The first half of the eighteenth century saw an increased interest in residential interior design and taste at the upper social levels. Interest in style and design also increased in the middling ranks, but for goods at more affordable costs. The middling ranks, not the elite, made up the largest part of the customer base for most upholders. Choices in how to spend one's money became more and more available.

The private and social lives of upholders were no different than those in the other trades and businesses. Most endeavoured to make enough money to give their children a basic education and, perhaps, send the oldest son to university. For those with the financial means, providing a daughter with a marriage settlement was prestigious, and a male upholder whose wife brought money to the marriage could help his business with new capital. With success came the expectation of living a private life commensurate with one's social rank. Sickness and death of young adults, children, and infants were also common events, even among the wealthy. It was not unusual for a widow to continue the upholding business of her husband. Bankruptcy would have been a major event for an upholder's family. Going from a secure position in the middling ranks to a lower rank because of bankruptcy would have meant a lower standard of living and less disposable income. Any public embarrassment resulting from bankruptcy and the public liquidation of the upholder's stock in trade was softened because bankruptcy was a common occurrence among all trades and businesses.[1]

Christopher Gilbert argued that Chippendale was hard-working, ambitious, and creative, even though business management was not one of his strengths.[2] Most upholders were ambitious, hard-working, and opportunistic. They wanted financial success and hoped to move into a higher social rank. According to Gilbert, Chippendale had social aspirations in mind when he dedicated his design book to influential patrons. It seems that Chippendale thought his reputation as an elite designer would cast him into a higher social rank beyond that of a tradesman, but moving into a higher social rank was difficult. The success that Robert Williams and John Trotter experienced was much the result of coming from a gentry background, a fact that Chippendale could not claim.[3] Financial success eluded Chippendale, but upholders who were financially successful could move into a higher middling order. Only a small number of upholders became wealthy enough to retire to a country estate, where, unless they came from a gentry family, social acceptance was not immediate.[4]

Irrespective of aspirations, most upholders remained in the middling rank of tradesmen. Some achieved a higher level within the middling order, but they were still of the middling rank. Upholders who achieved financial wealth and the means to purchase second homes probably were not self-made men. The case studies of Robert Williams and John Trotter point out that they were both younger gentry sons and apprenticed to well-established masters. Their respective networks of familial, social, and business connections enabled them to invest their profits in niche business lines and later in non-upholding businesses. Their accumulated wealth placed them in what can be called the 'commercial aristocracy'.

[1] Julian Hoppit, *Risk and failure in English business 1700–1800* (Cambridge: Cambridge University Press, 1987), 18–28. Hoppit explains that the social stigma of bankruptcy was two-part: personal failure and breaking one's word with creditors. There developed the concept of an honest bankruptcy versus the dishonest bankruptcy. Honest bankruptcy was caused by misfortune or events outside the debtor's control; dishonest bankruptcy occurred from theft, mismanagement, and dishonesty by the debtor.

[2] Christopher Gilbert, *The Life & Work of Thomas Chippendale*, Vol. 1 (London: Tabard Press, 1978), 4.

[3] Gilbert, *The Life & Work of Thomas Chippendale*, 3–4.

[4] Pat Kirkham, *The London Furniture Trade 1700–1870* (Leeds: Furniture History Society, 1988), 90–92.

The Upholders' Company was never an important company when comparing its size of membership with other London companies. This study found that not all upholders were members of the Upholders' Company. There were many who belonged to other companies or to no company at all. No attempt was made in this study to estimate how many upholders, livery company members or not, were practising the trade in London. The primary sources are unreliable for such an endeavour. For instance, Chippendale practised upholding but belonged to no company and promoted himself as a cabinet-maker. John Trotter was a member of the Joiners' Company but practised upholding.[5] Perhaps, one could estimate that the number of practising upholders in London was at least twice the membership number of the Upholders' Company, but this would be conjecture and have no basis in evidence.

Belonging to a livery company or not was a financial decision for upholders. By the mid-eighteenth century, the traditional advantages of livery company membership were becoming less important because there was little financial benefit. Also, it was not unusual for members of other livery companies to practise upholding, probably because the financial opportunities were sometimes greater in upholding than in other trades. Although having no livery membership was, in most instances, skirting the law, a few upholders operated in this way, knowing that the legal risks were minimal. Nonetheless, upholding as a trade continued to thrive as livery membership was losing its importance.

The Upholders' Company had advantages for members and the public at the beginning of the eighteenth century. The Company sought to protect the trade from interlopers and from those using bad materials and producing inferior goods, but this was largely unsuccessful. At the same time, the public was assured that goods purchased from Company members were of high quality. It also endeavoured to ensure apprentices received proper training. The Upholders' Company organized member funeral processions and provided modest financial sums for members needing short-term loans and for widows in need of money. By the end of the eighteenth century, a large number of practising upholders were not freemen of the Company. The paternalistic purpose of the Upholders' Company had ended. The Company became more of a social and

[5] Kirkham, *London Furniture Trade*, 136. Other notable London upholders and furniture-makers with no livery membership included William Hallett and John Cobb, who, like Chippendale, completed non-London apprenticeships.

philanthropic organization than a livery company representing the members and apprentices in the trade.

From the late-seventeenth century to the end of the eighteenth century, the business practices of upholders significantly changed. At the beginning of the century, most upholders were manufacturers, assemblers, and sellers of the goods needed to furnish a residential interior. Changing furnishing styles often required specialists to work with new methods and materials. Campbell elaborated on the specialized tradesmen that upholders employed to produce their goods. These included cabinet-makers, carvers, glass grinders, frame-makers, and screen-makers, among others. A large upholding business probably employed many of these specialists or used sub-contractors, such as gilders. Smaller firms would have subcontracted much of this specialized work. According to Campbell, the cabinet-maker was the upholder's right-hand man for all things mahogany and walnut.[6]

Around mid-century, the business model general upholders used included extra business lines because of their desire to earn more money. Another conclusion is that the eighteenth century was one of increased demand from consumers for household goods, as exemplified by upholders who adapted to eighteenth-century changes in taste and style, especially with furniture. Thomas Chippendale kept abreast of these changes and published his famous *Director* in 1754, which presented choices in design and style. Upholders were among the subscribers and able to copy these elite designs.[7] As the middling ranks grew and new goods replaced used ones, there developed a vibrant market for used household goods, giving consumers the option of purchasing quality used goods rather than new ones.[8] Upholders selling household goods to the middling ranks

[6] R. Campbell, *The London Tradesman* (London: T. Gardner, 1747), Campbell, 172–76.

[7] Thomas Chippendale, *The gentleman and cabinet-maker's director* (London: Thomas Chippendale, 1754), vii-x. The subscribers listed as upholders were: James Affleck, John Bladwell, Robert Barker, James Caddell (upholsterer); Collins, Henry Constable (upholsterer), Richard Dark (upholsterer); Elwick, Richard Farrer, Edward Good, William Hunter; Hardman, John Jeffries; Kitpin; Mainlove, William Miller, George Reynoldson, Paul Saunders (upholsterer); Sackham; Shane, Francis Say, and Richard Wright.

[8] Jon Stobart and Illia Van Damme, "Introduction," in *Modernity and the Second-Hand Trade: European Consumption Cultures and Practices, 1700–1900*, ed. Jon Stobart and Ilia Van Damme (Basingstoke: Palgrave Macmillan, 2010), 4–6; Clive Edwards and Margaret Ponsonby, "Polarization of the Second-Hand Market for Furniture in the Nineteenth Century," in *Modernity and the Second-Hand Trade: European Consumption Cultures and Practices, 1700–1900*, ed. Jon Stobart and Ilia Van Damme (Basingstoke: Palgrave Macmillan,

offered new and used items, aiming to maximize revenue potential through increased choices.

Readings in secondary sources allow one to conclude that the upholding trade evolved from a number of occurrences that, when accumulated, drove the upholding trade to adapt to changes in fashion and style, adopt new ways of conducting business, and enter new business lines. New general business models for upholders appeared. These were diverse in business lines and primarily driven by a desire for increased financial success. Overall, upholders were industrious, adaptable, fashion conscious, and business savvy.

Upholders wanting to increase their profits needed to adapt to changes in styles and materials. Not to do so meant having stock in trade that either did not sell or needed to be marked down in price. The research indicates that successful upholders consistently searched for ways to increase business revenue. Part of this transformation was selling convenience to the consumer. In funeral undertaking, for instance, they realized that there was a demand for fully managed funerals. Through reusing and renting some items and using their supply networks, upholders were able to provide a 'decent' funeral at a cost lower than if the items were gotten separately.

By the second-half of the eighteenth century, the London upholding trade had three distinct business lines: furniture-making, upholstery, and funeral undertaking. It was not unusual for upholders to concentrate on only one or two of these lines, and some found a specialty or niche business. A few even promoted items like window blinds or insect killer to supplement their income.[9]

In Chap. 2, the undertaking and funeral trade is categorized as a core business line for general upholders, along with furniture-making and upholstery. Undertaking and funeral management evolved into an

2010), 93–5; Jon Stobart, "Luxury and Country House Sales in England, c. 1760–1830," in *The Afterlife of Used Things: Recycling in the Long Eighteenth Century*, ed. Ariane Fennetaux, Amélie Junqua, and Sophie Vasset (New York: Routledge, 2015), 31–2, 34; Olivia Fryman, "Recycling Furniture in the Late Stuart Court (1689–1714)," in *The Afterlife of Used Things: Recycling in the Long Eighteenth Century*, ed. Ariane Fennetaux, Amélie Junqua, and Sophie Vasset (New York: Routledge, 2015), 89–92.

[9] *Gazetteer and New Daily Advertiser*, 20 July 1765. R. Adamson, upholder and cabinet-maker of Fenchurch Street, advertised he made Venetian window blinds. *Gazetteer and New Daily Advertiser*, 9 July 1765. John Muckleson, upholder and undertaker of Holborn, thanked his customers for using his services to rid their homes of bed bugs.

important business line for many upholders by the middle of the eighteenth century. Undertaking had been associated with upholders since the last part of the seventeenth century, when it started with a handful of full-time suppliers of funeral goods and services. It is not surprising that upholders began to dominate the funeral undertaking business during the first quarter of the eighteenth century. Funerals during that time used a lot of fabric, and upholders' skill in upholstery gave them a natural fit in that business line. One late seventeenth-century business practice that upholders adopted was the letting or renting out of certain funeral undertaking materials, especially those made of fabric. The ability to rent these materials gave individual upholders flexibility in deciding how deeply they wanted to be involved with funeral undertaking. By the second-half of the eighteenth century, many upholders were advertising undertaking, funeral furnishing, or funeral management. There were nuanced differences in these terms, although all three terms were connected to the business of death and burial. Only a few upholders were full-time funeral undertakers, even though many upholders advertised themselves as being in this facet of their trade.

The undertaking funeral management trade thrived because it was not costly for families and offered them convenience. A major convenience was that families could spend more time grieving and dividing the estate rather than making funeral arrangements. While upholstery and furniture-making were manufacturing and assembly business lines, funeral undertaking was partially a manufacturing and assembly business and partially a service business. Depending on an upholder's preferences, funeral undertaking services could include preparing the corpse for burial, selling coffins from stock or sourcing them, renting out or selling the needed fabrics for a respectable funeral, providing the processional hearse and carriages, and hiring the necessary burial attendants.

Political, economic, and social changes by 1690 allowed the funeral undertaking trade to emerge as a commercial business opportunity. It was a growth business at the beginning of the eighteenth century, but by the end of the century, the lack of pricing power signalled that funeral undertaking had become a competitive and high-risk business. During the course of one hundred years, funeral undertaking evolved from being a profitable growth business into a business line with moderate growth potential and low profitability. The business risks did not match the low investment returns. This mismatch resulted in a consolidation of funeral providers and the establishment of a separate funeral trade by the end of the eighteenth century.

Upholders' involvement in appraising, brokering, and auctioneering (Chap. 3) was part of the evolution of upholding in the eighteenth century. These services were ways for upholders to supplement their upholding income with minimal risk. The increase in consumerism near the end of the Seven Years' War was the catalyst for upholders entering these businesses as an extension of their core business lines of selling household goods. As the demand for these services increased, upholders looked to them as a revenue enhancement.

Sworn brokers and appraisers swore an oath to act fairly and honestly in their business dealings. It was a part-time or occasional business for them, and their strategy, it appears from the evidence, was to offer these services to supplement their upholding revenue. Appraising fees were standardized and not particularly appealing when one considers the risks of being required to purchase the goods if they failed to sell at their appraised value. Brokering could be as simple as taking used goods on consignment, but another route was to purchase used household goods and sell them in the shop or at auction.

There is no single reason that explains the increase in sworn brokers and appraisers after 1760. Between 1700 and 1760, only four upholders became sworn brokers. Fifty-eight upholders became sworn brokers from 1760 to 1800. The first possible explanation is that the Seven Years' War was coming to an end, although directly linking the war's ending to the increase is difficult. There is no apparent correlation between war and peace and upholder broker admissions other than that peace generally reduces business risk. Another possible reason for increased upholder broker admissions concerns the acceleration of consumer spending near the end of the war. As the elite and upper middling sorts increased their consumption of new and fashionable household goods, a surplus of used household goods was created. London's population growth from migration and immigration created a demand for these used goods. An additional explanation is that brokers of household goods were legally required to become sworn. Government regulation made acquiring this prestigious designation difficult. It is doubtful upholders became sworn solely because of the law as no evidence of increased enforcement of this law was found. The best explanation for the increase in upholders becoming sworn is there was increased demand for valuing and selling bankrupt estates and providing insurance valuations. A natural supposition here is that the increase in upholders becoming sworn brokers and appraisers made them seem more trustworthy. Nonetheless, upholders entered these business lines to earn more money. It may be that upholders were attracted to these service lines because it seemed like 'easy' money, that is earning money with minimal effort and risk.

There was also a notable increase in upholders advertising auctions by 1760. Upholders recognized that auctioneering was a growth business in which they could specialize as an extension to upholding. Because an upholder advertised an auction did not necessarily mean he/she was actually conducting the auction. Most upholders participated in auctioneering on a peripheral basis, acting as agents by providing information, answering questions, and handing out catalogues for the actual auctioneer, presumably for a small fee. There were few barriers to entering the auction business, which would have made it a very competitive activity. However, competition was lessened because operating a salesroom and hiring staff was expensive. Very few upholders became full-time auctioneers.

This research also found that upholders often acted as agents for their customers in a variety of personal ways by providing what might be called agency services for specific situations. For example, newspaper advertisements were placed by upholders on behalf of owners for the return of lost jewellery, watches, and wallets. It is possible these items had been pickpocketed, and a reward (ransom) would be paid for the return of the 'lost' item. Upholders also acted as agents for the selling and letting of land and buildings. If a customer needed a manager for their estate's deer herd or wanted to sell a pack of fox hounds, upholders were helpful in identifying interested parties. From these agency services, one can conclude that upholders were often seen as trusted advisers by their clients in areas beyond tastefully furnishing a residence.

Robert Williams was an apprentice upholder who eventually bought his master's business and developed a specialty in 'fitting out' East India Company (EIC) ship officer cabins. His account book reveals that he also had a substantial business in selling luxury household goods to EIC ship officers for their private trading in foreign ports. Williams eventually became the managing partner of a well-known bank, owned EIC ships, served as an MP, and owned two country estates. Williams's career trajectory and wealth accumulation were remarkable. Was he a self-made man? The research found that his father came from a lesser gentry family. His older brother, a former EIC ship captain and partner in the bank, gave Robert the business introductions he needed to enter these businesses.

'Fitting out' EIC officer quarters and selling household goods to ship officers for their private trading was a specialized extension of the upholding trade. However, Williams's entry into the banking business had no connection to the upholding trade. It was an opportunistic and profitable investment.

John Trotter, like Robert Williams, developed an upholding specialty. Trotter came from a minor Scottish gentry family and was apprenticed to Henry Williams, the royal joiner. (There is no known family relationship between Henry Williams and Robert Williams.) Trotter was appointed the royal upholsterer, a prestigious and profitable position. The goods he provided were varied and included bedroom items such as mattresses, blankets, and canopies. Trotter left the Great Wardrobe in 1761 and, subsequently, was best known as a military contractor, mainly supplying British army camp equipment that was shipped to North America, Germany, and throughout Britain. Army camp equipment contracting was an opportunistic business and a very difficult one to break into. Like Williams, Trotter cannot be called a self-made man. He had the advantages of being born into a gentry family, an apprenticeship with an elite joiner, and access to money from his mother, marriage settlement, and his cousins, the Coutts brothers.

Over the course of the eighteenth century, the London upholding trade evolved into a trade that did more than merely furnish residences. Upholders were the main purveyors of tasteful and stylish interior furnishings to the elite and middling ranks. They advised and assisted clients in furnishing rooms and even entire floors, and many understood how to create an overall theme through coordinating the use of furniture, upholstery, floor coverings, curtains, wallpaper, and decorative items. Upholders catering to the middling ranks also could furnish an entire space, often using sketches to allow their clients to visualize how a space would look. Beyond the furnishing of homes, many upholders were providing comprehensive funeral undertaking services at reasonable costs by the mid-eighteenth century. As it was with household goods, consumers of funeral goods and services now had choices in how to spend their money. Funeral undertakers offered convenience and all-inclusiveness for funeral goods and services rather than the family having to make the arrangements and acquire the necessary goods on their own. Toward the end of the Seven Years' War, some upholders added sworn appraiser and broker designations to their business expertise. These were service businesses that involved the valuing and selling of used household goods from bankruptcy, probate, and items replaced by new furniture. Appraisals for household insurance were also needed. Upholders also participated in the auction business, although few were the actual auctioneers. They mostly provided catalogues and answered questions about an upcoming auction. Finally, newspaper advertisements highlight how upholders were often trusted agents. A client could have an upholder, for instance, act as an intermediary for the return of property or the sale or lease of a residence.

Important conclusions about London's eighteenth-century upholders are made in this book. First, upholders were the main providers of residential furnishings, and they were profit-motivated. Not all upholders were members of London's Upholders' Company. Some belonged to the Joiners' Company or other liveries. Later in the eighteenth century, more and more upholders had no livery affiliation. The upholding trade was evolutionary, and upholders adapted to changes in fashion and material. Many upholders adopted new business lines to supplement their income, including funeral undertaking, broker and appraisal services, and auctioneering. Those offering these additional business lines were comprehensive upholders rather than general upholders. After the Seven Years' War, bankruptcy became a growing risk they all faced, especially because of the wide use of credit. By around 1760, upholders increasingly used newspaper advertising to promote their businesses. Convenience and service were important attributes of a successful upholder, and they often provided trusted agency services for their customers. Although most upholders were able to earn a respectable living as tradesmen, some did manage to become wealthy. Finally, the research found that those upholders who amassed great wealth probably came from a gentry background and had access to the money needed to take advantage of new business opportunities unrelated to upholding. Indeed, upholders created a new form of commercial, domestic service in eighteenth-century London.

Bibliography

I. *Manuscripts and Repository Sources*

The British Library, London

Mss Eur D1051. Account Book for the *Sulivan*.
Mss Eur D1051/7. Account Book for the *Hindostan*.

Dorset Record Office, Dorset

D289/F1. Robert Williams Warrant for the Pew No. 1B, St. Paul, Covent Garden.
Williams of Bridehead, Littlebredy, Archive fonds. D-WIB 1737–1924 Fanny Williams sub-series. D-WIB/C/1-6 1802–1817.

Guildhall Repository, City of London

Worshipful Company of Upholders in the City of London. *Meeting Notes of the Court of Assistants and Livery*.

S. Sanders, *The Eighteenth-Century London Upholder*,
https://doi.org/10.1007/978-3-032-08660-0

Hertfordshire Archives and Local Studies, Hertford

GH 723. Williams and Chassereau Accounting.
GH 1675-77. Account Book for the *General Coote*.
GH 851. Marriage Settlement between Robert Williams and Rev. Edward Aubery.
GH 1729. Stamp Office Legacy Duty on Residues of Personal Estates for Robert Williams.

London Metropolitan Archives, City of London

Reference Code: ACC/0426. Account Book of Robert Williams.
Reference Number: COL/CHD/FR/02/0689-0-696. Apprenticeship Indenture of John Trotter.
Reference Code: COL/BR/02/074-075. Index to Brokers' Bonds A-H and I-Z.
Reference Code: COL/BR05. Broker Sureties 1752–1813.
Sworn Broker Archives.

The National Archives, Kew

PROB 11/1166/325. Will of Francis Chassereau.
PROB 11/927/291. Will of Francis Chassereau (the Younger).
PROB 11/1159/4. Will of George Good, Auctioneer of Racquet Court Fleet Street. 2 November 1787.
PROB 11/1194. Will of John Trotter, Soho Square, Middlesex. 24 July 1790.
PROB 11/1552/502. Will of Robert Williams, Banker of Moor Park.
Series IR 1. Register of Duties Paid for Apprentices' Indentures, 1710–1811. Board of Stamps: Apprenticeship Books.
Lord Chamberlain's Appointment Books-Series II, 1755–1760. Reference: LC3/66. Royal appointment of John Trotter, 7 January 1756.
Lord Chamberlain's Appointment Books–Series II, 1760–1793.
Lord Chamberlain's Department 5/202, pp. 145–46, 8 May 1703, Order in Council excepting Household Officers from serving in local office.
Lord Chamberlain's Department, Great Wardrobe, Bill books: series II: tradesmen's bills etc. 10/10/1755-10/10/1756. Reference: LC 9/301.
Lord Chamberlain's Department, Great Wardrobe, Bill books: series II: tradesmen's bills etc. 10/10/1756-10/10/1757. Reference: LC 9/302.
Lord Chamberlain's Department, Great Wardrobe, Day Book, 17/11/1758-17/11/1760. Reference: LC 9/212.
Lord Chamberlain's Department, Great Wardrobe, Bill books: series II: tradesmen's bills etc. 10/10/1759-10/25/1760. Reference: LC 9/305.

Lord Chamberlain's Department, Great Wardrobe, Bill books: series II: tradesmen's bills etc. 10/10/1760-10/10/1761. Reference: LC 9/306.

Lord Chamberlain's Department, Records of Special Events. Funeral of Princess Caroline, daughter of George II, Funeral of Princess Elizabeth Caroline, and Funeral of King George II. Reference: LC 2/27.

Lord Chamberlain's Department, Records of Special Events. Coronation: George III and Queen Charlotte. Reference: LC 2/30.

Revenue Commissioners and Boards of Customs: Miscellaneous Books. Register of Seizures. CUST 21/75. No. 50, 3 July 1772.

Treasury Board Minutes. 1/12/1757-30/11/1760. Reference: T 29/33.

Treasury Papers. NORTH AMERICA: Provisioning: T 1/396. 28 June 1759. Memorial of John Trotter To Right Honourable Viscount Barrington, His Majesty's Secretary of War. Provisioning: Memorial of John Trotter asking payment for provisions supplied to America.

Surrey History Centre, Woking

Surrey History Centre, Woking. Properties of John Trotter in Epsom and Elsewhere: Deeds and Papers. SHC Ref. No. 186.

II. *Personal Correspondence with Author*

Powys-Lybbe, Timothy (heir general of John Trotter).

Williams, Sir Robert Philip, Bt., of Bridehead, Dorset (great-great-great-great grandson of Robert Williams).

III. *Newspapers and Periodicals*

Country Chronicle, September 1729.
Daily Advertiser, 1 April 1743.
Daily Advertiser, 17 June 1772.
Daily Advertiser, 26 February 1773.
Daily Advertiser, 7 December 1773.
Daily Advertiser, 17 September 1775.
Daily Advertiser, 21 October 1775.
Daily Advertiser, 2 February 1776.
Daily Advertiser, 16 February 1776.
Daily Advertiser, 18 October 1777.
Daily Advertiser, 12 February 1783.
Daily Courant, 17 February 1722.
Daily Courant, 31 January 1722.

Daily Post, 31 January 1722.
Daily Post, 27 February 1723.
Daily Post, 14 February 1732.
Gazetteer and London Daily Advertiser, 7 June 1763.
Gazetteer and New Daily Advertiser, 17 September 1764.
Gazetteer and New Daily Advertiser, 9 July 1766.
Gazetteer and New Daily Advertiser, 23 July 1766.
Gazetteer and New Daily Advertiser, 12 November 1766.
Gazetteer and New Daily Advertiser, 4 February 1768.
Gazetteer and New Daily Advertiser, 13 June 1768.
Gazetteer and New Daily Advertiser, 2 December 1768.
Gazetteer and New Daily Advertiser, 28 April 1770.
Gazetteer and New Daily Advertiser, 11 July 1771.
Gazetteer and New Daily Advertiser, 2 July 1772.
Gazetteer and New Daily Advertiser, 6 July 1772.
Gazetteer and New Daily Advertiser, 6 July 1772.
Gazetteer and New Daily Advertiser, 13 June 1777.
Gazetteer and New Daily Advertiser, 27 November 1777.
General Evening Post, 7–9 May 1751.
Gentleman's Magazine, Vol. XLI, 4 May 1771.
The Gentleman's Magazine: AND Historical Chronicle, January to June 1814, VOLUME LXXXIV.
Impartial Protestant Mercury or Occurrences Foreign and Domestick, 28 April–2 May 1682.
London Chronicle, 8–11 February 1766.
London Daily Post and General Advertiser, 17 January 1739.
London Evening Post, 23–25 June 1752.
London Evening Post, 18–20 January 1759.
London Gazette, 12–17 December 1774.
London Gazette, 25–29 November 1777.
Loyal Protestant and True Domestick Intelligence, 1 July 1682.
Middlesex Journal or Chronicle of Liberty, 8–10 October 1771.
Morning Chronicle and London Advertiser, 15 May 1773.
Morning Herald, 19 January 1789.
Morning Post and Daily Advertiser, 4 May 1775.
Morning Post and Daily Advertiser, 30 August 1776.
Post Boy, 8–11 February 1701.
Public Advertiser, 27 February 1755.
Public Advertiser, 29 March 1756.
Public Advertiser, 14 April 1769.
Public Advertiser, 4 December 1773.
Public Advertiser, 1 November 1775.

Public Advertiser, 31 January 1776.
Public Advertiser, 6 January 1777.
Public Advertiser, 3 November 1786.
Public Ledger, 14 October 1773.
Read's Weekly Journal or British Gazetteer, 4 August 1753.
Weekly Journal or British Gazetteer, 8 April 1721.
World, 23 January 1788.
World, 1 December 1788.

IV. *Unpublished Academic Work*

Perry, Rayne. *Pierre Langlois and the Eighteenth-Century Commode*. Glasgow: Unpublished Master of Letters Thesis at University of Glasgow/Christie's Education, 2011.

V. *Books published in the Seventeenth and Eighteenth Centuries*

Anon. *Funeral discipline: or, the character of Strip-Corps the dead-monger. According to the instructions of Paul Meagre, once mourner in chief to the funeral undertaker.* London: J. Roberts and A. Dodd, 1725.
Bailey, W. *Bailey's List of Bankrupts, Dividends and Certificates from the Year 1772 to 1793, Both Included with the Names and Residence of the Different Solicitors Under Each*. Vol. 1. London: T. Williams, 1794.
Campbell, R. *The London Tradesman*. London: T. Gardner, 1747.
Centlivre, Susanna. *A Bickerstaff's burying; or, work for the upholders. A farce; as it is acted at the theatres, with applause. By His Majesty's servants.* Dublin: S. Powell, 1724.
Chippendale, Thomas. *The gentleman and cabinet-maker's director…* London: Thomas Chippendale, 1754.
Cock, Christopher. *Bibliothecæ Bridgesianæ catalogus: or, a catalogue of the entire library of John Bridges*. London: J. Tonson and J. Watts, 1726.
———*A catalogue of Her Grace Kathrine Duchess of Buckingham's jewel's &c.* London: For the Author, 1744.
———*A catalogue of the entire collection belonging to Sir James Thornhill, late principal history painter to His Majesty, &c.* London: For the Author, 1735.
Farington, Joseph. *The Farington Diary*. Vol. VII, ed. James Greig, 1927. London: Hutchinson & Co., 1813.
Hardy, Charles. *A Register of Ships, Employed in the Service of the Honorable the United East India Company, from the Year 1760 to 1810*. Reprint. Memphis: General Books LLC, 2012.

Hogarth, William. *The Analysis of Beauty*. Reprint. Pittsfield, MA: The Silver Lotus Shop, 1909.
King, Gregory. *A scheme of the rates and duties granted to His Majesty upon marriages, births and burials*. London: Charles Bill, 1695.
Mortimer, Thomas. *Every Man His Own Broker*. London: S. Hooper, 1761.
———Merchant's Directory, *Being a Guide to all Men in Business*. 4th ed. London: J. Rivington and Son, 1783.
Planner, John. *The Town and Country Auctioneer's Guide, Containing the Abstracts of All the Acts of Parliament Relating to the Management and Collection of the Auction Duties*. London: T. Burton, 1797.
Rolt, Richard. *A new dictionary of trade and commerce, compiled from the information of the most eminent merchants, and from the works of the best writers on commercial subjects, in all languages. ... By Mr. Rolt, with the assistance of several eminent merchants*. London: T. Osborne and J. Shipton; J. Hodges; J. Newbery; G. Keith; and B. Collins, 1756.
Steele, Richard. *The funeral: or, grief a-la-mode: A Comedy*. 1701. Rev. ed. London: J. Tonson, 1723.
Waller, Thomas. *A general description of all trades, digested in alphabetical order: by which parents, guardians, and trustees, may make choice of trades agreeable to the capacity, education, inclination, strength, and fortune of the youth*. London: Printed at Crown and Mitre, 1747.
Walsby, John, Capt. *The ship's husband; a narrative; being a state of facts; addressed to the honorable Court of Directors of the East India Company; the ships' husbands, and commanders and others in that service*. London: Sold by T. Richardson, T. and J. Egerton, J. Ridgway, and H.D. Symonds, 1791.
Winstanley, Richard. *Silk throwsters, &c. A catalogue of ten pair of double Dutch silk mills, with reels, spindles, and iron-work complete, in very good repair* ... London: For the Author, 1787.

VI. *Secondary Books*

Addy, John. *Death, Money and the Vultures Inheritance and Avarice 1600–1750*. Abingdon: Routledge, 2013.
Agnew, David. *Protestant Exiles from France, Chiefly in the Reign of Louis XIV*. 3rd ed., Vol. 2. For Private Circulation, 1886.
Anon. *The English Reports*. Vol. XXXV. London: Stevens & Sons, Ltd., 1904.
Auber, Peter. *Analysis of the Constitution of the East India Company and of the Laws Passed by Parliament*. London: Kingsbury, Parbury, and Allen, 1826.
Ayres, David A.C. *Fripperers to Upholders*. London: Sustine Press, 2020.
Balen, Malcolm. *The Secret History of the South Sea Bubble: The World's First Great Financial Scandal*. New York: Fourth Estate, 2003.

Bannerman, Gordon. *Merchants and the Military in Eighteenth-Century Britain.* London: Pickering & Chatto, 2008.

Batchelor, Jennie and Kaplan, Cora. *Women and Material Culture, 1660–1830.* Basingstoke: Palgrave Macmillan, 2007.

Bayne, Robert. *Moor Park with a biographical sketch of its principal proprietors...* London: Longmans, Green and Co., 1871.

Beard, Geoffrey. *Upholsterers and Interior Furnishing in England 1530–1840.* New Haven & London: Yale University Press, 1997.

Beard, Geoffrey and Gilbert, Christopher, eds. *Dictionary of English Furniture Makers 1660–1840.* London: Furniture History Society, 1986.

Berman, Ric. *Schism: The Battle that Forged Freemasonry.* Eastbourne: Sussex Academic Press, 2013.

Black, Jeremy. *Culture in Eighteenth–Century England: A Subject for Taste.* London: Hambledon Continuum, 2007a.

———George II*: Puppet of the Politicians?* Exeter: University of Exeter Press, 2007b.

Bowett, Adam. *Early Georgian Furniture 1715–1740.* Woodbridge: Antique Collectors' Club, 2009.

———English Furniture *1660–1714 From Charles II to Queen Anne.* Woodbridge: Antique Collectors' Club, 2002.

Brewer, John. *The Pleasures of the Imagination.* London: Routledge, 2013.

Bucholz, Robert and Ward, Joseph. *London: A Social and Cultural History 1550–1750.* Cambridge: Cambridge University Press, 2012.

Burke, Bernard. *A Genealogical and Heraldic History of the Landed Gentry of Great Britain & Ireland.* Vol. II. London: Harrison, 1871.

Burke, John. *A Genealogical and Heraldic History of the Commoners of Great Britain and Ireland.* Vol. 1. London: Henry Colburn, 1836.

Carswell, John. *The South Sea Bubble.* Rev. ed. Dover: Alan Sutton, 1993.

Clouston, R.S. *English Furniture and Furniture Makers of the 18th Century.* London: Hurst and Blackett, Ltd., 1906.

Earle, Peter. *The Making of the Middle Class.* Berkeley: University of California Press, 1989.

Edwards, Clive. *Turning Houses into Homes: A History of the Retailing and Consumption of Domestic Furnishings.* London: Routledge, 2017.

Farrell, Stephen. *The History of Parliament: the House of Commons 1820–1830.* Ed. D. R. Fisher. Robert Williams, Jr. London: Cambridge University Press, The History of Parliament Trust, 2009.

Finn, Margot. *The Character of Credit – Personal Debt in English Culture, 1740–1914.* Cambridge: Cambridge University Press, 2003.

French, Henry and Rothery, Mark. *Man's Estate: Landed Gentry Masculinities 1660–1900.* Oxford: Oxford University Press, 2012.

Gibson, William. *A Brief History of Britain 1660–1851*. London: Constable & Robinson, Ltd., 2010.

Gilbert, Christopher. *The Life & Work of Thomas Chippendale*. New York: Tabard Press, 1978.

Gittings, Clare. *Death, Burial and the Individual in Early Modern England*. Beckenham: Croom Helm Ltd., 1984.

Heal, Ambrose. *The London Furniture Makers from the Restoration to the Victorian Era 1660–1840*. London: B.T. Batsford Ltd., 1953.

Holden, Kenneth. *Williams Deacon's 1771–1970*. Manchester: McCorquodale & Co. Ltd., 1971.

Holloway, Sally. *The Game of Love in Georgian England: Courtship, Emotions, and Material Culture*. Oxford: Oxford University Press, 2019.

Hope, Valerie, Birch, Clive, Gilbert, Torry. *The Freedom: The Past and Present of the Livery, Guilds and City of London*. Buckingham: Barracuda Books Ltd., 1982.

Hoppit, Julian. *Risk and failure in English Business 1700–1800*. Cambridge: Cambridge University Press, 1987.

Houlbrooke, Ralph. *Death, Religion, and the Family in England 1480–1750*. Oxford: Oxford University Press, 2006.

Houston, J.F. *Featherbedds and Flock Bedds*. London: Three Tents Press, 2010.

Jones, Emrys, ed. *The Welsh in London 1500–2000*. Cardiff: University of Wales Press, 2001.

Kirkham, Pat. *The London Furniture Trade 1700–1870*. Leeds: Furniture History Society, 1988.

Lane, Joan. *Apprenticeship in England, 1600–1914*. London: UCL Press, 1996.

Langford, Paul. *A Polite and Commercial People: England 1727–1783*. Oxford: Clarendon Press, 1989.

Learmount, Brian. *A History of the Auction*. London: Barnard & Learmount, 1985.

Litten, Julian. *The English Way of Death: The Common Funeral Since 1450*. London: Robert Hale Ltd., 1991.

MacQuoid, Percy. *A History of English Furniture*. London: Bracken Books, 1988.

McCracken, Grant. *Culture and Consumption*. Bloomington: Indiana University Press, 1988.

McKendrick, Neil, Brewer, John, Plumb, J. H. *The Birth of a Consumer Society: The Commercialization of Eighteenth-Century England*. Bloomington: Indiana University Press, 1982.

Mingay, Gordon. *English Landed Society in the Eighteenth Century*. London: Routledge and Kegan, 1963.

Mitchell, Ian. *Tradition and Innovation in English Retailing, 1700–1850*. Farnam: Ashgate Publishing Ltd., 2014.

Montefiore, Joshua. *A Commercial Dictionary: Containing the Present State of Mercantile Law, Practice, and Custom*. London: For the Author, 1803.

Mortimer, Thomas. *A General Commercial Dictionary Comprehending Trade, Manufactures, and Navigation.* 2nd ed. APPENDIX, No. II. London: Longman, Hurst, et. al., 1819.

Nevitt, T.R. *Advertising in Britain: A History.* London: William Heinemann Ltd., 1982.

Noble, Mark. *A History of the College of Arms.* London: J. Debrett, 1804.

Oliver, J.L. *The Development and Structure of the Furniture Industry.* Oxford: Pergamon Press, 1966.

Phillips, Henry. *Annals of the Worshipful Company of Joiners of the City of London.* London: Privately Printed, 1915.

Pickering, Danny. *The Statutes at Large from the Eighth Year of King William III to the Second Year of Queen Anne.* Vol. X. London: Joseph Benthan, 1864.

Raithby, John, ed. *The Statues at Large of England and of Great-Britain: From Magna Carta to the Union of the Kingdoms of Great Britain and Ireland.* Vol. IV. London: Eyre and Strahan, 1811a.

———*The Statues at Large of England and of Great-Britain: From Magna Carta to the Union of the Kingdoms of Great Britain and Ireland.* Vol. VI. London: Eyre and Strahan, 1811b.

Rothery, Mark and French, Henry. *Making Men: The Formation of Elite Male Identities in England, c. 1660–1900.* Basingstoke: Palgrave Macmillan, 2012.

Sargentson, Carolyn. *Merchants and Luxury Markets: The Marchands Merciers of Eighteenth-Century Paris.* London, Malibu: Victoria and Albert Museum in association with the J. Paul Getty Museum, 1996.

Shimbo, Akiko. *Furniture-Makers and Consumers in England, 1754–1851: Design as Interaction.* London: Routledge, 2016.

Smith, Hannah. *Georgian Monarchy: Politics and Culture, 1714–1760.* Cambridge: Cambridge University Press, 2006.

Snodin, Michael and Styles, John. *Design & the Decorative Arts: Georgian Britain 1714–1837.* London: V&A Publications, 2004.

Stanhope, Earl. *Life of The Right Honourable William Pitt.* New edition, Vol. II. London: John Murray, 1879.

Stobart, Jon and Rothery, Mark. *Consumption and the Country House.* Oxford: Oxford University Press, 2016.

Stobart, Jon and Van Damme, Illia, eds. *Modernity and the Second-Hand Trade: European Consumption Cultures and Practices, 1700–1900.* Basingstoke: Palgrave Macmillan, 2010.

Stuart, Raymond A. *My Ancestor Was an Apprentice.* London: Society of Genealogists Enterprises Ltd., 2010.

Taylor, Lawrence. *The History of Parliament: the House of Commons 1790–1820.* Ed. R. Thorne. Ref. Vols. 1790–1820. Robert Williams. London: The History of Parliament Trust, 1986.

Thompson, Andrew. *George II: King and Elector*. London & New Haven: Yale University Press, 2011.

Vickery, Amanda. *Behind Closed Doors: At Home in Georgian England*. New Haven & London: Yale University Press, 2009.

Ward, Joseph P. *Metropolitan Communities: Trade Guilds, Identity, and Change in Early Modern London*. Stanford: Stanford University Press, 1997.

Ward-Jackson, Peter. *English Furniture Designs of the 18th Century*. London: HMSO - Victoria & Albert Museum, 1958.

Weatherill, Lorna. *Consumer Behaviour & Material Culture in Britain 1660–1760*. Abingdon: Routledge, 1996.

Wiener, Martin. *English Culture and the Decline of the Industrial Spirit, 1850–1980*. Cambridge: Cambridge University Press, 2004.

Withington, John. *Secrets of Centenarian: What it is Like to Live a Century and Which of Us Will Survive to Find Out?* London: Reaktion Books, 2017.

The Worshipful Company of Upholders. *Worshipful Company of Upholders Financial History 1678–1939*. Reprinted 1999. London: Printed for The Company, 1931.

Wrigley, E.A. and Scholfield, R.S. *The Population History of England 1541–1871*. Cambridge: Cambridge University Press, 1989.

VII. *Articles and Chapters*

Allen, Richard B. "Satisfying the 'Want for Labouring People': The European Slave Trading in the Indian Ocean, 1500–1850." *Journal of World History*, Vol. 21, No. 1 (Mar. 2010): 45–73.

Aubin, Robert A. "Behind Steele's Satire on Undertakers." *Modern Language Association*, PLMA, Vol. 64, No. 5 (Dec. 1949): 1008–1026.

Bailey, Joanne. "'I Dye [sic] by Inches': Locating Wife Beating in the Concept of Privatization of Marriage and Violence in Eighteenth-Century England." *Social History*, Vol. 31, No. 3 (Aug. 2006): 273–294.

Beckett, J.V. "The Pattern of Land Ownership in England and Wales, 1660–1880." *The Economic History Review*, Vol. 37, No. 1 (Feb. 1984): 1–22.

Begiato, Joanne. "Beyond the Rule of Thumb: The Materiality of Marital Violence in England c. 1700–1857." *Cultural and Social History*, Vol. 15, No.1 (2018): 39–59.

Berg, Maxine. "From Imitation to Invention: Creating Commodities in Eighteenth-Century Britain." *The Economic History Review*, New Series, Vol. 55, No. 1 (Feb. 2002): 1–30.

Berg, Maxine. "Luxury, The Luxury Trades, and Industrial Growth." In *The Oxford Handbook of The History of Consumption*, edited by Frank Trentmann, 173–212. Oxford: Oxford University Press, 2012.

Berry, Helen. "Regional identity and material culture." In *History and Material Culture*, edited by Karen Harvey, 139–57. Abingdon: Routledge, 2009.

Bowen, H.V. "Investment and Empire in the Later Eighteenth Century: East India Stockholding, 1756–1791." *The Economic History Review*, Vol. 42, No. 2 (May 1989): 186–206.

Bowen, H.V. "Sinews of Trade and Empire: The Supply of Commodity Exports to the East India Company during the late Eighteenth Century." *The Economic History Review*, Vol. 55, No. 3 (Aug. 2002): 466–486.

Brooks, Colin. "Political Arithmetic and the Act of 1695." *English Historical Review*, Vol. 97, No. 382 (Jan. 1982): 31–53.

Cain, P.J. and Hopkins, A.G. "Gentlemanly Capitalism and British Expansion Overseas I. The Old Colonial System, 1688–1850." *The Economic History Review*, Vol. 39, No. 4 (Nov. 1986): 501–525.

Casson, Mark and Lee, John S. "The Origin and Development of Markets: A Business History Perspective." *The Business History Review*, Vol. 85, No. 1 (Spring 2011): 9–37.

Clark, J.C.D. "Religion and Political Identity: Samuel Johnson as a Nonjuror." In *Samuel Johnson in Historical Context*, edited by Jonathan Clark and Howard Erskine-Hill, 79–145. Cambridge: Cambridge University Press, 1994.

Clayton, Timothy. "Darly, Matthias." in *Oxford Dictionary of National Biography*, Oxford: Oxford University Press, 2004: NP.

Conway, Stephen. "British Governments, Colonial Consumers, and Continental European Goods in the British Atlantic Empire, 1763–1775." *The Historical Journal*, 58, 3 (2015): 711–732.

Craske, Matthew. "Plan and Control: Design and the Competitive Spirit in Early and Mid-Eighteenth-Century England." *Journal of Design History*, Vol. 12, No. 3, Eighteenth-Century Markets and Manufacturers in England and France (1999): 187–216.

Cressy, David. "Literacy in context: meaning and measurement in early modern England." In *Consumption and the World of Goods*, edited by John Brewer and Roy Porter, 305–19. London: Routledge, 1993.

De Vries, Jan. "The Industrial Revolution and the Industrious Revolution." *The Journal of Economic History*, Vol. 54, No. 2 (Jun. 1994): 249–270.

Derry, T.K. "The Repeal of the Apprenticeship Clauses of the Statute of Apprentices." *The Economic History Review*, Vol. 3, No. 1 (Jan. 1931): 67–87.

Edwards, Clive and Ponsonby, Margaret. "Polarization of the Second-Hand Market for Furniture in the Nineteenth Century." In *Modernity and the Second-Hand Trade: European Consumption Cultures and Practices, 1700–*1900, edited by Jon Stobart and Illia Van Damme, 93–110. Basingstoke: Palgrave Macmillan, 2010.

Elliot, J.E. "The Cost of Reading in Eighteenth-Century Britain: Auction Sale Catalogues and the Cheap Literature Hypothesis." *ELH*, Vol. 77, No. 2 (Summer 2010): 353–384.

Fine, Ben and Leopold, Ellen. "Consumerism and the Industrial Revolution." *Social History*, Vol. 15, No. 2 (May 1990): 159–179.

Fletcher, Holly. "Making Beds in early modern England: sleep, matter and environmental change." *Historical Research*, XX (2024): 1–22.

French, H.R. "The search for the 'Middle Sort of People' in England, 1600–1800." *The Historical Review*, Vol. 43, No. 1 (Mar. 2000): 277–293.

Fritz, Paul. "The Undertaking Trade in England: Its Origins and Early Development, 1660–1830." *Eighteenth Century Studies*, Vol. 28, No. 2 (Winter 1994–1995): 241–253.

Fryman, Olivia. "Recycling Furniture in the Late Stuart Court (1689–1714)." In *The Afterlife of Used Things: Recycling in the Long Eighteenth Century*, edited by Ariane Fennetaux, Amélie Junqua, and Sophie Vasset, 89–106. New York: Routledge, 2015.

Freyman, Olivia. "Rich Pickings: The Royal Bed as a Perquisite 1660–1760." *Furniture History*, 2014, Vol. 50 (2014): 119–136.

Gerhold, Dorian. "The Growth of the London Carrying Trade, 1681–1838." *The Economic History Review*, Vol. 41, No. 3 (Aug. 1988): 392–410.

Gilbert, Christopher. "The Early Furniture Designs of Matthias Darly." *Furniture History*, Vol. 11 (1975): 33–39.

Gilbert, Christopher. "Chippendale as Undertaker." *Furniture History*, Vol. 9 (1973): 114–118.

Gittings, Clare. "Sacred and secular: 1558–1660." In *Death in England: An Illustrated History*, edited by Peter C. Jupp and Clare Gittings, 147–73. New Brunswick: Rutgers University Press, 2000.

Glaisyer, Natasha. "Networking: Trade and Exchange in the Eighteenth-Century British Empire." *The Historical Journal*, Vol. 47, No. 2 (Jun. 2004): 451–476.

Grassby, Richard. "Material Culture and Cultural History." *The Journal of Interdisciplinary History*, Vol. 39, No. 4 (Spring 2005): 591–603.

Green, Georgina. "Valentines, the Raymonds and Company Material Culture." In *East India Company at Home, 1757–1857*, edited by Margot Margot and Kate Smith, 231–50. London: UCL Press, 2018.

Greig, Hannah and Vickery, Amanda. "The Political Day in London, C. 1697–1834." *Past & Present*, Vol. 252, Issue 1 (August 2021): 101–137.

Habakkuk, J.J. "Marriage Settlements in the Eighteenth Century," *Transactions of the Royal Historical Society*, 1959, Vol. 32: 15–32.

Harris, J.R. "Copper and Shipping in the Eighteenth Century." *The Economic History Review*, New Series, Vol.19, No. 3 (1996): 550–568.

Hartle, Robert, Jeffries, Nigel, and Pearce, Jaqui, "Household Assemblages Discarded by Moorfields Brokers: Material Culture in 18th-Century",

Transactions of the London & Middlesex Archaeology Society, Volume 72 (2021): 301–348.

Harvey, Karen. "Introduction." In *History and Material Culture*, edited by Karen Harvey, 1–25. Abingdon: Routledge, 2009.

Hay, Douglas. "Patronage, Paternalism, and Welfare: Masters, Workers, and Magistrates in Eighteenth-Century England." *International Labor and Working-Class History*, No. 53 (Spring 1998): 27–48.

Heckscher, Morrison. "Chippendale's Director: A Manifesto of Furniture Design." *The Metropolitan Museum of Art Bulletin*, Vol. 75, No. 4 (Spring 2018): 1–50.

Heller, Benjamin. "The 'Mene Peuple' and the Polite Spectator: The Individual in the Crowd at Eighteenth-Century London Fairs." *Past & Present*, No. 208 (Aug. 2010): 131–157.

Hoh-Cheung and Mui, Lorna. "William Pitt and the Enforcement of the Commutation Act, 1784 – 1788." *The English Historical Review*, Vol. 76, No. 300 (Jul. 1961): 447–465.

Houlbrooke, Ralph. "The age of decency: 1660–1760." In *Death in England: An Illustrated History*, edited by Peter C. Jupp and Clare Gittings, 174–201. New Brunswick: Rutgers University Press, 2000.

Hoppit, Julian. "Financial Crises in Eighteenth-Century England." *The Economic History Review*, New Series, Vol. 39, No. 1 (Feb. 1986): 39–58.

Hoppit, Julian. "Gregory King (1648–1712)." in *Oxford Dictionary of National Biography*. Oxford: Oxford University Press, 2004: NP.

Horrell, Sara, Humphries, Jane, and Sneath, Ken. "Consumption conundrums unraveled." *Economic History Review*, 68, 3, (2015): 830–857.

Innes, Joanna. "The King's Bench prison in the later 18th century: law, authority, and order in a London debtor's prison." In *An Ungovernable People*, edited by John Brewer and John Styles, 250–98. New Brunswick: Rutgers University Press, 1980.

Jenner, Mark. "Death, Decomposition and Dechristianisation? Public Health and Church Burial in Eighteenth-Century England." *The English Historical Review*, Vol. 120, No. 487 (Jun. 2005): 615–632.

Kellett, J.R. "The Breakdown of Gild and Corporation Control over the Handicraft and Retail Trade in London." *The Economic History Review*, New Series, Vol. 10, No. 3 (1958): 381–394.

Klein, Lawrence E. "Politeness and the Interpretation of the British Eighteenth Century." *The Historical Journal*, Vol. 45, No. 4 (Dec. 2002): 869–898.

Laurence, Anne. "Using buildings to understand social history." In *History and Material Culture*, edited by Karen Harvey, 103–22. Abingdon: Routledge, 2009.

Leunig, Tim, Minns, Chris, and Wallis, Patrick. "Networks in the Premodern Economy: The Market for London Apprenticeships, 1600–1749." *The Journal of Economic History*, Vol. 71, No. 2 (Jun. 2011): 413–443.

Levene, Alysa. "'Honesty, Sobriety and Diligence': Master–Apprentice Relations in Eighteenth- and Nineteenth-Century England." *Social History*, Vol. 33, No. 2 (May 2008): 183–200.

London Metropolitan Archives. *Sworn Broker Archives*, Leaflet No. 15.

McKendrick, Neal. "Josiah Wedgwood: An Eighteenth-Century Entrepreneur in Salesmanship and Marketing Techniques." *The Economic History Review*, New Series, Vol. 12, No. 3 (1960): 408–433.

McKendrick, Neil. "Josiah Wedgwood and Cost Accounting in the Industrial Revolution." *The Economic History Review*, Vol. 23, No. 1 (Apr. 1970): 45–67.

Milka, Amy. "Feeling for Forgers: Character, Sympathy and Financial Crime in London during the Late Eighteenth Century." *Journal of Eighteenth-Century Studies*, Vol. 42, No. 1 (2019): 7–25.

Miller, P.J. "Women's Education, 'Self-Improvement' and Social Mobility – A Late Eighteenth Century Debate." *British Journal of Educational Studies*, Vol. 20, No. 3 (Oct. 1972): 302–314.

Morgan, Kenneth. "Remittance Procedures in the Eighteenth-Century British Slave Trade." *The Business History Review*, Vol. 79, No. 4 (Winter 2005): 715–749.

Morrall, Andrew. "Ornament as evidence." In *History and Material Culture*, edited by Karen Harvey, 47–66. Abingdon: Routledge, 2009.

Nenadic, Stana. "Portraits of Scottish Professional Men in London, c. 1760–1830: Careers, Connections and Reputations." *Journal for Eighteenth-Century Studies*, Vol. 34, No. 3 (2011): 1–17.

Pearson, Robin. "Moral Hazard and the Assessment of Insurance Risk in Eighteenth- and Early-Nineteenth-Century Britain." *The Business History Review*, Vol. 76, No. 1 (Spring 2002): 1–35.

Pennell, Sara. "'All but the Kitchen Sink': Household Sales and the Circulation of Second-Hand Goods in Early Modern England." In *Modernity and the Second-Hand Trade: European Consumption Cultures and Practices, 1700*–1900, edited by Jon Stobart and Illia Van Damme, 37–56. Basingstoke: Palgrave Macmillan, 2010.

Pennell, Sara. "Consumption and Consumerism in Early Modern England." *The Historical Journal*, Vol. 42, No. 2 (Jun. 1999): 549–564.

Pennell, Sara. "Material Culture in Seventeenth-Century 'Britain': The Matter of Domestic Consumption." In *The Oxford Handbook of The History of Consumption*, edited by Frank Trentmann, 64–84. Oxford: Oxford University Press, 2012.

Pennell, Sara. "Mundane materiality, or, should small things still be forgotten?" In *History and Material Culture*, edited by Karen Harvey, 173–91. Abingdon: Routledge, 2009.

Philips, C.H. and D. "Alphabetical List of Directors of the East India Company from 1758 to 1858." *Journal of the Royal Asiatic Society of Great Britain & Ireland*, New Series, 73, (Oct. 1941): 325–336.

Ponsonby, Margaret. "Ideals, Reality and Meaning: Homemaking in England in the First Half of the Nineteenth Century." *Journal of Design History*, Vol. 16, No. 3 (2003): 201–214.

Randall, Richard H., Jr. "The French Taste." *Bulletin of the Museum of Fine Arts*, Vol. 60, No. 320 (1962): 46–55.

Rapp, Dean. "Social Mobility in the Eighteenth Century: The Whitbreads of Bedfordshire, 1720–1815." *The Economic History Review*, Vol. 27, No. 3 (Aug. 1974): 380–394.

Rugg, Julie. "From reason to regulation: 1760–1850." In *Death in England: An Illustrated History*, edited by Peter C. Jupp and Clare Gittings, 202–29. New Brunswick: Rutgers University Press, 2000.

Sanderson, Michael. "Literacy and Social Mobility in the Industrial Revolution in England." *Past & Present*, No. 56 (Aug. 1972): 75–104.

Sarin, Sophie. "The Floorcloth and Other Floor Coverings in the London Domestic Interior 1700–1800." *Journal of Design History*, Vol. 18, No. 2 (Summer 2005): 133–145.

Schmelzing, Paul. "Eight centuries of global real interest rates, R–G, and the 'suprasecular' decline, 1311–2018." *Bank of England*, Staff Working Paper No. 845, (Jan. 2020): 1–108.

Shammas, Carole. "Changes in English and Anglo-American consumption from 1550 to 1800." In *Consumption and the World of Goods*, edited by John Brewer and Roy Porter, 177–205. London: Routledge, 1993.

Sims, Ashley. "'Selling Consumption': An Examination of Eighteenth-Century English Trade Cards." *Graduate Journal of Visual and Material Culture*, Issue 5 (2012): 1–21.

Smail, John. "Credit, Risk, and Honor in Eighteenth-Century Commerce." *Journal of British Studies*, Vol. 44, No. 3 (Jul. 2005): 439–456.

Smith, Kate. "Sensing Design and Workmanship: The Haptic Skills of Shoppers in Eighteenth-Century London." *Journal of Design History*, Vol. 25, No. 1 (2012): 1–10.

Stobart, Jon and Van Damme, Illia. "Introduction." In *Modernity and the Second-Hand Trade: European Consumption Cultures and Practices, 1700*–1900, edited by Jon Stobart and Illia Van Damme, 1–15. Basingstoke: Palgrave Macmillan, 2010.

Stobart, Jon. "Gentlemen and shopkeepers: supplying the country house in eighteenth-century England." *The Economic History Review*, Vol. 64, No. 3 (Aug. 2001): 885–904.

Stobart, Jon. "Geography and Industrialization: The Space Economy of Northwest England, 1701–1760." *Transactions of the Institute of British Geographers*, Vol. 21, No. 4 (1996): 681–696.

Stobart, Jon. "In Search of Causality: A Regional Approach to Urban Growth in Eighteenth-Century England." *Geografiska Annaler. Series B, Human Geography*, Vol. 82, No. 3 (2000): 149–163.

Stobart, Jon. "Luxury and Country House Sales in England, c. 1760–1830." In *The Afterlife of Used Things: Recycling in the Long Eighteenth Century*, edited by Ariane Fennetaux, Amélie Junqua, and Sophie Vasset, 25–36. New York: Routledge, 2015.

Stobart, Jon. "Making the global local? Overseas goods in English rural shops, c. 1600–1760." *Business History*, 59:7 (2017): 1136–1153.

Tadmor, Naomi. "The Concept of the Household-Family in Eighteenth-Century England." *Past & Present*, No. 151 (May 1996): 111–140.

Tague, Ingrid. "Love, Honor, and Obedience: Fashionable Women and the Discourse of Marriage in the Early Eighteenth Century." *Journal of British Studies*, Jan. 2001, Vol. 40, No. 1: 76–106.

Thompson, E.P. "The Moral Economy of the English Crowd in the Eighteenth Century." *Past & Present*, No. 50 (Feb. 1971): 76–136.

Vickery, Amanda. "Women and the world of goods: a Lancashire consumer and her possessions, 1751–81." In *Consumption and the World of Goods*, edited by John Brewer and Roy Porter, 274–301. London: Routledge, 1993.

Wall, Cynthia. "The English Auction: Narratives of Dismantling." *Eighteenth-Century Studies*, Vol. 31, No. 1 (Fall 1997): 1–25.

Walsh, Claire. "Shop Design and the Display of Goods in Eighteenth-Century London." *Journal of Design History*, Vol. 8, No. 3 (1995): 157–176.

Walton, Karin. "The Worshipful Company of Upholders of the City of London." *Furniture History Society*, Vol. 9 (1973): 41–79.

Weatherill, Lorna. "The meaning of consumer behaviour in late seventeenth- and early eighteenth-century England." In *Consumption and the World of Goods*, edited by John Brewer and Roy Porter, 206–227. London: Routledge, 1993.

Whittle, Jane and Hailwood, Mark. "The gender division of labour in early modern England." *Economic History Review*, Vol. 73, No. 1 (Dec. 2018): 3–32.

Woodward, Donald. "The Background to the Statute of Artificers: The Genesis of Labour Policy, 1558–63." *The Economic History Review*, New Series, Vol. 33, No. 1 (Feb. 1980): 32–44.

VIII. *Electronic Sources*

The British and Irish Furniture Makers Online. https://bifmo.history.ac.uk/about/project (accessed 12 October 2020).

"Charles II, 1666: An Act for Burying in Woollen." in *Statutes of the Realm: Volume 5, 1628–80*, ed. John Raithby (s.l: Great Britain Record Commission, 1819). *British History Online*. http://www.british-history.ac.uk/statutes-realm/vol5/p598a (accessed 27 March 2017).
"Charles II, 1677 & 1678: An Act for burying in Woollen," in *Statutes of the Realm: Volume 5, 1628–80*, ed. John Raithby (s.l: Great Britain Record Commission, 1819). *British History Online*. http://www.british-history.ac.uk/statutes-realm/vol5/pp885-886 (accessed 27 March 2017).
"John Trotter" in British History Online. https://www.british-history.ac.uk/no-series/dict-english-furniture-makers/t (accessed 26 June 2025).
Chassereau family history. Familytreemaker.com, http://familytreemaker.genealogy.com/users/m/c/c/John-W-McCoy/BOOK-0001/0017-0007.html (accessed 3 December 2014).
City of London Livery Companies Commission. "Report of the Commissioners: Part 1," in *City of London Livery Companies Commission. Report; Volume 1*, (London: City of London Livery Companies Commission. Report; Volume 1, (London: Eyre and Spottiswoode, 1884), 7–20. British History Online. http://www.british-history.ac.uk/livery-companies-commission/vol1/pp7-20 (accessed 17 April /2017).
Eyre and Spottiswoode, 1884), 7–20. *British History Online*. http://www.british-history.ac.uk/livery-companies-commission/vol1/pp7-20 (accessed 17 April 2017).
Hannah Greig, "Faction and Fashion: The Politics of Court Dress in Eighteenth-Century England," *Apparence(s)* (6 August 2015): Abstract and Section 6, no page numbers. https://journals.openedition.org/apparences/1311#tocto1n (accessed 19 October 2021).
Joiners' Company records, 1640–1783, in British and Irish Furniture Makers Online. https://bifmo.history.ac.uk/find-people?keywords=&name=Hunt%2C+James&active_from=1750&active_to=1800&place=&occupation=joiner&source=All (accessed 28 September 2021).
Jones Lang LaSalle history of Richard Winstanley. https://www.lasalle.com/company/history (accessed 29 July 2021).
Kent, Henry. *Kent's Directory*. London: Richard and Henry Causton, 1774. 42nd ed. Ancestry.com. *U.K. and U.S. Directories, 1680–1830* [database on-line] (accessed 8 October 2014, Newberry Library).
Kent, Henry. *Kent's Directory*. London: Richard and Henry Causton, 1778. 46th ed. Ancestry.com. *U.K. and U.S. Directories, 1680–1830* [database on-line] (accessed 8 October 2014, Newberry Library).
Lawson, Philip Hugh. *Dictionary of Welsh Biography*. Anwyl family, of Park, Llanfrothen, Merionethshire. http://yba.llgc.org.uk/en/s-ANWY-PAR-1500.html (accessed 13 March 2017).

MeasuringWorth.com. (Converting past money amounts into today's money.) (accessed various dates).

Oxford English Dictionary. "fripper, n.". OED Online. December 2018. Oxford University Press. http://www.oed.com.oxfordbrookes.idm.oclc.org/view/Entry/74752?redirectedFrom=fripper (accessed 6 January 2019).

Oxford English Dictionary. "upholder, n.". OED Online. December 2018. Oxford University Press. http://www.oed.com.oxfordbrookes.idm.oclc.org/view/Entry/219963?redirectedFrom=upholder (accessed 6 January 2019).

Pirohakul, Teerapa. *The Funeral in England in the Long Eighteenth Century*. London: PhD Thesis at London School of Economics, 2015. http://etheses.lse.ac.uk/1076/1/Pirohakul_The_Funeral_in_England_in_the_Long.pdf (accessed 17 January 2016).

Trotter family history. Alexander Trotter of Kettilsheill, Berwickshire. http://powys.org/pl_tree/ps05/ps05_361.html (accessed 19 November 2020).

Trustees from the Turkey Company. http://www.british-history.ac.uk/survey-london/bk10/pp36-51 (accessed 23 November 2015).

Victoria & Albert Museum, London. "Pierre Langlois." http://collections.vam.ac.uk/item/O53325/commode-langlois-pierre/ (accessed 6 December 2014).

The Worshipful Company of Upholders of the City of London. Upholder Definition from "About the Upholders." https://upholders.co.uk (accessed 26 November 2018).

Index[1]

[1] Note: Page numbers followed by 'n' refer to notes.

S. Sanders, *The Eighteenth-Century London Upholder*,
https://doi.org/10.1007/978-3-032-08660-0

FSC
www.fsc.org
MIX
Papier | Fördert gute Waldnutzung
FSC® C083411

Kolibri 360 GmbH
Ferdinand-Jühlke-Straße 7
99095 Erfurt, Deutschland
produktsicherheit@kolibri360.de